Ayodhya

Celebrating
30 Years of Publishing
in India

'A momentous phenomenon that redefined India, the Ayodhya movement also incorporated ordinary people and their stories. These, alas, tend to either get relegated to footnotes or completely forgotten in the mega-narrative. Sutapa Mukherjee has rescued many of these forgotten voices from the condescension of history. Her vignettes of the movement will enrich our understanding of how the town of Ayodhya saw and imbibed the Ram hurricane.'—SWAPAN DASGUPTA, POLITICIAN AND COLUMNIST

'Sutapa Mukherjee's well-informed and illuminating book revisits the contemporary history of Ayodhya and its complex layers of unity and divisions. It breaks new ground by its detailed examination of the changing relationship between Hindus and Muslims in this historic city. Extensive interviews and conversations with activists of the Ram Temple movement and ordinary people demonstrate the vagaries of the social and economic changes taking place in Ayodhya. This passionate, engaged account is a must-read for those interested in understanding the problems of essentializing ideologies and grand narratives that ignore lived realities.'—ZOYA HASAN, PROFESSOR EMERITA, JAWAHARLAL NEHRU UNIVERSITY

'This is by far the most elaborate and incisive account of the Ayodhya controversy, taking us into the minds of the participants and others, and the growth of its diverse movements. Written in an amiable, accessible style and resonant with details, this book is a must-read for those interested in controversies around Ayodhya. The sleepy town of Ayodhya—some 79.8 sq. km with 4,51,000 people (according to the 2011 census)—will never be the same, even for the victors squabbling over the sports of legal victory. The book rightly ends with what it calls the "obvious prediction": "*Yeh toh jhanki hai, Kashi, Mathura baaki hai (This is only the trailer, Kashi and Mathura are still left).*"'—RAJIV DHAWAN, SENIOR ADVOCATE AND AUTHOR

Ayodhya

Past and Present

SUTAPA MUKHERJEE

HarperCollins *Publishers* India

First published in India by HarperCollins *Publishers* 2022
4th Floor, Tower A, Building No. 10, DLF Cyber City,
Gurugram, Haryana – 122002
www.harpercollins.co.in

2 4 6 8 10 9 7 5 3 1

P-ISBN: 978-93-5629-215-4
E-ISBN: 978-93-5489-592-0

The views and opinions expressed in this book are the author's own.
The facts are as reported by her and the publishers
are not in any way liable for the same.

Typeset in 11/15.2 Adobe Caslon Pro at
Manipal Technologies Limited, Manipal

Printed and bound at
Thomson Press (India) Ltd.

MIX
Paper
FSC FSC® C010615

This book is produced from independently certified FSC® paper
to ensure responsible forest management.

To my two mothers,
my Ma, Taruni Chatterjee,
and my Ma-in-Law, Mira Mukerjee—
who trusted me with almost everything

‘I am proud to belong to a religion which has taught the world both tolerance and universal acceptance. We believe not only in universal toleration, but we accept all religions as true. I am proud to belong to a nation which has sheltered the persecuted and the refugees of all religions and all nations of the earth.’

—Swami Vivekananda, *Addresses at the Parliament of Religions*

Contents

Introduction

Ayodhya—Divided It Still Stands

Since childhood, Ayodhya has intrigued me. As a Bengali settled in Lucknow, our family would often travel to Kolkata. On these to-and-fro train journeys, we would cross the Ayodhya railway station. Invariably, the place looked empty, except for the few sadhus who would sometimes hop onto the train. Most trains, such as the express ones, would not even stop there.

It seemed like such a disconnect that this small nondescript town was the birthplace of a powerful and culturally popular god, Ram. No tourists, no pilgrims, no activity—only a sleepy town that was neither on the state nor the national agenda.

Years later, post 1997, as a journalist covering the Ram Janmabhoomi movement for newsmagazines like *Outlook*, global news agencies such as Associated Press (AP) and Agence France-Presse (AFP), and online news portals like BBC, my extensive research and reportage convinced me of the various forms of cultural and civilizational divisions within Ayodhya.

Both the past and contemporary history of the town seemed to be steeped in layers of oppositions—the interplay between good and bad, right and wrong, positive and negative, peacetime and war, and light and dark—almost like the epic Ramayana.

I wanted to write about these issues. I wanted to capture the essence of Ayodhya in its philosophical, physical, social and spiritual aspects. None of the books, papers and articles I read focused much on the basic issues of this town that were varied and conflicted. Most saw these issues as either black or white, not black and white or, for that matter, shades of grey.

More than that, I wanted to tell the story of the town through its people and through their struggles, travails and foibles. At one level, the town's communities have clashed and fought over centuries. At the same time, their warmth and kindness have also flowed through every space, cutting across group divisions, positions and even political stances. I found the residents very amiable as individuals, but in groups, they would turn out as a different people, most of them fighting for a cause that they had very little knowledge about.

At a personal level, the love and respect I received from the locals and even outsiders, including leaders and Rambhakts involved in the movement, left a deep and indelible imprint on me. However, I was also bombarded with speeches and acts of hate. I met with violence and an attitude of distrust as a journalist. Through the pages of this book I, therefore, wish to acquaint the readers with the human beings who, over centuries and specifically in the last few decades, have found themselves immersed in the grand tales and narratives of the Ram Janmabhoomi movement.

This is an opportune time to do so. After the 2019 Supreme Court order—which resolved the age-old tussle between the various communities over the ownership of Ram's birthplace—the town is transforming and will finally emerge as a bustling pilgrim city like Kashi (Benares). I want to tell this story before the grand temple, tall statues, five-star hotels, mega-luxury malls and shining roads change Ayodhya.

Paradoxically, Ayodhya was a divided city since its inception. Yet, it was united in its unique way. One cannot understand the soul of this town with a straitjacketed view.

Now, there is little doubt that Ayodhya is ancient. In 1861–62, Alexander Cunningham, the founder of the Archaeological Survey of India (ASI), surveyed it. More than a century later, A.K. Narain of the Banaras Hindu University (BHU) concluded that those excavations proved that human habitation had existed in the town for 2,500 years.

However, the town was never the sole preserve of the Hindus. The Buddhists and Jains claim equal religious rights over Ayodhya. For these two religions, the place is as important as it is to their Hindu brethren.

Valmiki's Ramayana, as opposed to the later version by Tulsidas, states that Lord Ram was born in the eighty-first generation of the Ikshvaku dynasty of the Suryavanshis (solar genealogy). Hindu scriptures contend that King Ikshvaku was the son of the first human (Manu) and he founded the Raghuvanshi (another name for Suryavanshi) dynasty, the direct decedents of the Sun God, and ruled over Kosala. Ayodhya was the empire's capital.

The Puranas mention that there were sixty-four kings before Ram. The text gives the description of two dynasties, Videha and Vaisala, which belonged to the Suryavanshi lineage.

It was during the 'Golden Period' of the Guptas (AD 320–500) when religiosity was infused into this town. Ayodhya was identified, recognized and propped up as the birthplace of Lord Ram. It is in this era that Hinduism became predominant, both across north and east India. The traditions of Vaishnavism, Shaivism and Shaktism (focused on Devi worship) spread. The celebrated court poet of Vikramaditya (Chandragupta II), Kalidas, wrote his epic poem, 'Raghuvamsha', in Sanskrit, which, as the name suggests, was based on the dynasty of Lord Ram.

In modern times, the local guides tend to indicate that the quest for Ayodhya as a birthplace of Lord Ram began in the Gupta period (prior to AD 500). They tell stories from an ancient legend that describes how King Vikramaditya decided to rediscover the *janmasthaan* (birthplace). As per the legend, exhausted after a long journey, the king decided to rest by the River Sarayu. Accidentally, he was left behind by his companions. Suddenly from nowhere, a handsome prince, dressed from top to toe in black and mounted on a black horse, entered the river. When the horse and rider came out again a few moments later, an amazing change had taken place: the prince's mount, his clothes, his face were now all shining white. Taken in by such a strange transformation, the king wanted to know the reason behind it. The prince revealed his name as Tirthraj Prayag—thus personifying the ancient holy town of Prayagraj (formerly Allahabad). He explained that every year he carries with him countless sins from innumerable pilgrims who visit to take a dip in the Sangam in Prayagraj—the confluence of the three rivers, namely the Ganga, (the legendary) Saraswati and the Yamuna—to wash their sins away. From there he travels to the River Sarayu to cleanse their sins. Which is why the changeover from black to white. This made the River Sarayu even more effective than Prayagraj as a site of pilgrimage in a step towards salvation. Vikramaditya then pleaded with Tirthraj Prayag to give him some tasks and guide him so that he could complete them successfully. Fulfilling this request, he told Vikramaditya to once again re-establish the Ram Janmabhoomi. The king completed the assigned task with the help of the given directions and details. And finally, the exact site of the Janmabhoomi was discovered by setting free a cow which had recently delivered a calf. It is believed, as was foretold by Tirthraj Prayag, that milk began to flow automatically from her udders as soon as she reached the sacred spot. The local guides further try and convince the visiting pilgrims that soon after this holy incident, King Vikramaditya built a magnificent temple at the Ram Janmabhoomi, which was made of black touchstone and had eighty-four pillars. This anecdotal evidence has been partially backed by archaeological evidence of 2003 and 2020.

Cunningham and Narain also confirmed Buddhist presence in the area from the fifth century BC, or 2,500 years ago.[1] The Buddhists till date believe that the Mani Parvat mound in the town is a remnant of a huge stupa. It is a fact that Ayodhya is the ancient Saket, the city of Lord Buddha. Travelogues by the Chinese pilgrim Hiuen Tsang give vivid descriptions of Buddhist remnants during the seventh century.

In 492–460 BC, during the times of King Ajatshatru of the Maurya Dynasty, Saket was a trading town. Ajatshatru annexed several territories like Kosala and Kashi, which were close to his capital city of Magadh (Bihar).

Saket has been mentioned several times during the subsequent periods. After the Mauryans, Greek Demetrius I, who completed his emperor's—Alexander the Great—objectives, crossed through Punjab, Saket and Mathura to seize Pataliputra (Patna).

In 1993, a Kushan inscription was found in the Rabatak village of Afghanistan which read, 'In the year one, it has been proclaimed unto India, unto the whole realm of the governing class including Koonadeano (Kaundinya, Kundina) and the city of Ozeno (Ozene, Ujjain) and the city of Zageda (Saketa) and the city of Kozambo (Kausambi) and the city of Palabotro (Pataliputra) and so long unto the city of Ziri-tambo (Sri-Champa).'

Chinese and Tibetan historians have also mentioned how King Kanishka fought with the King of Soked (Saket). Jain texts associate Ayodhya with the birthplace of their first-born Tirthankara

8,400,000 years ago,[2] and that of the fourth Tirthankara, 5,000,000 years ago.[3]

The Jains believe that the place was visited by saints like Parsavanath and Mahavira. Jain pilgrims still visit the town to offer prayers at the eight well-maintained Jain temples that even now stand tall in this town.

Clearly, for the first 1,000 years (500 BC to AD 500) at least, and even later, the town was a melting pot of several religions. Various communities lived amicably, despite invasions by kings and the rise of new and different empires.

In the next 1,000 years, the religious mix of the town changed. While Ayodhya continued to be important for the Buddhists and Jains till the eighth century at least, the number of Hindu residents increased, or became predominant.

There is little doubt that Hinduism, after initially losing out to Buddhism, was on the ascendancy from the eighth century onwards throughout India. Some historians think that Adi Shankaracharya—historians disagree on his lifetime and diverge on the period when his philosophy became popular—was responsible for this. There are, however, others who give credit to different Hindu philosophers for propagating the religion.

Whatever may be the truth, in reality, across India, there was Hindu rejuvenation between AD 700 and 1100. In some ways, the Hindus were consolidated. In others, they remained divided, but enjoyed a sense of commonality. In fact, the sects of Ayodhya may trace their histories to this period when the town became home to thousands of Ramanandi sadhus—a demography that later gave rise to several orders and *akhara*s across the country.

One of the priorities of the Hindu philosophers of this era was to appropriate Buddhism and somehow take Hinduism to a more acceptable level among the masses. Such philosophers, including Shankaracharya, travelled across India to achieve this objective.

Being the recognized birthplace of Lord Ram, Ayodhya was obviously influenced and transformed by these movements.

Coincidentally, it was around this time that India caught the attention of Muslim invaders. The route was carved by Muhammed Bin Kasim in AD 712, then came the plunderers Muhammad Ghori (AD 1000–1027) and Mahmud of Ghazni (AD 1175–1206), followed by the Delhi Sultanate.

Chistu Rajamony wrote in his PhD thesis that 'the early settlements of Muslims in Ayodhya suggest that the first Muslim invasion of Avadh, present-day Ayodhya, occurred before 1030. Within two centuries, Ayodhya became the headquarters of a Muslim province in the Delhi Sultanate.'[4] Rajamony further mentions that the first Mughal Emperor, Babar, defeated the ruler of Ayodhya in a battle and appointed Mir Bagi Tashqandi as the governor of the Ayodhya region, who built a mosque in Ayodhya in 1528. 'From 1528 until the British period, Ayodhya was under Islamic rule.'[5]

Thus, in the second half of the thousand-year period between AD 500 and 1600, Hindus and Muslims became integral parts of the town. Like the former, the newcomers also attached great religious prominence to Ayodhya—they too began to trace back possible significant associations the town had with their theological beliefs. Even today, the local Muslims refer to the town as 'Khurd Mecca' (Little Mecca), which links the place to the most revered one on earth for them. Like the position that Lord Ram's birthplace has in the hearts of the Hindus, Ayodhya signifies crucial connections with Prophet Muhammad for the Muslims.

When I met Mohammed Umar, the grandson of Zahoor Ahmed, the *mutawalli* (trustee of the Waqf) of Babri Masjid and the first Muslim to witness the events that placed the idol of Ram Lalla within the mosque premises in December 1949, he took me for a visit to the Naughazi Mazar—meaning 8.19-metre-long tomb.

Muslims believe that their preacher Hazrat Nuh is buried here. Nuh is for Muslims what Noah, the famous Biblical character, is for Christians. Apart from this, there are scores of other ancient Muslim graveyards of Sufi saints, as well as dilapidated mosques, across Ayodhya. Many of them are believed to be there from AD 1000–1500.

The next seminal inflexion points in Ayodhya's religiosity came in the 1500s, when Babur reached India and set up the Mughal empire. It is believed that in 1528, the commander-in-chief of his army, Mir Baqi, constructed the Babri Masjid. The mosque became a place for prayers for Muslims and, over the years, one of hatred for the Hindus. One can easily say that it is from those days that the religious complexion of the town changed dramatically.

Even to this date, it is common among large sections of people to look at the Mughals as the invaders. It is a historical fact that many of their rulers did commit atrocities against the Hindus and destroyed temples during their long reign of three centuries. At the same time, it cannot be denied that the Mughals also believed in religious and other forms of assimilation.

A few Mughal emperors even went out of their way to ensure that Hindus and Muslims lived amicably. Rules and laws were changed to protect the social, economic and religious rights of the Hindus. Hence, the two communities lived in a constant love–hate relationship—love in some geographical spaces and hatred in the others.

As an individual, I am rather ambivalent. I am well aware of certain acts of the emperors that show them in an unkindly light. At the same time, Babur, who has become a portrait of hatred for many Hindus now,[6] was a symbol of love and kindness for me and my contemporaries from what emerged of his character from our school lessons. My early memories go back to the 1970s, when we schoolgirls were in awe of the man's grit as we read of the difficulties he overcame during his journey to India—the way the emperor faced and countered challenges both on the personal and administrative fronts.

As a child, in those years, I was most taken in by his love for his son, Humayun. The history teacher would beautifully relate to us the way Babur passionately and ceaselessly paced around Humayun's bed when the boy was extremely sick. Babur checked in on his son day and night and prayed that Allah should cure him and, if need be, transfer the illness to the father. This was at a time when the emperor struggled to find his bearings as a ruler–founder of a new empire in a new land. This story moved me to tears. To me, more than an emperor, he was an ideal father.

The positive impact of the Mughal reign cannot be ignored. The rulers constructed mini-societies across cities and regions, where Muslims and Hindus lived in harmony. Deep economic connections between the two communities, which are witnessed even today although in a diluted form, led to social coexistence. Or was it the opposite?

Rules, laws and social order enabled the two communities to interact with each other, and there was a sense of religious freedom. Tensions and riots erupted regularly, but they were curbed immediately. The emperors did not encourage these rifts because they were interested in a long-term investment in India. They did not envisage themselves as mere invaders or plunderers and the people from the two communities were made aware that they had to live together, and their lives depended on each other.

Unlike Lucknow or Delhi, Ayodhya did not see the same levels of economic integration. Some professions were dominated by Muslims and in others Hindus held a prominent place. But it was evident in those years that both the religious communities were involved in each other's spiritual activities. Even today, there are Muslims whose livelihoods depend on the prosperity of the thousands of local temples. They sell flowers and other products that are used by the Hindus in their religious, cultural and daily rituals.

Differences existed and surfaced on and off, but there were no recorded disturbances of importance. In fact, one of the first known riots between the two communities was in 1855, a few months before the Muslim province of Awadh was annexed as Oudh by the British.

It is ironic that the tensions began over Hanumangarhi, a Hindu temple which was built on the land donated by a Muslim, Nawab Abul Mansur Safdarjung, the second ruler of the Awadh kingdom. The Hindu *bairagi*s (recluses/saints) wished to expand their territory. A Sunni zealot, Shah Ghulam Husayn, began a crusade against Hanumangarhi. He alleged that the bairagis had usurped the land of the Qanati (makeshift) masjid, which dated back to the reign of Mughal Emperor Aurangzeb and was inside the Hanumangarhi premises. The Hindus overpowered the Muslims in the ensuing battle, and the former killed several members of the latter. It was at that time that the focus of the Hindus shifted to the Babri Masjid as many Muslims took shelter in its premises during these skirmishes. In another incident, Maulawi Amir Ali of Amethi (Uttar Pradesh) and Maulawi Ramzan Ali organized Sunni Muslims and gathered them in their town. They planned a 95-km march from Amethi to Ayodhya. Thousands were supposed to join this group in Faizabad.

However, the local Shia administration took proactive precautions and blocked off the bridge that led to Ayodhya from Faizabad. At the latter town, the Sunnis were met by their Muslim opponents, the Shias, who were armed and had the support of the soldiers supplied by a few Shiite landlords in the area. The Sunnis lost.

Despite these tensions between Hindus and Muslims, as also Muslims and Muslims, there was general peace. In reality, during India's First War of Independence against the British in 1857, local Hindu and Muslim leaders joined hands, raised an army and battled the colonial soldiers. Two of the popular Indian revolutionaries, one from both communities, were even hanged in Ayodhya after the British won the war.

Both Hindus and Muslims did complain against either the expansive tendencies of the temples or the mosques, respectively. But it was done in an overall live-and-let-live spirit. The two communities knew that while they could tussle for religious dominance, they had to coexist in the same small town.

According to some historians, the real divide between Hindus and Muslims started in earnest after 1857, and largely because of the deliberate divide-and-rule policy of the British. The colonialists realized that they had to create a wedge between religious communities, ethnic groups and caste sections across India. They did it successfully, which was also evident in Ayodhya.

It was around this time that the British used the excuse of proactively stopping possible violence to build grilled enclosures and allocate marked areas for the Hindus and Muslims in the disputed Babri Masjid–Ram Janmabhoomi premise. Officially, it allowed the two communities to offer prayers separately and without any visible disturbances. In practice, it accentuated the divisive feelings between them. The bickering and disputes continued.

Over the next few decades, the British administration regularly intervened as a third-party intermediary in any dispute that broke out to settle them appropriately. For example, in 1934, a riot erupted over the slaughter of a cow in the neighbouring village of Shahjahanpur. In Ayodhya, enraged Hindus demolished one of the domes, which was already in a dilapidated state, of the Babri Masjid. The British reacted and rebuilt it with the help of a Muslim contractor. The Hindus were asked to pay fines to finance this.

The British-inflamed tensions between the two communities reached a new climax just after India's independence. In December 1949, a group of Hindu sages sneaked into the Babri Masjid and placed the idol of Ram Lalla under the main central dome. The event was dubbed as the miraculous return of the lord to his birthplace, the place where he truly belonged. Obviously, this disturbed the existing peace in the town. Hindus and Muslims were pitted against each other, more so than ever. Yet they still coexisted and went along with their lives.

But, among certain Hindu sections, there was a renewed energy and enthusiasm to correct a (perceived) historical wrong. Babri Masjid, as also Ram Janmabhoomi, became a pressing issue between the two communities. Among the Muslims, there were efforts to retain the centuries-old status quo.

Despite these tensions, the residents of Ayodhya chose the legal path to confront each other or to change the situation on the ground, rather than succumbing to violence. The 1949 incident showed that the local administration played into the hands of the Ramanandi sadhus, which left the Muslims high and dry. This was also a period when senior politicians brazenly took to supporting the Hindus, isolating the Muslims.

Despite the agitated stance by political parties like the Hindu Mahasabha, the people of Ayodhya were inclined to patiently wait for a legal verdict.

A slew of litigations ensued for seventy long years, which finally landed at the doors of the Supreme Court as various title suits, or petitions, to claim that the disputed property belonged to the Hindus, Muslims, or Lord Ram himself (represented by Ram's *sakha* or best friend), were filed. Final hearings began on 6 August 2019 and after a long-drawn-out forty-day hearing, the judgment was ultimately pronounced on 9 November 2019.

Even as they fought in the various courts, the Hindus and Muslims mingled with each other. Among the first legal litigants were Ram Chandra Paramhans, mahant of the Digambar Akhara, and Hashim Ansari, popularly addressed as Hashim chacha by the Ayodhyawasis.

The former was a respected Hindu saint and the latter a well-known supporter of Muslim causes. And above all their religious differences, they remained best friends till their last breath!

On their litigation dates in Faizabad Court, they travelled together and came back in the same vehicle after intense debates in the courtroom. Theirs was an iconic friendship that is still remembered by all sections of people in the town. It will remain a legend that symbolized the mutual trust and love that the two communities shared. Outsiders may forget it, but the residents, despite anxieties, still look up to and believe in that friendship.

What truly changed the physical space of Ayodhya was the decade of the 1980s. Prior to that period, most local residents still believed in happy coexistence and hoped for a peaceful solution to the religious dispute. However, that decade saw a huge influx of outsiders—politicians, civil servants, religious leaders from both communities, spiritual and philosophical heads, as also the millions of *karsevak*s (religious volunteers). They were the ones who transformed the soul, heart and mind of this town forever.

This happened for several political, economic, social and religious reasons. At the political level, 1977 was a pivotal transition point. It was the first time that the Congress lost a national election. Among the parties which witnessed an ascendancy was the Bharatiya Jana Sangh that was later to become the Bharatiya Janata Party (BJP). The Jana Sangh was a crucial partner in the ruling coalition that emerged from the 1977 general elections, the Janata alliance.

Suddenly, in the 1980s, the BJP realized that it had a shot at political power, not just at the Centre but also in the northern states. To change the electoral equations, it needed to consolidate Hindu votes. It had to break the existing arithmetic. The Congress won the various elections because of the combined support of Muslims, Dalits, women voters and several backward classes.

Given its legacy and baggage, the BJP initially consolidated the upper-caste segments. It used patriotism (doused with religious fuel) to rouse the people. Its strategies included the call for a fight to restore and rebuild Hindu temples destroyed by Muslim rulers, focus on ancient Hindu-centric cultural and civilizational practices and aiming for support from the historical span of Bharat that stretched from Iran to Indonesia, and Afghanistan to Sri Lanka.

Somehow, the fight to reclaim Ram's birthplace in Ayodhya clicked. This was possibly because of the social milieu in north India. Of the two grand epics, the Ramayana and Mahabharata, most traditional and conservative families were aware of the former, and rituals based on it were observed in many homes. In contrast, the story of the Mahabharata and the teachings of the Bhagavad Gita were complex and thus less followed by the masses.

When the state-owned broadcaster, Doordarshan, serialized and aired the Ramayana in the late 1980s, it became an instant success. On Sunday mornings, people stayed indoors to watch the serial and the streets were empty. Within a short span the social popularity of Lord Ram grew.

Not many people realize, but Ram, unlike Krishna or other gods, has a north–south footprint in the country. The lord's travels during his years in *vanvaas* (exile) stretched southwards from Ayodhya and stopped at Sri Lanka, where he defeated Ravan. Hence, people in most Indian states were aware of the god, and the simple, loving message of the mythology.

Several peripheral organizations of the Rashtriya Swayamsevak Sangh (RSS), the umbrella that supported the BJP, immediately used the prevailing environment to make inroads within society. They succeeded in north India. The Vishva Hindu Parishad (VHP) became the dominant force that tried to consolidate the Hindus. It descended on Ayodhya and changed the town permanently. The locals feel almost dominated by the VHP, which as time rolled by, took over the nooks of the town and became the sole decision-maker.

At an economic level, the 1980s saw the first, although uneven, waves of reforms and liberalization. After Rajiv Gandhi of the Congress became Prime Minister in 1984, he allowed freer and cheaper imports, joint ventures between Indian and foreign firms in sectors like automobiles, and started the Information Technology (IT) revolution.

In the 1984 Lok Sabha polls (assembly elections), though the BJP won only two seats (out of 543), its might grew nationally and it readied itself to counter the Congress. Simultaneously, the RSS and its tangential entities tried to revive Hindutva. The Ram Janmabhoomi movement became the focal religious point of convergence.

The Congress's desperate appeasement of the Muslims for votes, through such instances as the Shah Bano case—one of the legal milestones protecting Muslim women rights—and the subsequent law that was framed, helped create more divisiveness between the Hindus and Muslims. Movements by the VHP were juxtaposed with similar congregations by conservative Muslim organizations.

Along with the VHP, the momentum was stoked by the RSS, BJP and Bajrang Dal over the decade spanning the 1980s. The legal efforts intensified even as these entities aimed to bring together Hindu religious sects and groups. The efforts culminated in the shattering events of 1992.

In December 1992, millions of karsevaks gathered in Ayodhya, broke the security cordon and demolished Babri Masjid. The centuries-old mosque was razed to the ground. There were outcries of political and religious conspiracies. But that came later. Without a structure, the disputed property was ready for a new temple of Lord Ram, and that too at his birthplace.

One may think that by the time of the demolition, Ayodhya would have been internally divided and the two communities would have been at each other's throats. That was not the case. Most of the clashes, riots and conflicts before and in 1992 were largely instigated by outsiders. The people of Ayodhya felt emotionally and spiritually conflicted, even as many of them took part in the riots—but they were yet not in a state of physical unrest.

The best way to reveal this social atmosphere is through the story of V, who wishes to remain anonymous. I met him on one of my frequent trips to Ayodhya in 2019–2020. Since our first meeting he affectionately addresses me as *didi*, meaning older sister.

V shifted to the town from Basti, which is another small town about 60 km from Ayodhya. His father was extremely religious and when V was an eight-year-old boy, the family decided to settle at their ancestral house in Ayodhya. As a child, V visited the disputed area, not out of any religious compulsions but to play with his friends. They played *gilli-danda*, hide-and-seek, climbed trees and ate fruits—indulged in all activities that any child of his age enjoys. His friends belonged to both the communities as is the case even till date.

On the morning of 30 October, to prevent the karsevaks from reaching the Babri Masjid, the police barricaded the 1.5-kilometre-long lane that led to the sixteenth-century-old mosque.

'Ayodhya was in an unprecedented security cordon. Curfew had been imposed. Yet, sadhus and karsevaks marched towards the structure.

'By noon, police received orders from then Chief Minister Mulayam Singh Yadav to open fire at the karsevaks. The firing led to chaos and stampede. Police chased down the karsevaks in the streets of Ayodhya.

'Another round of clash erupted on November 2 ... The karsevaks would not be deterred. The security forces responded by opening fire the second time in three days.

'Many died in the clashes. Official records showed 17 deaths ... [sic]'[7]

V now strongly believes that the *karseva* in 1990, when the police on orders from the then chief minister of Uttar Pradesh, Mulayam Singh Yadav, shot to death many religious volunteers, changed the equations between the two communities in Ayodhya.

Charged with anger towards Yadav for having ordered the firing on the holy karsevaks, V joined the VHP to avenge the transgression. He took part in subsequent rallies and processions and was also there when the Babri Masjid was demolished in 1992. He was witness to the scene where scores of karsevaks climbed the three domes with poles and pickaxes.

He was both elated and disheartened when the domes came down. He was proud of the fact that the VHP had achieved its objective. He did feel a bit dejected that he could not reach right up to the mosque and help the other karsevaks as he could not find a way to reach the spot. He could only stay with the crowd and watch the happenings as a bystander from a distance.

Around 5 p.m. that evening, after the demolition, as he trudged back with a local VHP head and a few karsevaks, he heard screams—a group of Hindus were screaming for help, shouting that the Muslims had begun to fire. They immediately sped to the spot, Tehri Bazaar, a locality that has always been dominated by Muslims. What V saw was in contrast to what they had heard a few minutes ago—it was the Muslims who were under attack. In V's words, 'In that instant, something within me tripped and snapped. I shouted out a lie, almost in reflex, "*Bhagho, bhago, police aa rahi hai* (Run, the police are coming).'" He added that the outcome was exactly what he had hoped for—all his companions and other Hindus immediately fled from the spot and the Muslims were saved.

But something lingered on in the deepest part of V's heart. While he was fine with the demolition, he failed to fathom the lust, frenzy and madness of his fellow Hindus. They were after all karsevaks, devout Ram *bhakt*s. How could they stoop so low?

Once it was dark, V trooped down to his favourite place in Ayodhya, the Manas Janamsthali Mandir, a temple dedicated to the poet Goswami Tulsidas, who inked the Ramayana in a common man's dialect. A couplet from the Ramayana written on a tin board caught his attention. It read:

Par hit saris dharam nahi bhai,
aur pad pidha sam nahi adhmai.

Translated in English, it means: 'There is no better religion than service to other, no crime worse than inflicting pain on others.'

V stopped associating with the VHP or the Ram Janmabhoomi movement post that evening. Then on, he was on his own quest along with a few of his friends. Like him, most locals wanted to wash their hands off the conflict that had made their lives complicated just because they were the people of the town where Ram was born!

As far as the BJP was concerned, after the demolition it gained political power at the Centre for several years. Ayodhya simmered but did not burn because the late Atal Bihari Vajpayee, former Prime Minister, was keen to show his secular, rather than strident, face to the world.

The top brass of organizations like the VHP, as well as the umbrella RSS, were steeped in anger, desperation and frustration at Vajpayee's behaviour. But there was also a feeling within the highest level in the RSS that it was better to keep the Ayodhya issue alive, rather than build a temple there and lay it to rest for good.

In the new century, when the BJP unexpectedly lost power at the Centre, it was again on the back foot. Hence, it once more started to make the right noises about the Ram Janmabhoomi. The 2002 riots in Gujarat, and tensions in other parts of the country, also kept the fire alive.

What shows the uncertainty of the first decade of this century was the Allahabad High Court order on the disputed property: It divided the area into three—equal portions to the three main claimants, the Hindus, Nirmohi Akhara and Muslims. The claim of the lord himself, that he was the real owner of the place, was not considered by the high court.

The social fabric changed again when the BJP romped back to power with a majority of its own in the 2014 national elections. By then, and after that year, several states were painted in saffron colours. The BJP made inroads into the western, eastern and southern parts of the country, apart from the northern ones.

Logically, the Supreme Court judgment of 2019 reflected this new reality. It awarded the disputed property to Lord Ram. Rifts were created yet again. In Ayodhya, while the Muslims feel more alienated and uncared for than ever before, many of the Hindu sages also do not see eye to eye with the VHP. Most locals of this town feel that their little abode is no longer with them. It has been hijacked by the politicians to meet certain ends with whatever means that suits them best.

1

The Polestar of Faith and Belief

'God is always the upholder of justice'

—MAHATMA GANDHI[1]

Travelogues are powerful. They capture the past. They can also carve the future! Get hold of a good travelogue and there is no end to enjoying the excitement it brings along. These are mostly read out of lurking passions to know the hitherto unknown. Whatever may be the reason, it is a great feeling to be one with the observer on a journey, to understand different people, their intentions and their various triumphs and tribulations.

You embark on a virtual journey to many lands through the writer's words that bring forth minute details of people, their culture, the landscape, along with a liberal sprinkling of anecdotes. Then there are those travel stories that take the readers through a time machine into different realms of history—the panorama, flora and fauna, artwork and architecture, events and personalities which include lives of commoners, rogues, emperors and empresses, pretty courtesans and court jesters.

For most Indians, the first experience of a travelogue is from their school days. Invariably the curriculum has history textbooks with chapters that include tales of the two famous Chinese travellers, Hiuen Tsang and Fa Hien, who travelled on foot to India to delve into and learn from the land of their lord—Gautama Buddha.

In 2019, these and dozens of other travelogues on India were gleaned, neither for pleasure nor for any academic study but for an unusual reason—to locate the exact birthplace of a god and whether the followers' belief in its location, which was long-standing and stretched across centuries, held any water. The five judges' bench of the Supreme Court was on a mission to establish Lord Ram's janmasthaan.

Ironically, some of the travel writers, and the millions of readers, had little or no idea whether Ayodhya was indeed Lord Ram's birthplace. Through possible restless days and nights, the five judges meticulously dug out details from varied literature ranging from ancient, medieval to modern eras to reach a conclusion to a question that had bogged politicians, spiritual leaders, several communities and, of course, dozens of judges before them for more than 150 years.

In their lengthy judgment, they included pages and excerpts from the travel records left by well-known names such as Fa Hien, Hiuen Tsang, Guru Nanak, William Finch and Joseph Tiefenthaler.

Like the two Chinese travellers, most of the others did not come to India, nor visit Ayodhya, for the love for Ram. They were there either because they yearned to know more about their own religions or on some other project assigned to them by their seniors.

Hiuen Tsang and Fa Hien toured India in the fourth and seventh centuries, respectively. The former (AD 399) visited in the quest of Buddhist texts, the latter (AD 627–643) too, with the same intention, traversed the original Silk Route before reaching his destination. Their travel records are great historical treasures as they detail the way Buddhists lived and practised the religion in the land of their lord.

These two travelogues provide insights into the cultural, social and political aspects of the kingdoms they came across in south Asia. The opening passage of Fa Hien's *A Record of the Buddhist Kingdoms* tells us that his primary purpose was to procure texts related to monastic rules (Vinaya).[2] It is interesting to note that neither of the Chinese pilgrims scripted their experiences; these were later recorded and preserved through oral and written relay by monks.

Hiuen Tsang, who came when Emperor Harshavardhana was in power, portrayed the king as someone who 'is virtuous and patriotic; all people celebrate his praises in songs ... His renown was spread abroad everywhere, and all his subjects reverenced his virtues. The empire having gained rest, then the people were at peace. On this he put an end to warlike expeditions and began to store up in the magazines, the lances and swords. He gave himself up to religious duties; he prohibited the slaughter of any living creature. He himself set the example and ordered all his people to abstain from flesh meat, and he founded Sangharamas wherever there were sacred traces of religion.'[3]

It was from Kannauj that Hiuen Tsang headed south-east for the kingdom of 'O-yit-to' (Ayodhya), which was 'six hundred li (300 km)' away. He mentioned, 'There are here about one hundred temples with several thousand priests, who study both the Small and the Great Vehicle.'

When he left Ayodhya, Hiuen Tsang wasn't aware that death hovered around him, and this could have been the last destination in his life. 'The Master of the Law left the kingdom of Ayodhya, having paid reverence to the sacred traces, and following the course of the river Ganges, proceeded eastward, being on board a vessel with about eighty other fellow-passengers.

'After going about a hundred li, both banks of the river were shrouded by the thick foliage of an Asoka Forest, and amid these trees on either bank were concealed some ten pirate boats. Then these boats, propelled by oars, all at once burst forth into the midstream. Some of those in the ship, terrified at the sight, cast themselves into the river, whilst the pirates, taking the ship in tow, brought it to the bank. They then ordered the men to take off their clothes and searched them in quest of jewels and precious stones. Now these pirates pay worship to Durga, a spirit of heaven, and every year during the autumn, they look out for a man of good form and comely features, whom they kill, and offer his flesh and blood in sacrifice to their divinity, to procure good fortune. Seeing that the Master of the Law was suitable for their purpose, both in respect of his distinguished bearing and his bodily strength and appearance, they exchanged joyful glances, and said, "We were letting the season for sacrificing to our god pass by, because we could not find a suitable person for it, but now this Sraman is of noble form and pleasing features—let us kill him as a sacrifice, and we shall gain certain good fortune."'

A dacoit pulled out a scythe. At that very moment, lightning ripped through the sky. This was followed by a strange miracle. An unexpected typhoon clobbered the strong trees, dust blinded the travellers and pirates and the river was wild. Everyone was terrified. The attackers were on their knees; they apologized to the monk. They said that the miracle was a warning from the goddess that they were about to commit a sinful sacrifice. They shouted *Jai Ma* again and threw their scythes. The dacoits bowed and begged for forgiveness. The weather calmed down, the attacked and attackers chatted like friends, and finally headed towards their separate destinations.[4]

The other volume of travel tales brought up during the hearings in the apex court was those from the *Janamsakhis*, a legendary biography of Guru Nanak, the founder of Sikhism. When the authors of the *Janamsakhis* described the journeys made by Mardana and Nanak Dev, they would have never imagined that centuries later extracts from these texts would be produced as evidence in the Supreme Court. The text was mentioned to establish the importance of Ayodhya in 1511.

Rajinder Singh, a resident of Faridabad, Haryana, claiming to have interest in the study of religious, cultural and historical books on Sikhism, appeared as a witness and brought out the fact that 'Guru Nanak Devji, after getting the appearance of God on the auspicious day, *Bhadrapad Poornima*, 1564-Vikrami = 1507 CE prepared him for going on pilgrimage. Then he went to Ayodhya via Delhi, Haridwar, Sultanpur, etc. Almost 3–4 years have passed in this journey. Similarly, Guru Nanak Dev went on pilgrimage to see Shri Ram Janam Bhoomi Mandir in 1567–1568 Vikrami = 1510–11 Christian era. It is mentioned here that invader Babar has not invaded India by that time.'[5]

According to the *Janamsakhis*, the saint and his inseparable friend and companion, Mardana, started their journey across the Himalayan foothills and Gangetic plains to cover as many *teerth sthaan*s (holy places) as they could within a year. They chose destinations where God, in various avatars, had revealed himself in human forms. Having no other option in those years, the two friends travelled only by boat and foot.

The last lap of this trail was a difficult one—the night air was bitterly cold and, apart from an occasional owl, the sound was that of the moving oars. Mardana donned an ochre *fatua* (long loose shirt) and a loosely tied matching turban. Nanak, as always, remained unperturbed, comfortable in his traditional white flimsy flowing robe. Seated calmly, he gazed up at the stars above, oblivious of the chill.

As usual, Mardana, off and on, got anxious about the food ration they carried, 'What if it was not enough?' Nanak ensured that they carried a surplus stored in two large sacks and a few smaller ones. The other accessory the duo treasured during their travel was Mardana's *rubab* (a string instrument).

They reached Ayodhya at dawn, wore their clogs, and walked on a mud path. Faraway, they spotted a few locals busy with their daily early morning chores. As the two friends reached closer, a few couples with cows, who were out to exchange milk for groceries and other victuals, looked suspiciously at the two strangers. After a few questions, another couple offered the two friends some tea; Nanak could not hold himself back and requested milk instead, which was his favourite drink and staple diet in those years.

Soon, the inquisitive neighbours gathered under a banyan tree with *dholak*s and cymbals, and a spontaneous religious congregation began. While the locals sang *bhajan*s, Mardana reflexively strummed on the rubab's thick strings. The instrument aroused curiosity, as the residents hadn't seen anything like it before. 'What is this?' 'How is it made?' 'Where do you get these?' The two friends answered all the queries happily. Then came the requests for songs. Mardana plucked on his rubab, and Nanak sang.

Although the apex court noted that the extracts from *Janamsakhis* produced as evidence do not identify the exact place of Ram Janmabhoomi, it establishes the fact that Nanak visited Ayodhya for *darshan* (visiting a holy place and deity). It also revealed the possibilities of pilgrims visiting Ayodhya before 1528 (when the Babri Masjid was built).

'The Brahmakund Gurudwara near the janmabhoomi stands as a testimony that Guru Nanak visited Ayodhya,' claimed Gyani Guljit Singh, a resident Khalsa, while showing me around the gurudwara. He pointed at a well and recounted to me the story of how Nanak created it miraculously when one of his devotees was thirsty. He requested me to sprinkle some water from the holy well on my head. 'You will carry back the Guru's blessings.' I followed his instruction; the water, these days, is mechanically drawn out by an electric motor. The gurudwara, situated on the banks of the Sarayu River, is clean and very well maintained. We meditated for a while and then proceeded to see the relics of some of the gurus who later visited Ayodhya.

Later, we passed through some tunnels into a cavern, which appeared to be a combination of a museum and a temple. The Mukhya Granthi told me that Guru Tegh Bahadur and Guru Gobind Singh also visited this town. To date, the weapons used by the Sikhs to fight the Muslims at the request of a bairagi sadhu, Baba Vaishno Das, in 1708, are kept on display. Alongside are a brocade jacket, turban and footwear (*khadau*) apparently used by Guru Tegh Bahadur.

Then there were travelogues scripted during the British Raj, which the Supreme Court justices also sifted through.

William Finch, a renowned astronomer and cartographer, reached India with Captain Hawkins, the commander of *Hector*, the first East India Company (EIC) ship. It docked at Surat (Gujarat) on 24 August 1608, and the duo's assignment was to sign a treaty with Mughal Emperor Jahangir. Hawkins returned to England, but Finch delayed his departure to explore the country. He visited Ayodhya between 1608–1611 and was fascinated with the Hindu's piety for Lord Ram. He witnessed Hindu devotees offering prayers within the premises of a mosque that locals believed was erected over a Hindu temple devoted to the god. Records prove that Finch travelled on eastwards to Sultanpur, which is about 70 km from Ayodhya. The locals told him stories about how the lord appeared in a human form to witness and experience the '*tamasha*' of this world and relieve it of demons and mischief-makers.[6]

In the following century, a European Jesuit priest, Joseph Tiefenthaler, visited Ayodhya. He deviated from his initial missionary work and became a cartographer. He lived in India for thirty-eight years (1743–85). His famous book, *Historisch-geographische Beschreibung von Hindustan* (The Historical and

Geographical Description of Hindustan), has forty illustrations, including maps and city plans, most of which were drawn by him. It is from Tiefenthaler that we received the first drawings of the routes of the rivers Ganga and Ghagra. His work on the latter river possibly took him to Ayodhya.

According to Tiefenthaler's account, which differs from the usual narrative, Aurangzeb (1618–1707) demolished the Ramkot fortress, including the house that was considered the birthplace of Ram. A mosque with three domes was constructed there. However, Tiefenthaler added that 'others say that it was constructed by "Babor [Babar]".' The Hindus continued to offer prayers at a mud platform that marked the birthplace of Rama. Tiefenthaler was well-versed in Persian and Sanskrit. Evidently, he did not find an inscription on the walls of the mosque, stating that it was constructed under Babar's orders.[7]

According to the Supreme Court bench, 'Travelogues and gazetteers contain loose fragments of forgotten history. The evidentiary value to be ascribed to their contents necessarily depends upon the context and is subject to a careful evaluation of their contents.' The verdict also states, 'Our analysis has included in the balance, the need for circumspection, as we read in the accounts of travellers and gazetteers a colonial perspective on the contest at the disputed site.' Remarking on writings of Tiefenthaler in the eighteenth century and Robert Montgomery Martin in the early nineteenth century, the court stated that these 'record the prevalence of Hindu worship at the disputed site. They also reference special occasions such as Ram Navmi during which Hindu devotees converged upon the Janmasthan from distant areas motivated by the desire to offer prayer to Lord Ram.'

The courts stressed: 'The oral and documentary evidence shows that the Hindu devotees of Lord Ram hold a genuine, long-standing and profound belief in the religious merit attained by offering prayer to Lord Ram at the site they believe to be his birthplace.'[8]

Reactions to the usage of such travelogues and oral descriptions by different witnesses called for mixed reactions from the legal fraternity. Faizan Mustafa, vice chancellor, National Academy of Legal Studies and Research (NALSAR) University of Law, Hyderabad, opines that though the court said in its order that its decision would be on the basis of title, not faith, eventually it relied on old travelogues, which were questioned by historians, and concluded that it was people's faith that Lord Ram was born under the demolished mosque's central dome in Ayodhya.[9]

To get deeper into the realms of history it is always worthwhile to dig into the past for concrete corroborations. The archaeological evidence from the disputed site in Ayodhya helped the judges to a great extent to come to their final decision.

In 1989, the UP state government acquired 55,674 acres of land beyond the Babri Masjid to build a Ram Katha Park. The aim was to 'create an experience of the cultural aspect emerging from the great epic, Ramayana'.[10]

In June 1991 when the land around the Babri Masjid was levelled, there were reports of Hindu religious relics being found below which even included part of an arch. Rakesh Tewari, who was the state director of the archaeology department in those years, had taken an inventory of the unearthed objects and deposited them at the Ram Katha Kunj under the custody of the district commissioner.

The Allahabad High Court, in order to get sufficient archaeological evidence on the issue, enquired 'whether there was any temple/structure which was demolished and the mosque was constructed on the disputed site' as stated on page 1 and further on page 5 of their order dated 5 March 2003. It had given orders to the Archaeological Survey of India (ASI) to excavate at the disputed site where the ground penetrating radar (GPR) survey suggested evidence of anomalies which could be structure, pillars, foundation walls, slab flooring, etc., which could be confirmed by excavation.[11]

Way back in January 2003, a GPR survey was conducted by Tojo Vikas International at the behest of the Allahabad High Court. The report stated that there were 'anomaly alignments' spread across the main platform of the 'disputed structure', the north and south of the sanctum sanctorum stretching right up to the Ram Chabootra area. It suggested the presence of construction at a depth of up to five and a half metres under the rubble.

Based on these initial findings, the task of further investigation was placed under the ASI in March 2003.

I visited the site during those days. Everything was handled with extreme diligence and the utmost care, including the equipment they used, be it the knives, spades, crowbars or the baskets where the findings were placed. All the work staff had newly made identity cards. Labourers who were hired put their thumbprints on the register maintained by the ASI. Those who were literate proudly signed. Most of these workers perceived themselves as involved in a prestigious *sarkari* (government) job and worked with a certain sense of pride.

The survey began on 15 March 2003. The *mazdoor*s sweated in the blazing heat of the summer and mechanically, yet attentively, carried out the instructions of the ASI experts. The scene brought back T.S. Eliot's lines from 'The Waste Land', 'April is the cruellest month, breeding Lilacs out of the dead land, mixing Memory and desire …'

Each trench was supervised by an archaeologist. Specific scientific methods had to be maintained while they were digging. Eager journalists waited patiently for an archaeologist to reach their temporary office with the day's findings. Not many questions were entertained.

Initially, the work started with about fifty labourers, who were mostly locals. They dug up things that had been buried for centuries. Though they came to the site at 8 a.m., the work would begin a couple of hours later due to the formalities and thorough frisking that they had to go through. Repeated reminders were given to them to keep their identity cards safely. Some of them reached an hour earlier to pray to their lord, who sat mutely under a fuchsia-coloured temporary plastic cover. The pilgrims during these months made their visits through the caged corridor, the only passage left for them to visit the temple while the digging carried on.

Inquisitive travellers sometimes tried to flick aside the thick scarlet curtain covering the iron rod partition to block the excavation area. Cops were posted to prevent such acts. Added security from the Central Reserve Police Force (CRPF) was also present at the site.

The lives of the hardworking labourers seemed somewhat paradoxical. They were all on an unknown quest; some of them were uneducated yet involved in a scientific search. Many were humble but burdened with a lofty task. There was confusion, and still, the focus remained. Most were indifferent, yet had to be diligent.

The ASI team dug out the trenches throughout the disputed area, only leaving the patch where the deity was housed untouched, with a safe distance of 10 feet from the makeshift temple, as instructed by the high court. The excavation was conducted in phases.

As reported by me in *Outlook*, 'On 20 April, the Archaeological Survey of India (ASI) came across two graves—the first in trench number F9 and the second stretching from the separation wall of F9 to the adjacent E9 trench towards the south of the makeshift temple. The graves, in fact, have been unearthed in the area where there were hopes of finding the grand Ram Temple that Babar is alleged to have demolished to build the mosque in 1528. The items discovered in the 40 days of digging by the ASI team clearly point to a Muslim habitation as early as [the] 13th to 14th century.'[12]

At this juncture there were several papers and reports by eminent archaeologists and academicians openly casting doubts on whether the excavations could bring forth any credible evidence pointing to the existence of a temple.

The excavations and findings were all documented on camera and video. In five months, the ASI excavated ninety trenches and, within fifteen days of the completion of work, it submitted a report on 22 August 2003.

In early 2020, when I met the ex-ASI director, Rakesh Tewari, in Lucknow, he seemed amused by the initial assumptions made by both academicians and journalists. 'Is anyone contesting the fact that Muslims lived in these locales?' he simply asked.

'I must admit that most writers with left-wing leanings write really well and are largely read. I love reading their papers, but that's where it ends for me,' he explains. And then he asked, possibly in a sarcastic manner, 'Have you read anything from those famous historians after the later findings were excavated?'

In the final report submitted by the ASI on 22 August 2003, it has been mentioned that, 'Now, viewing in totality and taking into account the archaeological evidence of a massive structure just below the disputed structure and evidence of continuity in structural phases from the tenth century onwards up to the construction of the disputed structure along with the yield of stone and decorated bricks as well as mutilated sculpture of divine couple and carved architectural members including foliage patterns, amalaka, *kapotapali* doorjamb with semi-circular pilaster, a broken octagonal shaft of black schist pillar, lotus motif, circular shrine having *pranala* (water chute) in the north, fifty pillar bases in association of the huge structure, are indicative of remains which are distinctive features found associated with the temples of north India.'[13]

In the 2019 Supreme Court judgment, Justice Sudhir Agarwal opined: 'Archaeology provides scientific factual data for reconstructing ancient historical material, culture and understanding.' Archaeology, he stated, 'is a multi-disciplinary scientific subject and requires a team of workers for effective results. Excavation of ancient sites is one of the major works of Archaeologists. As it is a scientific discipline, it uses scientific methods in its working'.

Partially based on the archaeological evidence, the judgment clarifies that 'if a place of worship belonging to a particular religion is demolished, it would remain a place of worship for that faith. If it was proved that a temple on a disputed site was forcibly demolished for the construction of a mosque, the temple would continue to be treated as a temple.'[14]

The 2003 excavations were not the first ones in Ayodhya. They have been carried out at irregular intervals ever since the ASI was established in 1861.

Soon after taking over as the first director-general (DG) of the ASI, Alexander Cunningham surveyed Ayodhya in 1862–63. His primary interest was to identify historical places mentioned in the Buddhist pilgrim records of Hiuen Tsang and Fa Hien, which he also did in the case of what he called Ajudhya. He noted three mounds as places of great antiquity (Mani Parbat, Kuber Parbat and Sugriva Parbat) and identified them respectively as two stupas (domed Buddhist structures)—the first of Ashoka, the second supposedly containing the hair and nails of the Buddha—and the third mound as a monastery. He also recorded oral traditions and places associated with the Ramayana story, among which are mentioned the Janam Asthana or birthplace temple of Ram. What is noteworthy is that Cunningham (1871: 321) wrote, 'There are no high mounds of ruins covered with broken statues and sculptured pillars such as mark the sites of other ancient cities, but only a low irregular mass of rubbish heaps, from which all the bricks have been excavated for the houses of the neighbouring city of Faizabad.'[15] However, Cunningham still left the issue open-ended. 'He referred to several Brahmanical temples but mentioned that they were all of modern construction, perhaps built on the sites of older temples destroyed by Muslims. What is remarkable is that although he referred to the existence of a Janam Asthana temple, it had no connection to the Babri Masjid; he made no mention at all of the latter. In other words, while he recorded several traditions associated with Ram, nowhere did he refer to the Babri Masjid as standing on the spot of a destroyed temple.'[16]

In 1889–1891, German archaeologist Alois Anton Führer conducted another survey. He, in his documents, stated that the Ramayana-era city was destroyed after the death of Brihadbala, and was rebuilt by Vikramaditya. He also wrote that most of the existing Hindu and Jain temples in the city were modern, although they occupied the sites of the ancient temples that had been destroyed by Muslims.

The five Digambara Jain temples in this town were built in 1781 to mark the birthplaces of the five Tirthankaras, who are said to have been born in Ayodhya. A Svetambara Jain temple dedicated to Ajitanatha was built in 1881.

'Based on local folk narratives, Führer wrote that Ayodhya had three Hindu temples at the time of Muslim conquest: Janamasthaan (where Rama was born), Svargadvaram (where Rama was cremated), and Treta-ke-Thakur (where Rama performed a sacrifice). According to Führer, Mir Khan built the Babri mosque at the place of Janmasthanam temple in 1523. He stated that many columns of the old temple were utilised to construct it. These pillars were of black stone, called *kasauti* by the natives.'[17]

Janet Spector, an American archaeologist, noted in her book, *What This Awl Means* (1993), 'It is only natural for an archaeologist to imagine stories about the past.' She describes how the field team often spent its leisure time conceiving possible scenarios about the people who produced the remains found at a site. In the case of

Ayodhya, Janet's theory was reversed; the epics had already triggered the perceptibility of the nation, and every detail unravelled was being tested for its ability to fit into the collective imagination.[18]

Over the decades it became most important for the legal fraternity to decide upon Ram's exact birthplace. For this, the apex court turned the pages of a few important Hindu scriptures. Its judgment mentions scriptures like the Puranas and Valmiki's Ramayana to prove that Ayodhya was Lord Ram's birthplace. *The Skanda Purana, Vaishnava Khanda* and *Ayodhya Mahatmya* mention and describe Ram's Janmasthaan. So did the Ramayana and Tulsidas's *Ramcharitmanas.*

The order stated: 'There is, in other words, no dispute before this Court in regard to the faith and belief of the Hindus that the birth of Lord Ram is ascribed to have taken place at Ayodhya, as described in Valmiki's Ramayana. What is being disputed is whether the disputed site below the central dome of the Babri Masjid is the place of birth of Lord Ram.'[19]

The word 'faith' has been used 213 times in the verdict. The Ramayana is such a vital part of Indian society that no one can escape the stories and shades, people and perceptions, traditions and travels detailed within its 24,000 verses.

However, there are still those who are not convinced by this part of the judgment. Noted historian Dwijendra Narayan Jha, in an interview with The Wire, said, 'There is no evidence to show that Ayodhya was a Hindu pilgrimage centre in ancient times. And it had not emerged as one even as late as the 18th century. Tulsidas, the celebrated author of the *Ramcharitmanas*, does not mention Ayodhya as a pilgrim centre. He suggests that it was not Ayodhya, but Prayag (Allahabad) that was to him the principal place of pilgrimage.'[20]

Once the Supreme Court concluded that the Lord's birthplace was under the central dome of the demolished mosque, there was the matter of the limitation statute. Under the Limitation

Act, 1898, which governs a suit for possession of any immovable property, the period of limitation is a maximum of twelve years. This implies that if no action is taken by the aggrieved party for twelve years, the person cannot claim back a dispossessed property. In the case of Lord Ram's temple and birthplace, the event possibly happened thousands of years ago before the birth of Christ. How could a court of law deal with it in this century?

The Supreme Court felt that the time under the limitation statute began from the date of the dispossession or discontinuance of the use of the property.

According to the claims made by the Nirmohi Akhara, the discontinuance of the use of the Lord Ram Temple happened on 5 January 1950, after the acquisition of the property by the government. It filed the suit on 17 December 1959, which was within twelve years.

On the question of whether the suit filed by the Sunni Waqf Board fell under the limitation act, the court ruled in the board's favour. The reason was that the Muslims argued that they were dispossessed of the place of worship by a deliberate act of the Hindus. This happened in December 1949, when a group of Hindus placed the Ram Lalla idol under the central dome of the mosque and the local administration stopped the *namaz*.

In the next year, the disputed site came under the government's management. This dispossession was within twelve years, as the Sunni Board filed its specific suit in 1961.

Such arguments related to possession and dispossession came under the ambit of Article 142, which empowers the Supreme Court to 'pass such decree or make such order as is necessary for doing complete justice in any cause or matter pending before it, and any decree so passed, or orders so made shall be enforceable throughout the territory of India'.

This article encompasses a suit for possession of immovable property. By implication, it can deal with cases in which the property owner is dispossessed of the land. And also, cases where the owner discontinues the possession for some reason. Of course, there needs to be evidence of prior possession by the plaintiff as well as the dispossession or the discontinuance of possession while the plaintiff was in possession. The period of limitation of twelve years begins from the date of dispossession or discontinuance.

The other aspect of interest in the Ram Janmabhoomi case was the presence of God as a juristic person, but as the apex court stated, 'At the heart of the legal dispute in the present batch of appeals is the question whether the first and second plaintiffs in Suit No. 5—Bhagwan Sri Ram Virajman and Asthan Sri Ram Janam Bhumi, Ayodhya—possess distinct legal personalities.' Are Hindu idols or deities legal persons?

A legal person, whether living or non-living, animate or inanimate, is an entity that holds certain rights and duties under the laws of the land. Such an entity shall be able to enforce legal relationships with similar persons.

The history of having a god in the form of a deity or idol as a juristic person in Indian courts dates back to the eighteenth century. During this period, there were serious and several challenges to the Hindu practice of donating and dedicating properties to temples and idols. English judges during colonial rule adopted the doctrine that Hindu idols possessed legal personality. This was because they had to apply Hindu law to religious endowments.

In 1919, a Hindu bequeathed his lands to the idol (or *thakur*) of Shri Radhakrishnaji. A dispute ensued between the descendants of the donor and the managers/*shebait*s of the idol. The former alleged that the latter mismanaged the place of worship and denied access to the public. The donor's family wanted the property to be declared as a 'public temple'. The scope of the original will was in question. A legal precedent that was set in this case was that after he had donated his lands and properties, the donor lost claims and rights to his donations and endowments. Henceforth, the legal rights rested with the idol and the real beneficiaries of the act were the devotees and worshippers. In such a case, the 'proper maintenance' is seen as how to 'enable the worshippers to achieve the spiritual benefit'.[21]

In the *Vidya Varuthi Tirtha vs Baluswami Ayyer* (1921) case, the court held that the deity, in Hindu Law, has been given the status of a legal or juristic person and is vested with the capacity of receiving gifts and holding property. To conclude, it can be said that gods are recognized as persons only for lawful purposes and thus named as 'Legal/Juristic Person'. But a deity is considered so only after its public consecration. Such deities enjoy property rights, are liable to pay taxes, can fight legally and can also be sued. However, they do not have any fundamental rights.[22]

In the case of *Yogendra Nath Naskar vs Commissioner of Income Tax, Calcutta*, by deciding that a Hindu idol (or deity) fell within the definition of an individual under Section 3 of the Income Tax Act 1922, Justice Ramaswami, on behalf of a three-judge bench of this court, held: 'The correct legal position is that the idol as representing and embodying the spiritual purpose of the donor is the juristic person recognised by law and in this juristic person the dedicated property vests.'[23]

He added: 'Neither God nor any supernatural being could be a person in law. But so far as the deity stands as the representative and symbol of the particular purpose, which is indicated by the donor, it can figure as a legal person.'

Hence, through the above arguments, in 2019 the Supreme Court established the legal rights and personality of an idol. It then decided whether Bhagwan Sri Ram Virajman, the embodiment of Lord Ram, could be considered as the owner of the disputed property in Ayodhya.

First, the court said that the Hindus had faith and belief in Lord Ram and the idol. This was a personal matter, and 'it is not for this Court to scrutinise the strength of their (Hindus') convictions or the rationality of their beliefs beyond a prima facie examination to ascertain whether such beliefs are held in good faith'.[24]

Second, the court decided that there was both oral and documentary evidence to establish that there was 'a long practice of Hindu worship' at the disputed site. It added that 'Devotees converged upon the area from across the country to celebrate Ram Navami, the birthday of Lord Ram, for centuries. Among them were the Nirmohis and Nihangs.'[25]

The Supreme Court judgment expounded, on such a legal personality as determined by legal precedents, the idol per se is not important. Even an abstract idea can be conferred with a legal personality, the same as a specific idol. The judgment clarified that 'In the case of Hindu idols, legal personality is not conferred on the idol simpliciter but on the underlying pious purpose of the continued worship of the deity as incarnated in the idol. Where the legal personality is conferred on the purpose of a deity's continued worship, moving or destroying the idol does not affect its legal personality. The legal personality vests in the purpose of continued worship of the idol as recognised by the Court. It is for the protection of the continued worship that the law recognises this purpose and seeks to protect it by the conferral of juristic personality.'[26]

In the months preceding the Supreme Court's final order, there were several times when the court master hailed, 'Ram Lalla Virajman!' At those moments, the omnipresent God was represented by his sakha, that is, his closest friend down on earth, Triloki Nath Pandey.

This unique association reminded me of other divine–human friendships—Moses had Rameses, Jesus had Lazarus, Krishna had Sudama, Sun had Phoenix, Horus had Sobek, et al.

There are other lists of enthralling, apocryphal and, most often, inspiring friendships to be found in the world of fiction. For every Daenerys, there is a Jorah; every Frodo Baggins has a Sam; Calvin cannot chase his dreams without Hobbes; Captain Kirk requires Mr Spock; Sherlock Holmes feels lost without John Watson.

Together, these friends break hurdles that come in the way of quests. Loyalty, tenacity and devotion are the key characteristics between these friends.

Almost in the same way, when Lord Ram could not defend himself as it was impossible for him to make an appearance in an earthly court, a sakha came forward to help! This friend decided to argue on behalf of the lord and presented all the necessary evidence in the court.

Triloki Nath seemed to be a perfect choice. For around a decade, he played the part with grit and guts. Finally, on 9 November 2019, he reclaimed and won back Ram's lost paradise, Ayodhya.

This method of the gods and mortals helping each other to gain justice has been a part of Hindu mythology long before our legal system came up with this provision. In one such myth, God himself appeared as a witness to help out his devotee. Let us, for the moment, travel to the famous Sakshi Gopal Temple located 20 km from Puri, Odisha. Gopal is another name for Lord Krishna. It is believed that a devotee must visit this temple after completing the pilgrimage at the famous Puri Jagannath Temple.

The story behind the Sakshi Gopal Temple revolves around a young man who desperately approached Gopal for help. Once upon a time, the local village headman was taken ill, and nobody cared to look after him save this young man. The headman recovered under his care. And as a token of gratitude, he promised to marry his daughter to the youngster who had helped him recuperate.

Time passed, and the chief showed no signs of keeping his promise. When reminded of it, he challenged the young man to produce a witness to validate his demand. No human turned up, and finally, it was Lord Gopal who, taken in by the youth's devotion and honesty, volunteered to become the witness.

The lord told the young man that he would follow him to the headman's house, but the youth should not turn around. While crossing a mound of sand, the young fellow could not hear the God's footsteps and looked back. At that moment, Gopal turned into a stone statue. It is believed that a temple was built on this spot. 'Sakshi Gopal' means 'Witness Gopal'.

In her essay in the book *Religious Rights*, Ratna Kapur writes, 'Although the concept of idols as Juristic persons originally developed in Roman law, over the years, it has been developed by Indian Courts as one based on the religious customs of the Hindus themselves.'[27]

In 1989, when the title case moved out of the Faizabad civil court to the Allahabad High Court, the deity, Bhagwan Sri Ram Virajman, became a litigant. A retired judge of the Allahabad High Court Deoki Nandan Agarwal filed a lawsuit (Suit No. 5) on the Lord's behalf.

Deoki Nandan belonged to a Vaishnav family that was committed to Lord Ram. He had spent his childhood in Faizabad, the twin and adjoining city of Ayodhya. Later, he served as a senior advocate and then as a judge in the Allahabad High Court. After retiring from this prestigious post, in 1983, he went back to Faizabad to gather relevant documents and revenue records that would help him prove that the 'disputed land' was Ram's birthplace. On 1 July 1989, he filed a writ petition at the Lucknow bench of the Allahabad High Court seeking for an appointment in the role of Ram Lalla's sakha. At that time, Deoki Nandan was the working president of the VHP, an affiliate of the RSS that spearheaded the movement to construct a Ram Temple in Ayodhya. When Deoki Nandan, Lord Ram's sakha, died in April 2002, his position was taken by Thakur Prasad Verma, a history professor at the Banaras Hindu University (BHU). Later in 2008, Verma requested to be relieved from the role of Ram's sakha as he felt he could not carry on the responsibility since he was not keeping too well. Two years later, Triloki Nath Pandey, another senior VHP leader, was entrusted with the task, and he most willingly and gladly took up the role of Ram's closest friend in the court. He explained that since Ram Lalla was a minor and a deity he needed his 'sakhas' to represent him in the court.

Triloki Nath preferred to call Ayodhya his home and not Buxar, where his wife lives with the rest of the family. 'I am a married man, but I am a VHP leader first. My priority is towards spreading Hindutva, and I want to remain true to my vows and job.'

I had met him a few days after the Supreme Court verdict was announced. After spending ten days in Delhi to attend the court and visit lawyers and other party people, he was back in Ayodhya. He was seated at his favourite spot, a place at the end of a long corridor at the VHP office in Karsevakpuram, where he also met visitors.

Dressed in an off-white flannel kurta-pyjama and woollen jacket, he looked stern, observant and purposeful. As I awaited my turn, two VHP members discussed functions to be organized over the next few days, including the felicitation of some of the Supreme Court judges.

From planning functions at Karsevakpuram, Triloki Nath's attention drifted to the latest *Panchjanya* (24 November 2019)—a Hindi weekly magazine published by the RSS. Deendayal Upadhyaya, who was an RSS *pracharak* (worker), launched it in 1948 in Lucknow. The latest cover had a beaming picture of Uttar Pradesh Chief Minister Yogi Adityanath.

The headline screamed, '*Ab Mili Hai Ayodhya ko Pehchan* (Finally, Ayodhya Has Been Recognized)!' I picked up a copy. The lead story was titled '*Mandir Wahin Banega* (Temple Will Be Built There)', and there was another story on how the Gorakhspeeth, from where Adityanath traces his roots, played a role in the efforts to construct the temple.

An opinion piece, '*Faisle Par Rai* (Opinion on the Verdict)' had a list of quotes by important people, including one from Prime Minister Narendra Modi. He stated, 'The Apex Court has given its verdict on Ayodhya, and this should not be interpreted as a win or loss for anyone. Be it *Rambhakts* (followers of Ram) or *Rahimbhakts* (followers of Rahim), at this hour, the feelings of *Bharat Bhakti* (love for India) should rule. My appeal to the people of this country is that they should maintain peace and brotherhood.'

Triloki Nath offered me lemon tea with a plate of bhujiya (a snack made of gram flour). A framed photograph of Ashok Singhal and a framed picture with 'Aum' written on it adorned the wall adjacent to where Triloki Nath was seated. A little behind his chair was a large table. On top of that stood a wooden model of the Ram Mandir. On one of the walls at the end of the wide corridor was a wooden rack with pictures and idols of gods and goddesses. The corridor had a wide opening on the entrance side, which was covered with iron grills. Heavy tarpaulin sheets were used in place of curtains to keep away the winter cold.

'You seem to be looking at my mandir?' he asked and immediately added, 'But my favourite goddess is not there. She is none other than Bharat Mata. She is a mother to even Ram and Krishna, and she is a mother to everyone living in this country. As a Bengali, you would surely know that the origins of Bharat Mata can be traced back to a play by a Bengali nationalist, Kiran Chandra Bandyopadhyay, which was first performed in 1873.'

Triloki Nath expressed joy over the verdict, '*Hriday mein hillole aa gaye* (Ripples of happiness filled my heart).' I asked him how it felt to be a close friend of the lord. 'It may sound strange, but I dreamt of the lord almost every night during the last decade when I represented him in the court and stood on his behalf. He has blessed me amply, and even the entire nation has his blessings.'

Triloki Nath was born in a Vaiṣhnav family in Buxar. The family members were ardent followers of Ram. The only festival, he recollected, that he enjoyed as a child was Ram Navami. '*Hamare yahan yeh tyohaar bade dhoom dhaam se manaya jata tha* (This festival was celebrated with great pomp at our place),' he said nostalgically.

He added that he would also eagerly wait every year to watch the Ramlila. This enactment would take place in a school ground close to his house. This fondness for Ram and his love for religion prompted him to join the RSS in Baliya district in 1964. From then on his main task was: '*Logon mein Hindu gaurav sthapith karna* (To reinstate the pride of being a Hindu among the people).'

Triloki Nath refused to talk about his education. But it is a known fact that he completed his graduation in 1978. 'What worth do these certificates carry? I don't even have my birth certificate. All these papers tie one down and make us slaves of some industry.' He added, '*Seva ke liye koi certificate ki darkar nahi hota hai* (You do not need any certificate to do social work).'

In 1977, when Emergency was imposed in the country, Triloki Nath was sent behind bars as he was an active RSS worker. A couple of years after his release, from 1981 onwards, he worked as the head of the Sanskrit Raksha Yojna (Sanskrit Defence Scheme). Dutifully, he promoted the ancient Hindu language in schools and within the RSS. A year later, he became a member of the VHP. His excitement that day was palpable as he discussed the Ram Janmabhoomi *andolan*.

'It was in 1984 that this movement started. *Hum sab ne yeh soch liya tha ki ghulami ki kalank ko hatakar hum Ramji ke liye mandir nirman karenge* (We decided to bring an end to the tarnished structure that symbolized slavery and build a temple for Ram).' He spoke about how Kameshwar Chaupal laid the foundation stone on 9 November 1989. He called it a '*rochak ghatana*' (interesting incident) as the task was carried out despite the government's diktat. 'Saints from all over and around 25,000 members from Bajrang Dal ensured we would succeed in our mission.'

Within the court premises, Triloki Nath was involved in the Ram Janmabhoomi case as a *pahrokar* (pleader) since 1994. He said, 'That gave me good experience of the proceedings, so I was prepared and could take up the task as Ram Lalla's sakha when the charge was conferred upon me on 8 February 2008.'

It took close to eleven years before Triloki Nath was able to restore the lord's property—it was clear after the Supreme Court's judgment that the Ram Temple was a given.

On 1 March 2020, I heard that Triloki Nath had a heart attack. He was admitted to the All-India Institute of Medical Sciences, New Delhi. I called to find out how he was faring. Someone informed me that he was in the ICU. After a week, I called again. This time, a familiar voice said, '*Jai Shri Ram.*' Ram's sakha was out of danger and seemed to be recovering well. We chatted for a bit; I could sense the same affection and enthusiasm even over the long-distance call. 'Glad to know you are feeling better,' I said. 'If I have helped Ram Lalla, he ought to help me,' he replied confidently. A year and a half later, on 24 September 2021, Triloki Nath breathed his last.

The day-to-day hearings that began on 6 August 2019 ended on 16 October 2019.The final verdict was pronounced at 11.02 a.m. inside Court 1 of the Supreme Court, which is the Chief Justice's court room. The hearing had continued for a period of forty days at a stretch, the second-longest in the Supreme Court's history. In this period, everything appeared as usual—the wooden chairs, the judge's highchair and table, shelves laden with books, the bright lamps fixed on the ceiling and, of course, the many portraits of ex-Chief Justices of India hung on the wooden-panelled walls, mutely watching the proceedings. But there was one difference that needs a mention—even within the courtroom, the nation appeared divided. One of the lawyers, who had attended a few of the hearings, said, 'It was a strange experience for many of us. This was the first time I noticed that within the courtroom the lawyers stood with the side they represented and supported.'

Besides the commoners and sages crowding outside Court 1, there was a bevy of camerapersons. Reporters made a beeline to take bites. The judgment was sure to make global headlines.

The next day's newspaper headlines revealed their ideological leanings. 'In the name of Ram, the site is now Hindu Sthan'; 'Temple gets site, mosque a plot'; 'Temple set in stone'. A few dailies even used interesting puns, 'Ram Mandir within site'; 'Lord gets his land; Muslims a fragile piece'. Most of the Hindi dailies welcomed the verdict openheartedly. They celebrated the decision of the Supreme Court without any hesitation and came up with headlines like, '*Ayodhya Ram ki (*Ayodhya is Ram's abode)'; '*Ramlalla hi virajman* (Ramlalla will be seated)'; '*Asli malik Ram Lalla. Mandir yahin banega* (The real owner is Ram Lalla; the mandir will be built here only)'; and '*Shri Ram*'.

Across the country, there was peace. Or was it a lull?

Prime Minister Narendra Modi's appeal for harmony made its way to every nook. Addressing the nation in his monthly *Mann ki Baat* (Inner Thoughts) programme, that is aired on the state-run All India Radio and Doordarshan, he requested the people to maintain peace after the verdict. He referred to the earlier high court's decision, which was accepted by the country. He thanked the people for their maturity and asked them to uphold self-control.

In Ayodhya, after the order, life carried on at its usual pace—devotees continued to visit the temples and bhajans filled the air. There were subtle and symbolic celebrations in some places though. The marble statue of Valmiki, which earlier lay dust-laden in a discreet corner of the government sales outlet en route Hanumangarhi, was newly polished and adorned with a saffron tilak and fresh marigold garland. Over his shoulders sat a brand-new crisp saffron stole with 'Jai Sri Ram' printed all over.

At one of the important traffic crossings, the TV *Ramayana*, was aired. Hindus congratulated each other. A handful of Muslims joined in the salutations, though most of them preferred to stay indoors. For them, Babri Masjid was lost forever.

On 9 November 2019, Abdul Ansari, a ninety-year-old Muslim who lives in Gadiwan Tola, a Muslim locality in Ayodhya, was extremely tense. He is a very pious man—though he can barely walk, he never fails to offer his daily prayers. After his prayers that morning, the nonagenarian sat with his son, Munna. 'I asked my brother to run the stationery store we own as I had to stay back to tell my father what was going on, on the TV. You see, he is a little short of hearing,' explained his son, Munna, to me.

The father stared hard at the screen till the verdict was pronounced and then silently crawled back to his bed. No prayers or dinner that day, only sleep. No one ever asked him why he never spoke about the verdict. In fact, he never spoke unless necessary since that morning.

The birth anniversary of the Prophet a few days later turned out totally uneventful. Within a few hours after the verdict, several events that had been planned for Milad-un-Nabi were cancelled. As a curfew was declared, it was impossible to have a procession, which was a usual event. A day before the Supreme Court decision, strings of lights were hung in the Chowk area. All of them were silently removed the following day.

The winners took it all; the losers stood small.

2
Splintered Peace

'I consider myself a follower of Islam, Christianity, Zoroastrianism and every other religion because I am a true Hindu. All religions are equal and they are founded on the same faith.'

—MAHATMA GANDHI[1]

'Why are you here? What do you want? Are you from the media? You guys only come to us to take sound bites! What do we gain from it? It doesn't change anything for us,' Basheer Ahmed, a *paduka* (wooden clog) maker who looked like he was well into his sixties, sharply shouted out. His anger took me by complete surprise. I let his anger dissipate as he continued to work with his mechanical saw in a large basement room in Babu Bazaar, Ayodhya.

The room was dark and dingy. The iron frames and railings were rusted and dampness hung heavy from the low ceiling. Thick wooden scraps were spread all over the floor.

In between his work, he observed me intently while I stood around quietly watching him. He took his time before he asked somewhat gently, 'Do you want to go up and sit comfortably at my son's store just across the road?' I nodded in approval as I moved quickly towards the dark stairway, hoping he would not change his mind again.

We clambered up, walked across the street and sat on a rickety wooden bench in front of a small store. Basheer ordered two cups of milky and syrupy tea and finally flashed a smile, exposing his tobacco-stained teeth that only added to his unkempt appearance. He noisily slurped the tea, enjoying each sip, kept the cup away and then suddenly rolled up his pyjama to show me a dreadful wound draped in a dirty bandage.

'You see this? It is a broken bone. I have no money to get it plastered, but who cares?' I am told that Basheer received the injuries just a week ago, on his way to the mosque. On that dawn, he was standing in a queue outside a public washroom en route to the mosque. He shares more details, 'At that early hour, at dawn, there was a man with his face covered who came up to me and suddenly started beating me up. I fell down. Some known people picked me up and dropped me home, on their bike. My family members ran to register an FIR but that was not an easy task.' He added, 'Those men then threatened to burn down our house and kill us. They even told us that they would uproot us Muslims from here. They even beat my son Asif. That man who beat me up, an upper-caste Hindu, has several cases registered against him but despite all such charges, he moves around freely.'

This altercation happened within a couple of days after the apex court's order on Ram Janmabhoomi. Basheer's twenty-four-year-old son, Asif Mohammed, also present at the shop, listened on to his father's story. It was evident from his nonchalant stance that he had heard it many times before. He preferred to remain quiet and concentrate on his work instead.

In his store, Asif sells all items required for a Hindu puja, which includes prayer beads, yellow-and-red strings, vermillion, glass bangles, incense sticks and so on. There are some cosmetics too, like lipsticks and kohl sticks with fancy but misspelt brand names painted on the cases. All the wares are neatly spread on the plastic tabletop. Bordering these on the right are notebooks, ball-point pens and cellphone cases with 'Jai Shri Ram' printed on most.

After completing his Class VIII from a local school, Asif gave up on studying further as he felt it was more important to help his father, who had lately found it challenging to work for long hours as he would earlier. The son was rather well dressed and stood out in contrast to his father, both in his clothing and demeanour—that day, he donned a pair of yellow earphones, and as I complimented him on his style, he smiled and confessed that he loved Bollywood stars, Salman Khan in particular. His sense of clothing clearly revealed his efforts in emulating his favourite star—a black oversized T-shirt and matching drainpipe trousers, glitzy copper streaks running through his thick black crop, and it was difficult not to notice the big black earstud in his left ear!

Asif would have left Ayodhya a long time ago. But with ageing parents and hungry mouths to feed at home, he was 'stuck here, leaving everything to destiny'. The father agreed. 'We have no other option; we cannot do much, we dare not. Things were hugely different for us till the early eighties.' He proudly held up a wooden clog from an adjacent shelf. 'You see this? I used to be respected because of this footwear. These are used by most sadhus and *mahant*s, and also given as offerings in most temples here. Despite my skilled craftsmanship, like the others from my community, I have been treated like a slave ever since the VHP entered our town twenty years ago, in the late eighties.'

Basheer has been chiselling out clogs for forty-five years. These days, age has slowed him down. He earns a rupee per clog, which makes his monthly earning around Rs 1,000 only. His hands are a testimony to his hard work, cracked with years of nailing, cutting and wood-sawing.

These padukas or khadaus are made of scrap wood from the trees of honey (*mahua*), mango or black plum (*jamun*), depending on the availability. The wood is then cut into different sizes and carved to give it the right shape. A wooden peg is fixed at the front portion of the clog so that the big and index toes can slip comfortably on either side of it.

According to Hindu traditions, both animal skin and leather are taboo for any religious activities. Hence, the Hindus either walk barefoot or wear wooden padukas during rituals or inside holy premises. There is also a ritual to offer clogs in temples, especially those devoted to Lord Ram. In Ayodhya, these wooden clogs have a special status since Ram's younger brother, Bharat, ruled the kingdom by symbolically placing the lord's padukas on the throne when Ram was sent to exile for fourteen years.

I said thanks to Basheer and Asif, and walked down the street. About 500 metres away, there are small tailoring shacks where men were seated at their sewing machines, busy stitching tiny frocks cut out of yards of brightly coloured Chinese silk fabric. These pretty dresses are then sent to different localities where women add finishing touches to them with gold laces, fancy buttons and strings. Devotees buy these bright and blingy skirts to dress up the idols in their homes and even offer them in the temples.

A few kilometres further down the street is Tehri Bazaar, a Muslim locality. Asif had directed me to this area earlier in the day. Reaching the houses in this slum, which are glued to one another, needs special skills—one has to jump across a broad open drain, walk on dusty mud paths and continuously whisk away mosquitoes and flies. A few houses have boards prominently placed that declare that they were built under the Pradhan Mantri Awas Yojna—the central government's welfare scheme that took off on 25 June 2015, intending to provide pucca houses to eligible beneficiaries by October 2022.

There is a strange sanctity amidst the squalor. Children play in the crummy by-lanes; men happily stand in small groups, exchanging notes and laughing; and the women all appear to be indoors.

My eyes caught a group of women peering from inside one of the houses as they briefly held up their dupattas to take a look at me. I walked up to the door and brazenly peeped inside—a dozen women were sitting and stringing marigold flowers. It is Parveen's house, I learnt. She was the oldest in her family. The rest of the people in her house were family members and neighbours. They were initially cagey in their response. They discussed something among themselves in hushed tones, after which Parveen offered me a seat.

When they asked my name, I decided to make up a Christian one, and all at once, they appeared absolutely comfortable. Rabia, a young girl, placed a plate of dalmoth (savoury mixture) along with two pieces of mithai and a water bottle beside my chair, and even gave me a tight warm hug. The women seemed happy as they sat in a circle, stringing together the yellow–orange marigolds, adding bright glazy paper leaves at regular gaps. This family has been in this business for generations, I was told. Florists from nearby nurseries drop flowers by the kilos, depending on the need of the day.

These garlands of various lengths are mainly sold outside the Ram Temple and Hanumangarhi. Business is profitable, especially on Tuesdays when Hindu worshippers visit Hanumangarhi, during the wedding season, and even during the three annual melas (fairs) held in Ayodhya—the Ram Navami fair held on the Lord's birthday in April, the Shravan Jhula fair in July–August and Kartik Purnima in November.

These Muslims try and stay happy among themselves despite their challenging lives and paltry incomes. Since the late 1980s, the Muslims remain huddled together in a few slums. Most men from this vicinity work on daily wages at the nearby brick kilns or construction sites. A few have even purchased rickshaws on bank loans and make money by pulling them in the town's busy parts. It is visibly a very close-knit community. 'We deliberately stick to each other since 1990, when for the first time our space was infiltrated by thousands of karsevaks. These men who are supposed to be Rambhakts loudly proclaimed their hatred towards us Muslims. In those years, we would be petrified at their very presence,' explained one of the women. Parveen told me that there were fourteen Muslim families in the locality—three Qureshis and nine Ansaris, besides a couple belonging to other castes.

Most Muslims in Ayodhya are either Qureshis or Ansaris.

A Tata Institute of Social Sciences (TISS) working research paper by Khusheed Akbar states that the Ansaris and Momins are from the *julaha* weaving community, and are mainly spread across Bihar, Uttar Pradesh and other parts of India. Julahas are one of the largest occupational *biradari*s (communities) among the Muslims.

The julahas claim to be the descendants of Ayub Ansari, a companion of Prophet Muhammad. Some trace their origin to the Ansar tribes of Arabia. Scholars contend that these weavers converted to Islam; they were among the first ones to do so. Through modern education and other means, Ansaris improved their status over generations.

Qureshis slaughter animals as a profession. They are known by different titles such as Kasai, Chikwa, Bakarkasab and Badekasab. Some believe that they are the descendants of the Arab tribal king,

Qassa, who settled in different parts of India, along with other kings and their soldiers. Others admit that they are converted Hindus.

There is a theory that the Qureshis hailed from a Hindu caste, Khatik, which is engaged in dealing with meat, hides and animal skins. Field observations indicate that they are well-off due to their links with lucrative businesses. But the educational status is low among them.[2]

However, the presence of Muslims in Ayodhya can be established from more than a thousand years ago. It was ruled by Muslim sultanates in the twelfth century. In the pre-Islamic days, the town was believed to be the burial site of Prophet Shis (Seth) and Islamic missionary Hazrat Nuh. In fact, Ayodhya was considered by the Muslims to be 'Khurd Mecca (Little Mecca)' because it was the burial site for a large number of holy apostles and religious leaders from the community.

As I sat among the women of Tehri Bazaar and watched them laugh, talk and go about their business, a man in a black cloak walked in. He looked and sounded authoritative. Noticing me, he said, 'I forgot to introduce myself. I am Advocate Mohammed Ansari.' A typical Indian quirk of prefixing the profession to the name! He claimed he was a fan of Emperor Aurangzeb, the sixth Mughal ruler. He justified his love for the emperor. 'He lived like a true Muslim. He despised the spendthrift and self-indulgent rulers, which is why he even imprisoned his father, Shah Jahan. He wanted to propagate the spread of Islam and, in the process, he constructed several mosques.'

Advocate Ansari dodged questions about the mosques that were built after pulling down temples during the reign of Aurangzeb. He promptly changed the topic when I brought this up and instead complained that he could not settle in Pakistan after the 1947 Partition because the family was not wealthy enough. 'My family did not have the money to shift. Besides, at that time, we felt we would be treated well here. Today, I blame the Sanghis for having embittered us. The rift between the Hindus and Muslims in Ayodhya has been created mainly by them.'

His scorn included both Hindus and the moneyed Muslims. In Ayodhya, the latter has even grabbed vast areas of the available Waqf properties. Finally, he ended with a prophecy. 'But wait and watch, in a century or two, there will be a Muslim rule yet again, and this cruelty will be avenged.'

Like Advocate Ansari, there are numerous Muslims whose hearts and minds still remain divided between India and Pakistan. Nothing epitomizes this internal division more than the gentleman's game of cricket. It is not a rare sight in an Indian city, town or village, to see Muslims celebrate Pakistan's victory over India.

When Pakistan wins, the loud cheers from the Muslims reverberate through colonies where they are in sizeable numbers. As a couple of examples, we have Mohammad Ali Street in south Mumbai and Park Circus in central Kolkata.

Such sentiments of Muslims being the 'other' in their own country, meaning Pakistani, are even fanned by Hindu politicians, leaders and senior officials, who time and again ask the Indian Muslims to 'pack their bags and go to Pakistan'. On 20 December 2019, Akhilesh Narayan Singh, a senior police officer from Meerut, a town in western Uttar Pradesh, allegedly shouted at a group of Muslims who were protesting against the amended Citizenship Act asking them to 'go to Pakistan'.[3]

'Veteran actors Naseeruddin Shah and Aamir Khan have been called "traitors" by senior leader of Rashtriya Swyamsevak Sangh (RSS) Indresh Kumar. "They may be good actors but they don't deserve respect as they are traitors. They are like Mir Jafar and

Jaichand."'[4] Jafar was the Bengal army commander under Nawab Siraj ud-Daulah but during the Battle of Plassey, he betrayed the nawab and helped the British. In return, he was amply rewarded and made the nawab in 1757 after the victory of the British. Jaichand, who is still disregarded for treason, had joined the raider Muhammad Ghori when the latter wanted to attack the Rajput king, Prithviraj Chauhan, in the Second Battle of Tarain (1192).

In 2010, Shiv Sena supremo late Bal Thackeray labelled Shah Rukh Khan, the famous Bollywood star, as a traitor. The actor's fault was that he wanted Pakistani players to be allowed to play in Indian Premier League (IPL) matches. 'On a day when Bal Thackeray labelled him a "traitor", Shah Rukh Khan on Saturday stuck to his comments on Pakistani players in IPL saying there was nothing "anti-national" and ruled out meeting the Shiv Sena supremo on his own to sort out the controversy.'[5]

In 2015, Yogi Adityanath, then a member of Parliament (MP) from Gorakhpur (current chief minister of Uttar Pradesh), slammed Shah Rukh Khan and compared the celebrity with the mastermind behind the 2008 Mumbai attacks, the Jama'at-ud-Da'wah (JuD) chief, Hafiz Saeed. 'I am saying these people are speaking in a terrorist's language. I think there is no difference between the language of Shah Rukh Khan and Hafiz Saeed,' he said.[6]

Immediately taking advantage of the situation, the JuD head posted a flurry of tweets, inviting the actor to make Pakistan his new home. SRK's folly was that he had joined a protest by the intelligentsia, which urged people to return official awards to make a point against the growing communal intolerance within the country.

This feeling of otherness even made its way into the school syllabi. Most students are not aware of leaders like Maulana Abul Kalam Azad, who was an erudite scholar and senior leader of the Indian National Congress during the Indian independence movement. The youngsters have no clue about the Urdu poet and Indian freedom fighter Maulana Hasrat Mohani who coined the oft-used phrase, '*Inqalab Zindabad*' in 1921, or even the poet Muhammad Iqbal who wrote '*Saare jahaan se achha*', a song invariably played to celebrate India's glory.

On 7 July 2020, the central human resources department (HRD) ministry made significant deletions from the syllabus for secondary and senior secondary schools. These included chapters related to the concepts and values that were important in understanding the character and goals of modern India's social, cultural and political life.

Reacting to these omissions, Prof. Jagmohan Singh, chairperson, All India Forum for Right to Education, a non-governmental organization, clearly stated that, 'The deletions in the syllabus are aimed at clearing the ground for advocating the Hindutva concept of the Hindu Rashtra for which the present regime is aggressively working.'

One can say that the policy of 'Divide and Rule' that the British started has survived through more than seven decades of India's independence. Sadly, we forget that India is appreciated globally because of its secular culture.

Al-Biruni (after 1050), who translated Sanskrit classics into Arabic, wrote in his monumental *Kitab fi tahqiq ma li'l-Hind* that there were many barriers that separated the Hindus from Muslims, but they were based on either political reasons or linguistic differences. Without an iota of doubt, his statement stands true even in the twenty-first century.

Salman Khurshid wrote in his book, *Visible Muslims, Invisible Citizens*, that the 'sad thing is that people are still looking for political gains from unfortunate events by distorting truth and thus discouraging any honest appraisal of historical facts. Let me, therefore, say for the record that the use of violence for political reasons is deplorable—it is no less than a hate crime. It is not that the identity and ethnicity of the victim is in itself determinative, except to the extent of underscoring the motive. All the violence is reprehensible and must not be condoned or given an alibi.'[7]

How does one convey these thoughts to the likes of Advocate Ansari, who still cannot forgive the Hindus and repeatedly says, 'The trauma the Hindus put us through in 1992 still haunts me. Our houses were set ablaze by a crowd of fanatic karsevaks in the night.'

Ansari's eyes turned red as he remembered the night when he realized that a Hindu could no more be his friend. He narrated how his Hindu neighbours, who were childhood friends, provided kerosene, oil and wood to set the Muslim houses in the area on fire. His tears are those of hurt and resentment for the deception. 'I never dared to question them. To date, I have not. We are a small number in Ayodhya. There is no way we can fight them.' Since then, he maintained minimum formalities with his Hindu associates in town. He feels comforted by the fact that several families in Ayodhya had sent off the women and children to other places before the carnage had taken place that year. There are many Muslims in Ayodhya who are still as pained as him.

Nafreen's story is heartrending. About 500 metres from Babri Masjid, the thirty-five-year-old was immolated by karsevaks. Sayyad Muhammad Asif remembers the tragedy of his *bhabhi* (cousin's wife). 'She was ill, bedridden and could not be shifted to a safer place. The frenzied Hindu crusaders saw her helplessly lying on the bed. Despite that, they set her house on fire and burnt her alive.'[8] Asif felt that it was fortunate he had at least sent the other women and children of the family to a relative's house in an adjacent district on 1 December 1992.

Asif remembered sadly, 'We knew there was going to be barbarism in the coming days. We quietly stood and watched the savages screaming "*Jai Shri Ram*", and burning the pages of the Holy Quran. They defaced several *mazars* (graves) and damaged many mosques.' On 6 December 1992, when the Muslims gathered for the morning namaz, the imam prayed for their safety. Asif recollected, 'The local religious heads that morning were not concerned about the mosques and graveyards, but our lives.'

Asif's house was looted and burnt. This incident happened around 11 a.m. on 6 December 1992. He narrated it with tears in his eyes, 'My brother ran away before the mob reached our house. He stood behind the house and quietly watched it reduce to ashes. It took us six long years to rebuild the house and make it liveable.'

Asif shares more details, 'After about ten days we were given some compensation, amounts varying from Rs 4,000 to Rs 20,000, from what the government called the interim relief fund. Besides this initial monetary help there was no more support from the government. The administration also asked us to lodge FIRs, which we did against all those "unknown people".' He continued with his laments, 'In those years there were no CCTVs, and it was next to impossible to trace the ones who had caused us so much of damage and pain.' He further added, 'Even today, we have no one to protect us. Our so-called Muslim leaders made this conflict into a money-making business. Most have self-indulgent interests, and they will always be safe in their positions, be it as an advocate or politician. The only weapon we have with us is silence.'

Asif suddenly enquired, 'Can you tell how are we connected to Babur? I still haven't understood.' This question was on top of his mind because, in those days, the Hindu mob called out slogans that spelt out the intention of the crusaders. One of the slogans stated, '*Hum aaye hain Babur ko barbaad karne, aaj unke santano par badla lenge* (We have come to destroy Babur, today we shall take revenge on his children).' Like him, most Muslims in Ayodhya are left wondering how they are related to Emperor Babur, as assumed by the Hindu fanatics.

In their paper, 'Ayodhya, Archaeology and Identity', Reinhard Bernbeck and Susan Pollock wrote,[9] 'The 1992 destruction of the mosque becomes a direct response to a perceived wrong of 500 years ago; bringing the past very near to the present helps to legitimate revenge for past injuries. Ironically, Muslims living in India today are in many cases not even the descendants of the Mughal invaders of the Middle Ages but rather members of low Hindu castes who have converted to Islam.'

According to a report published by the Human Rights Watch,[10] 'Although the Uttar Pradesh government and the national government of India had an adequate warning about the intentions of the *karsevaks*, they did not attempt to prevent the destruction of the Babur Mosque at Ayodhya. As the mosque was being destroyed, local police from Ayodhya as well as the Provincial Armed Constabulary [PAC; the Uttar Pradesh state police] stood by. During the following hours, *karsevaks* rampaged through Ayodhya's Muslim neighbourhoods, violently attacked Muslims, looted their shops, and set fire to their homes. Local police and the PAC neither protected Ayodhya's Muslims nor stopped those who perpetrated the violence. National police forces intervened only after the mosque had been destroyed and the local Muslim population had suffered widespread violence.'[11]

BBC's former India correspondent, Mark Tully, affirms the same in his book *India in Slow Motion*. Describing the scene of destruction on 6 December 1992, he writes, 'Above the raucous slogans and the bellowing of conch shells, we heard a leader of the BJP shout through a microphone, "Police, don't interfere!" He needn't have worried, the police had no intention of interfering. The last line of defence retreated from the mosque holding their wicker shields above their heads as protection from the stones raining down on them.' He further adds that as the police moved away, two young men managed to swiftly crawl right up to the 'the top of the mosque's central dome, hoisted a saffron flag, and started hacking away at the old mortar. That was the last we saw of what was known as the Babri Masjid, the mosque of the emperor Babur.'[12]

Having no other option, few local Muslims have forgotten, forgiven and moved on. The most apt example is that of Parveen, the garland-maker, whom I met at Tehri Bazaar. She is realistic and optimistic, unlike her neighbour, Mohammed Ansari. She prefers to hold on to happier memories. 'We feel grateful to the police. I must say that in December 1992, a large number of them were stationed in our locality and gave us the protection we needed. Maybe it was beyond them to control such a huge mob.'

It is another matter that despite the promises of safety and security by the government officials, the Muslims temporarily shifted to the nearby towns of Faizabad and Sultanpur, both in 1990 and 1992, and came back after months when normalcy returned.

Parveen's attitude displeased Ansari, who shouted at her angrily in my presence, '*Aapi* (older sister), don't talk like a traitor. I am an advocate, and I know it all.' He carried on, 'The cops pretended to do their duty, but their heart was with the Hindus. Simultaneously, the local rich Muslims were interested in filling their coffers instead of extending help to us. They are into politics and have the least concern for people like us.'

According to Ansari, the Muslim leaders who 'pretended' to fight for the Muslims in the Ram Janmabhoomi cases were opportunists (he added an abusive word that cannot be repeated here) who wished to gain political mileage.

A massive bungalow, a little behind the Ram Janmabhoomi site. The high black steel gate has spikes on the top, and two sentries guard it. Haji Mehboob is dressed in a crisp white kurta and has a sense of royalty around him. He is calm, composed and contemplative. Cimba, his pet Labrador, snuggles at his feet, the only companion Haji has this evening. He has just come back from a meeting with a few members of the All-India Muslim Personal Law Board (AIMPLB). The board wants to file a review petition before 9 December 2020 against the recent Supreme Court judgment on the Ayodhya dispute.

The AIMPLB shot into prominence because Islam provides a guide for the followers in the matter of 'life, belief, prayers, social behaviour, civil conduct, personal and social relationships, family affairs, and personal life'. Its website clarifies that such 'Personal Law' does not stem from practices, conventions, customs, decisions, experiences, advice and preachings. 'In fact, the fountainhead of the social order and Personal Law of Muslims is the Book (Quran) revealed by Allah and the Sunnah (of the Prophet).'

The website mentions that it is for this reason that the Muslims believe that the Personal Law is 'not merely a cultural issue or an issue of customary practices ... Rather it is an issue which concerns the safeguarding and conservation of their religion.'

Given this backdrop, Haji Sahib is in a dilemma; the Muslims seem divided. 'I have had enough. I sincerely want closure. Let's see how far we can go with our discussions. Undoubtedly, I did say that I shall accept the court's decision, but at the same time, I cannot refuse the people of the board if they want me to join them for a review.'

Among Muslims, the review petition has become a controversial issue. Hashim Ansari's (the first litigant) son, Iqbal, who has no love lost for Haji Mehboob, had told me, 'Those who want to go for a review are doing it because they want to create a political standing and remain in the limelight.'

Even the Sunni Waqf Board, a party in the litigation, decided against a review petition on the ground that the judgment brought the centuries-old issue to a closure. It is important to note that the AIMPLB was not a party in the suit, although it took up the role of an organizing body during the legal hearings.

The Supreme Court on 19 December 2019 'dismissed all the petitions seeking review of its November 9 verdict in Ayodhya land dispute case.

The five-judge bench headed by Chief Justice S.A. Bobde and comprising justices D.Y. Chandrachud, Ashok Bhushan, S. Abdul Nazeer and Sanjiv Khanna, which took these review pleas for consideration in-chamber, rejected them after finding no merits.'[13]

I want Haji Mehboob to cheer up. I prod him to talk about his earlier years. 'Long ago, when I was a toddler, there were frequent riots in Delhi, where we lived. From the mother's side, my grandfather felt it was safer to shift to a peaceful town. My father, Haji Phenku, took his advice, and we landed in his estate in Ayodhya.'

As they were devout Muslims, the family members took care of the Babri Masjid and even gave donations for its maintenance. Haji Phenku worked as the muezzin and was one of the five defendants named in the suits filed by Hindus in the Babri Masjid case.

I realize that he wishes to be left alone; on many occasions, aloneness helps most. Yet just before I leave, I tell him what Iqbal Ansari believes, '*Inhone toh apni dukaan khol dee masjid ke naam par* (They opened their businesses in the name of the mosque).' Haji replies in a surrendering tone, 'I know most Muslims believe we let them down.'

Jafaryiab Jilani, another Muslim who shouldered the Ayodhya case on behalf of the Muslims, is also somewhat unpopular among the ordinary Muslim folks in Ayodhya. I meet the advocate in Lucknow at the Amiruddaula Islamia Degree College, Lalbagh, where he is the acting manager. His office is in a basement, well organized and clean. He has several officials to assist him.

He sits on a swinging chair amidst shelves stacked with books and files. Angry over the divided opinions among Muslims, especially after the verdict, he blurts out, 'Do not ask me about those who were only excited about seeing their names in newspapers and participating in TV shows. I attach no importance to them, whether they be an ex-vice chancellor, ex-senior government officials, or sitting chairman of Shia Waqf Board. None of them made any contribution in the legal battle.'

Jilani does not name anyone, but the advocate who spearheaded the case, adds, 'This is why they have no following. I have the following and trust of most Muslims.'

Commenting on the judgment, he says, 'We decided to obey the law, and we respect the verdict. But that does not mean that we keep quiet when the errors in the judgment are obvious.'

For example, he points out, 'The placement of the idols in 1949 was totally illegal.' He fails to understand how the idols turned into deities without rituals. He adds, 'It is strange that idols that were forcibly and stealthily placed inside the premises can claim possession of a place that is more than four hundred years old. The Muslims are acquainted with Hindu laws. Presumptions that prayers in the mosque were not held before 1857 goes against Mughal history. The Muslim leadership feels that the attitude of the court was opposed to the legal system.'

Jilani's memory is like that of a computer. He chronologically speaks of his role in the case. It was thirty-seven years ago, in 1983, when he accidentally stumbled into the Ayodhya issue. Loitering around in the District Court, Faizabad, he took the file from the court reader, who maintained the custody of case files since no one appeared in the case, though it was listed several times. That was how Jilani learnt about the existence of Babri Masjid in Ayodhya.

Things began to roll out, and he was drawn in. Within a year, he received a letter written on a postcard from Hashim Ansari. It stated that a local Congress leader and MP, Nirmal Khattri, planned to light lamps in the mosque to celebrate Prakash Utsav (lighting ceremony) to mark the day the idols were placed in December 1949.

Jilani then discussed the issue with Mushtaq Ahmad Siddiqui, a senior advocate who was involved in the case. Jilani and Ansari were asked to come to Faizabad. The former took the bus to the city the very next Sunday. Hashim rode on his bicycle from Ayodhya to reach Siddiqui's house. This was the first time that Jilani saw the mosque.

Ali Mian, the president of the AIMPLB and chief of Nadwa, a college for Islamic studies in Lucknow, asked Jilani if he managed to get hold of the legal documents. At that point, Jilani only had notes of three or four pages.

Ali Mian procured all the certified copies from the Faizabad Court after a payment of Rs 2,000, a princely sum in those days. The two held a press conference in Lucknow and apprised the media of the Muslims' views regarding Babri Masjid.

In 1985, Veer Bahadur Singh, the chief minister of Uttar Pradesh, summoned Syed Farhat Ali, a retired IAS officer and chairman of the Sunni Waqf Board. Mata Prasad, home secretary, UP, was present when Farhat Ali announced that 'Muslims will not give away the mosque'. Veer Bahadur Singh was told that Muslims would not withdraw their suit, filed by the Uttar Pradesh Sunni Central Board of Waqfs, later the Sunni Waqf Board, along with eight Muslims in 1961. They claimed possession of the mosque.

Jilani also revealed that Veer Bahadur Singh had a discussion with the Muslims and tried convincing them to give up the claim on the Babri Masjid. The same day, an inspector from the Intelligence Bureau visited Jilani, and asked for copies of the plaint. When asked for a reason, the inspector said that the Centre wanted the details. According to Jilani, 'After Farhat Ali refused to give away the mosque, the district judge, Faizabad, unlocked the mosque on 1 February 1986.'

It has rained through the night, and the morning is cold. Bablu, a local electrician, is sitting out basking under the warm sun with his Hindu colleagues at Shringar Market. He is diplomatic and conscious of what he says and where, like most of his clan in this town. 'We cannot make any comments on the decision of the Supreme Court [on the disputed property].' His friends nod and carry on with their banter. Bablu offers me chai and urges me to walk up to his shop. Away from the crowd, the meekness is replaced with anger. 'We cannot express our feelings in front of the Hindus. We are in the minority, and they have all the power. The VHP gets to know everything. We don't want another riot; we have had enough.' He remembers the days when the Hindus and Muslims lived amicably and forged genuine friendships. But things have changed over the last two decades. The politicians created a massive wedge between the two communities, which seems impossible to bridge.

Bablu and I walk in pregnant silence. We stop in front of a *surma* (kohl) shop. 'Meet Mohammad Umar, whose grandfather was in charge of the Babri Masjid when the idols were shifted inside on 22 December 1949,' Bablu says, introducing me to the shop owner. The two decide to walk me to a graveyard, where we sit on a *charpoy* under a tamarind tree. The trees around sway and bend as if to pay obeisance to the buried. Brighter green graves pop up from the green grassy ground.

Umar's words add to the calm atmosphere. 'The trees acknowledge Hazrat Nuh, who lies here.' A local legend says that Nuh was buried here. Both Hindus and Muslims visit this mazar to seek blessings. People still believe that Allah will protect them in the same way that he protected his devotees during the ancient apocalypse.

Umar's grandfather (Dada), Mohammad Zahoor Ahmad, was one of the early complainants in the Ram Janmabhoomi–Babri Masjid case. According to Umar, Zahoor worked as the *mutawalli* of the Babri Masjid.

Umar relates, 'Dada was shocked to see the idols of Ram and Sita when he entered the masjid on 23 December 1949. He told us stories about how the police lathi-charged the Muslims who had gathered for their namaz that morning and spared the Hindus who came in large groups to see the idols and offer prayers. After my grandfather passed away, my father, Farooq Ahmad, replaced him in the court proceedings.'

As children, Umar and his friends went to the disputed site on bicycles to climb the guava trees and pluck fruits. They would play there for hours together. 'Everything was normal till the police took over the place in 1990. We were forced to get used to the barricades put up everywhere in this town. Over the past two decades, we have learnt to get over the earlier nostalgia,' he says. Muslims like Umar and Parveen have learnt their lessons.

Later that evening, I meet Sadiq, popularly known as Babu Tailor. He says he can never forget how his house was set on fire in December 1992. His expression changes and tears well up in his eyes as he talks about those years. Like the other Muslims, Babu too had sent his family to a relative's house in 1992. He stayed back and witnessed the dastardly incident.

Later, the media used his quotes regularly and he, too, is familiar with several reporters. During this particular trip, which was after the Supreme Court judgment, I realize that though he still sits in his 'tailoring shop' every day, he is now assisted by his son, who manages the show. Even as I visit him this time, there are a few mahants from Hanumangarhi who place their orders with Babu. They are old clients who love Babu's cuts.

'You only see the sadhus now at my shop. But in 2005 and 2006, I stitched clothes for Ram Lalla and his brothers, Lakshman, Bharat and Shatrughan, who reside in the Ram Temple,' he declares. He has no clue and is still bemused why the Ram Temple's *pujari* changed his mind in 2006 and placed his tailoring orders with someone else.

Not that he misses those 'pious' orders, but the act convinced him that there is bigotry towards his community.

Babu acknowledges, 'As far as stitching those clothes was concerned, it was not out of any *shraddha* (devotion) for Ram, as the media has been reporting. I took up the task as it was good for my business. I had more clients as more and more people came to know about my tailoring trade and as an after-effect I earned more.'

Ayodhya signifies how a place of worship can change human equations. It can transform nobodies into kingpins and kings and reduce good people into cynics.

The Muslims who have made Ayodhya their home appear disinterested in discussing all the conflicts that took place between the two communities for centuries together over the ownership of the Babri Masjid–Ram Janmabhoomi temple. What upsets them is the hatred that the Hindus nurture towards their community till date for what a Mughal emperor allegedly did centuries ago.

While interviewing the local Muslims in Ayodhya, it is almost vital that I meet Iqbal Ansari. I head for Hashim Ansari's house. Iqbal, his son, who replaced his father in the legal battle after the latter's death in 2016, is unlike most other Muslims here. '*Bilkul, mandir banna chahiye* (Of course, the mandir should be constructed),' he asserts dramatically.

Iqbal is flashy and loud, a man who loves attention. He welcomes me inside, and I sit on a plastic chair placed among a couple of others in the square living room. His father's photograph hangs within a green plastic frame on a wall beside a mirror. There is dust on the photo; the mirror is spotless. Iqbal's son, who is in his early twenties, is just back after a haircut. He heads to the mirror and runs his hand through his trimmed crop. He poses and tries a few styles and then walks inside. My gaze shifts to the photograph, and I travel back in time.

Always dressed in a white kurta-pyjama, Hashim Ansari would typically have a *gamcha* (a flimsy towel in red and white) hanging loosely from his shoulders. The pungent smell of his beedis was not easy to endure, but his profound philosophy was. Born to a tailor, he took up the same profession when he was only twelve years old. He and his father would stitch clothes for the gods in the different temples. In return, they were served the khichdi prasad which took care of their daily meals.

I tell Iqbal I was fond of his father. His response takes me by complete surprise, '*Walid bahut saal pehle guzar chuke; ab hum hee sab kuch hain* (Father died years ago, now I am everything).' He was unabashedly trying to shift the focus from his father to himself, which pushed me further into the past. Hashim was a humble man. He was above religious conflicts and had Hindu friends. The only people he despised were the VHP members who he held responsible for all the troubles that brewed in his town.

The Muslim litigant, who went to the court to fight for Babri Masjid, did not mince words. I remember him often telling journalists, 'This one man (ex–Prime Minister Narasimha Rao) could have prevented the incidents on 6 December 1992, but he had no will. We suffered, as did the entire nation. Life in Ayodhya will never be the same ever again.' Remarking on his father's belief, Iqbal Ansari says, 'Of course, my father was right as PM Narsimha Rao was fully aware of what was happening in Ayodhya, like anyone else in his place would have been.' He then quickly adds, 'You see, in those years I would hear my father discuss many such issues, but I really never paid much attention as I was too young to comprehend politics.' Suddenly, Iqbal's tone changes and he declares aloud, 'Anyway, the final judgment was based on the faith of the Hindus, and we too have accepted the decision of the apex court.'

Hashim was right. After the demolition, 'life in Ayodhya' was never the same; it lost its peace, slow pace and tranquillity. People remained divided. Since the 1990s, life in the temple town was guided by official passes, curfews and the ordinary people were apparently guarded by thousands of khaki-clad securities round the clock.

I get back to the present and find a deep contrast between the father and son. Iqbal, unlike his father, was dressed in trendy clothes—loose purple pants rolled up to the ankles, grey socks tucked in dusty black boots and a salmon-pink shirt. He has a narrow face with shifty eyes, a stubbled beard and sports a semblance of a moustache. He sprints around the room restlessly, talking nineteen to the dozen. He looks like an Indianized Charlie Chaplin.

'Hindus, go ahead and make the temple!' He points outside his door. 'I have three acres of land here; I can arrange for two more acres. We can build a mosque right here.' He suggests a name for the new mosque, Ayodhya Masjid. His logic: it is best to name it after a place, not a person, as experience shows that a personality can create trouble even after several generations and centuries.

'One has to be careful about the names of places of worship. I am for peace.' Pause. 'Madamji, just like you, people from all over the world ask for my opinion on the final verdict.' He looks around the room as if there is a vast audience. Finally, he ends with a profound, almost jingoistic statement, '*Jis mulk mein hum rahte hain, us mulk ke hum wafadar hain* (I am loyal to the nation where I reside).'

There are two visitors besides me, one of them responds meekly, '*Ji bilkul, aap to ek world celebrity hain* (Yes, you are a world celebrity).' With the aplomb of a true celeb, Iqbal smiles back. Pause. This time he condemns his brethren. 'They are lazy; they curse Hindus. When they are hungry, they shamelessly visit a temple for prasad.' The man has surely forgotten his roots.

Two guards stand in their posts outside his house. They have a series of questions for all visitors. Iqbal loves their presence and makes it obvious when he haughtily declares, 'The security is for the VIPs who visit, as it is for me. One cannot take risks.'

This last statement reminded me of Hashim again. A few sentries were posted outside his house as well, as directed by the state government. He would be somewhat embarrassed with all the attention given and often explain, 'I have no enemies; maybe the government believes that the VHP leaders do not like me. And these guys are posted here; I have to endure them, and so have you.'

The Waqf Board's involvement in Ayodhya possibly predates the country's independence. The doctrine of Waqf among Muslims, both the competing sects of Shia and Sunni, is centuries old. The word means an endowment, generally a property, which is used 'solely for the purposes recognized under Islamic Law as pious, religious, or charitable'. It is managed by a mutawalli, who can be assisted by a committee.

In India, the laws related to Waqf were passed by various legislators since 1913. In the United Provinces (later Uttar Pradesh), there were two acts passed in 1923 and 1936. When the Muslim community expressed unhappiness at the working of the second act, it was replaced by the UP Muslim Waqf Act, 1960. In 1995, the central government implemented an overarching act, which was amended in 2013.

Most state-level Waqf Boards are controlled by Sunnis; only two states, UP and Bihar, have Shia Waqf Boards due to sizeable populations of the Shia sect. From the 1940s, the Sunni and Shia sects have battled over the control and ownership of the Babri Masjid in Ayodhya.

According to Waseem Rizvi, who hails from Old Lucknow and was the chairman of the UP Shia Waqf Board (2015–20), 'When the Sunnis claimed the Babri Masjid in the 1940s before Independence, the Shias protested against their assertion in the Faizabad Court.'

Both the Sunni and Shia sects accept that the mosque was built by Mir Baqi, who was a Shia, which indicates that the subsequent mutawallis of the masjid were (obviously) Shi'ites. Hence, this sect finds it 'incomprehensible' that a Waqf created by a Shia could become a Sunni one. But, for an inexplicable reason, the Shia Board did not pursue the legal case. Based upon the observation of an official administrator, the Sunnis laid claim on the property and structure.

In the Supreme Court judgment in 2019, the Shia claim was rejected because it was more than seven decades old. And the Sunni one was dispensed with because the sect couldn't prove ownership beyond any reasonable doubt.

After spending a week in Ayodhya in early 2020, I left for Lucknow. Ayodhya's Babu Tailor had reminded me of my tailor, Hafeez, in Janpath Market, whom I would often visit when we lived in the state capital. I dropped by at his shop to catch up after a long gap. Hafeez was a favourite with the fashionable women and girls of Lucknow. I sipped from the glass of Coke that was offered, and we talked of old times. He seemed least interested in the Babri Masjid case.

From there, I headed to the Chowk area in Old Lucknow to buy a couple of *chikankari* sarees. I saw women sowing beautiful designs on yards of soft fabric. They reminded me of the women stringing flowers in Parveen's house.

A trip to this beautiful city is incomplete without kebab from the famous Tunday, so I packed a fair amount to carry for friends and family back home.

On the way to the airport, I passed a huge hoarding gently ordering all visitors to the city, '*Muskuraiye ki aap Lucknow mein hain* (Smile that you are in Lucknow).' I smiled, feeling proud of India's syncretic culture, commonly referred to as the Ganga-Jamuni *tehzeeb*, attributed to the Muslim Nawabs and, thankfully, still not tampered with within the city of Lucknow.

3
Ram Resurrected

'Raghupati Raghava Raja Ram, Patit Paavan Sita Ram'

Ayodhya is like most of the modern–traditional religious cities and towns in India. Unlike many, it still awaits the construction of an international airport, besides other modern amenities. At present, the nearest airfield is the Chaudhary Charan Singh Airport, Amausi, Lucknow.

From there, it takes almost three hours to reach Faizabad, the twin companion town of Ayodhya. There are no plush hotels in the former, but a visitor can enjoy a comfortable and pleasing stay, thanks to the hospitality and helpfulness of hotel staff in most places. Nothing in Faizabad, the district headquarters of Awadh, indicates that Lord Ram's abode is next door, except the fleet of tourist buses at the parking areas of hotels. Clearly, the town is a part of a cultural journey.

In Faizabad, you notice the impact that economic reforms have had on Tier-2 and Tier-3 towns. Almost everything indicates the cliché of the bourgeoisie of such towns in an age of consumerism. There are a few spaces that can be dubbed shopping malls. If you are from a metro or a more extensive city, you may think of them as large departmental stores. Some cafes sport fancy European names. Kebabs and biryani stalls are found on most street corners, with banners exalting the food in Urdu. One can spot a few gyms and diet centres, too, with ads that scream out their benefits from gaudy kiosks.

A narrow road connects the twin towns, and a speed of 20–30 km/hr on it is considered fast. As one can imagine, Ayodhya is a 'vegetarian' place, as Lord Ram's followers, who are Vaishnavites (followers of Lord Vishnu), think of non-vegetarian food as unholy. Of course, as far as questionable habits go, there is one herbal intoxication available here—*ganja* (marijuana). I remember way back in 2001 a Naga sadhu telling me during my visit to the Maha Kumbha Mela at Allahabad, 'This divine intoxicant makes the sadhus feel that they are in heaven!'

On this connecting road, motorcycles, three-wheelers and cycle-rickshaws are the preferred mode of transport, besides cars and buses that indicate the influx of travellers. It takes a while before one reaches the gigantic concrete gateway that welcomes the pilgrims: *Pawan Nagri Ayodhya aagman par aapka hardik swagat hai* (You are heartily welcome to the holy town of Ayodhya). There is another line inscribed under the initial entryway, taken from the fifth section of the *Sundar Kand*, which is the only part of the epic Ramayana where the hero is Hanuman and not Lord Ram. The line reads, *Choupayi prabisi nagar keeje sab kaja. Hridayrakhi Kosalpur Raja* (By entering the city of Ayodhya belonging to King of Kosalpur, use your heart to perform your tasks).

The word 'Ayodhya' has Sanskrit origins and is formed by joining two words, '*a*' and '*yodhya*'. While '*a*' means no, '*yodha*' means 'one worthy of a war', the two put together would translate into 'one not to be fought', thus invincible. Given the bloodshed it has seen in ancient and modern times, it sounds ironic, hollow and a bit shallow.

Within Ayodhya, that measures 79.8 sq. km in area, Lord Ram, and his loyal devotee Hanuman stare at you from every possible quarter. There is a Ram Medical Store, Ram Sweets, Ram Dresses, Ram Bridal Make-up, apart from Hanuman Electric Stores, Pawanputra Sweets, Maruti Yoga Centre, among many more.

The hippest brands—fakes and duplicates, mostly—are juxtaposed with saffron stoles and headbands bearing Lord Ram's name. That the ruling hue of the town is saffron, there can be no doubt—the garment stores sell saffron-coloured towels, shorts, sarees, salwar suits, kurtas and undergarments. In the sweet shops, the white barfis (milk cakes) appear to be struggling to garner some attention as they rest under the pressure of the enormous mounds of saffron-coloured laddoos (sweet balls made from gram flour). Carts that sell flowers and garlands have every shade of saffron overflowing from their wooden tops. The chosen flower here is marigold, in all possible shapes and sizes.

With a population of 451,000 (Census 2011), Ayodhya houses thousands of temples. 'An official gazette from the British era suggests that Ayodhya was once a proud home to close to 5,000 big and small temples. But decades of neglect followed by communal tension has wiped out almost half of them.' The newly created Ayodhya Municipal Corporation has identified about 182 dilapidated temples which may collapse any time.[1]

However, the town is more expansive in spiritual terms than its temples. It has structures related to several religions—Hindu, Jain, Buddhist, Sikh and Islam. The town was, and in several cases continues to be, an important pilgrimage centre for these religions. Interestingly, most of them have their versions of the Ramayana, which mention Ayodhya and Lord Ram in their own intrinsic ways.

In the Jain Ramayana, the town is mentioned as Saket, where King Dasarath ruled and had four queens—Aparajita, Sumitra, Suprabha and Kaikeyi. Aparajita's son Padma was later known as Ram, Sumitra's son Narayan was Lakshman, Kaikeyi's son was Bharat, and Suprabha's Shatrughan. The Jains believe that it was Lakshman who killed the demon Ravan and, hence, both went to hell. In their next births, they will be honest and good, and attain salvation.[2]

Ayodhya is home to five of the twenty-four Jain Tirthankaras of the present cycle—the first Rishabha-nath, the second Ajita-nath, the fourth Abhinandan-nath, the fifth Sumati-nath and the fourteenth one, Ananta-nath. Of the Tirthankaras, twenty-one belong to the Ikshavaku dynasty, which is the dynasty of the Hindu God Ram.

In the Buddhist version of Ramayana, which is known as *Dasaratha Jataka*, the story is the same as in Valmiki's epic. But there are two differences. King Dasarath sent Ram, his wife, Sita, and brother Lakshman to the forest in a bid to protect them from his ambitious third wife, Kaikeyi. There is no mention of Sita's abduction by Ravan in these texts.

Ramayana finds a place within the Sikh holy text, the Guru Granth Sahib, as well. In it, the characters have spiritual and metaphorical significance only—Ravan depicts ego, Sita stands for intellect, Ram is the inner self and Lakshman represents mindfulness.[3]

According to historians, there are 300 versions of the Ramayana, and each has its local flavour and interpretation. The Indian tribes such as the Bhils, Mundas, Santhals, Gonds, Sauras, Korkus, Rabhas, Bodo–Kacharis, Khasis, Mizos and Meiteis, each have their own adaptations, which reflect the local lifestyle and culture. For example, in Assam, where hill women are skilled weavers, Sita is characterized as a fine weaver.[4]

The epic established itself even in distant lands—Myanmar, Indonesia, Cambodia, Laos, the Philippines and China.

In his paper, 'Ayodhya, India: Cultural Landscape and Perspectives for Inclusive Heritage Development', Sarvesh Kumar elaborates the inclusive and secular nature of this town. 'Ayodhya for a period of over two thousand years has borne witness to the presence of Jainism, Buddhism, Shaivism, Vaishnavism, and Islam too. Therefore, Ayodhya consists of the sacred and religious places for Hindus together with Jains, Buddhists, Sikhs, and Muslims too. Ayodhya is also a sacred and important place for Koreans because it is the birthplace of legendary foremother from whom the royal dynasty got succession.'[5]

In February 2000, a large Korean delegation visited Ayodhya and conferred a unique status to it. The Koreans believe it is a kin city of Kim-Hae, a prosperous South Korean town.

Kim-Hae's mayor, Song Eun Bok, renewed a link that is 2,000 years old. A medieval monk, Iryon (1206–1289), wrote that there was once an adventurous princess from Ayodhya who sailed the high seas. Her ship was damaged in a storm, but she did not stop until she reached the distant and famed Land of the Morning Calm (Korea). Here, she fell in love with a handsome prince, married him and lived happily ever after. The prince was from Kim-Hae. The Koreans believe that the origins of the powerful Kim clan can be traced to this marital bond.[6] 'Several historical Korean stories tell the story of an Indian princess—Suriratna—who married a South Korean king and started a dynasty.' Besides, 'Some Chinese-language texts claim that the then King of Ayodhya had a dream where God ordered him to send his 16-year-old daughter to South Korea to marry King Kim Suro.'

During the visit of the Korean delegation, Mayor Song received a warm welcome with the traditional tika and *namavali*s (stoles with

Ram printed on them). The temple town's administration and its mahants took turns to make the foreigners comfortable.

The chairperson of the Ayodhya municipality handed over a symbolic golden key to the town to the mayor. This was followed by the presentation of a model of the proposed Ram Janmabhoomi temple. 'We thought the new millennium was the ideal time to revive the old bond,' said Song in his speech.

South Korean Prime Minister Kim Jong Pil addressed a letter to the 'Rajah of Ayodhya', Bimalendra Mohan Pratap Mishra, which stated: 'I am the 72nd descendant of King Kim Suro of the Garak Kingdom.'[7]

Even today, the banks of the Sarayu River are dotted with places of worship that belong to various religions and stand as silent testimony to the town's secular fabric.

One of the most imposing structures here is the Jain temple dedicated to Sri Ananta-nath (the endless), at the Rajghat. He was the fourteenth Tirthankara and born in Ayodhya on the thirteenth day of the month of Vaisakha (in the Georgian calendar, it begins mid-April and ends mid-May). The temple has the Tirthankara's statue in copper colour. He is in a seated posture. There is an ornate umbrella in silver over his head. The inside arcs have beautiful designs, both painted and embossed. The temple also has a massive hall with marble flooring, where devotees offer prayers. The Sarayu flows silently beside this serene grandeur.

A little further up the lane is the famous gurudwara of Ayodhya, the Brahmakund Sahib. Gyani Guljeet Singh Khalsa, who lives with his family, looks after both the administration and rituals of the gurudwara. He is usually dressed in a white kurta that reaches a little below his knees, white pyjamas and a black turban that matches the belt across his chest that holds his kirpan.

We talk about the 2019 Supreme Court's judgment. He proclaims that three Sikh gurus, Guru Nanak, Guru Tegh Bahadur Singh and

Guru Gobind Singh, visited this 'holy place'. Enthusiastically, he takes me to the different parts of the gurudwara. These include a cave, tunnel and a well that is believed to be created miraculously by Nanak. A tiny glass room exhibits the ninth guru, Guru Tegh Bahadur Singh's bow and arrows, shield, cymbals and footwear.

Guljeet Singh is happy with the court verdict and that Guru Nanak's visit to Ayodhya was a part of the evidence. Talking about the future Ram Temple, he says, 'We are delighted that the lord will finally be inside a grand temple.' And then he flits to the past, 'Do you know Baba Vaishnavdas Ji, a senior mahant of Ayodhya, wrote a letter and invited Guru Gobind Singh to help fight the Muslims, who were always creating trouble for the Hindu devotees visiting the Ram Janmabhoomi? Since the Mughal period the Hindus and Sikhs have worked together to liberate the Ram Mandir from the Muslims' He then brings up the fanaticism exhibited by Mughal Emperor Aurangzeb, 'We all are aware how the Hindus were harassed during his rule.' Ayodhya was no exception. The Mughal sent his general, Jabaz Khan, to subjugate the Hindus. The 10,000 *chimtadhari* (Hindu sages who used tongs as weapons) along with the Sikh soldiers defeated the Mughal army in just seven days. The Khalsa adds, 'The Sikhs were always ready to rescue the Hindus from the Muslims. The Mahants often reached out to them, and they would reach the temple town to fight out the Muslims.' He then shows a few paintings and illustrations of Guru Gobind Singh's visit to Ayodhya as a child in 1672.

Of course, when one talks about the presence of various religions in Ayodhya, we cannot forget the sixty-odd mosques. Given this diverse religiosity, it seems like a wonder that the town became a Hindu nationalist symbol. How did a place that was inclusive and accommodative become one of exclusion? How was love replaced by hate? One can blame the events in the past few decades or even go back a couple of centuries. But the transformation started way before the British.

The Ramayana was first written in Sanskrit by Valmiki between the fifth century BC and the first century BC. Through the ages, even though it became popular and was read by the upper-caste Brahmins at rituals and ceremonies, the story didn't have a strong connect with the masses. Most sections in those years did not understand the language, which was used only by the upper-caste Brahmins. The commoners thus recited it robotically.

Back when Valmiki wrote the epic, Sanskrit was the most commonly used language in northern India. As we saw earlier, the book became a preserve of several religions and regions, with each one having its own versions.

However, what is the most popular one now is the epic poem, *Ramcharitmanas*. Tulsidas, who scripted this version began to write it in 1574, or almost 2,000–3,000 years after Valmiki. The exact date of the writing is mentioned within the text as the ninth day of the month of Chaitra, which is Ram's birthday, and celebrated as Ram Navami. Tulsidas, who was also a Sanskrit scholar, chose to rewrite his version in a popular language, Awadhi, which continues to be a spoken dialect in several regions of north and central India. *Ramcharitmanas* has seven *kand*s (sections), consisting of poems and couplets and is in the form of a narration related by Lord Shiva to his wife, Goddess Parvati.

For historians, Tulsidas's (1532–1623) is a significant period. By this stage, Hinduism had revived and reached the masses mainly due to the Bhakti cult. Prior to this, Adi Shankaracharya, in the eighth century, had put in all his mind and might to the revival of Hinduism by travelling through the length and breadth of the country. It must be noted that for centuries together, 600 BC to 1300 AD, Jainism and Buddhism, which technically branched out of Hinduism, were more popular among the masses.

Shashi Tharoor, a former diplomat and now politician, wrote that by the eighth century, 'Subsequently Hinduism had become paralysed by its own inflexible practice of orthodoxy, ritualism, and formality, and in retreat before the rise of the reform movements challenging it, notably those following the ascetic Mahavira (599–527 BC) and the other-worldly Gautama Buddha (563–483 BC), whose followers branched out into new religions distinct from the *Mimamsa* Brahmanism practiced by mainstream Hindus. Both new faiths flourished for several centuries, as Hinduism descended into esoteric disputes …'[8]

Adi Shankaracharya (788–820; his dates are disputed) is believed to be the spiritual brain behind Hinduism's revival in the eighth century. His Advaita Vedanta was the philosophically robust response to that era of confusion, integrating diverse thoughts and Hindu practices into a philosophy based on the Vedic dictum of 'One Truth, many dispositions', wrote Tharoor.

Dr David Frawley, an American Hindu teacher, believes that in his short life of thirty-two years, Shankaracharya 'fundamentally changed India. Shankara is best known for his promulgations of Vedanta in its Advaitic or non-dualist form, but this is just the crest jewel of his many lofty achievements.' He adds that the philosopher-guru 'revived Hindu dharma overall, marking a new era in its expression'.[9]

In his spiritual journeys, says Tharoor, Shankara traversed India's 'length and breadth three times'. His travels 'took him from the southernmost tip of the country (he was born in Kerala) to Kashmir in the north, Gujarat in the west, and Odisha in the east'. He debated with scholars everywhere and preached his beliefs.

Dr David Frawley wrote, 'Shankara organised four great mutts across India (Dwarka, Puri, Sringeri, and Joshimutt). He is said to have renovated the char dham, or the four main Himalayan temples of Badrinath, Kedarnath, Gangotri, and Yamunotri. He reorganised Hindu worship into the five deity lines of Shiva, Vishnu, Devi, Ganesha, and Surya. His hymns or stotras to all the main Hindu deities remain commonly chanted in pujas and temple rituals in the north and south India.'[10]

By the sixteenth century, when Tulsidas rewrote the Ramayana, Hinduism was back on track marked by a cultural unity across the country. However, by that time, India witnessed waves of invasions from outsiders. The Muslim Mughal empire was well-established by then. Hence, even as Hinduism reclaimed its dominance and despite the decline of Buddhism and Jainism, Islam was on an upsurge. The fight, therefore, was mainly between these two communities.

So, it was logical for many Sanskrit scholars, besides poets like Tulsidas, to make further attempts to popularize Hinduism. Accessible myths and parables were the best way to achieve this objective. And as a consequence, over the next few centuries, Lord Ram emerged as one of the popular gods in north and central India. More importantly, the recital of *Ramcharitmanas* became quite common in millions of Indian homes.

As a geographical place, Ayodhya saw its ups and downs between 500 and 1500 CE. Historian Hans Bakker recorded this in his research. During the golden Gupta period and the reign of either Emperor Kumaragupta or most possibly his successor, Skandagupta (455–467), the capital of the kingdom shifted from Pataliputra in Bihar to Ayodhya in Uttar Pradesh. Under King Narsimhagupta, the empire was devastated by the invading outsiders, the Huns. By the middle of the sixth century, the political centre in north India shifted to Kannauj, and Ayodhya fell off the radar. It possibly retained its regional power but was never the centre, as it used to be. After a hibernation of half a millennium, the city reappeared, transforming into a place of religious significance.

Hans Bakker in his essay, 'Ayodhyā: A Hindu Jerusalem: An Investigation of "Holy War" as a Religious Idea in the Light of Communal Unrest in India' mentions', 'It is only in the eleventh and twelfth centuries that Ayodhya develops into a pilgrimage-centre in which the spot where Rama was born, the Ramajanmabhumi, is the main attraction. A coincidence? Or is there some intrinsic connection between the Muslim invasions and the rise in importance of this god as a symbol for traditional Hindu values? In any case, there can be no doubt that as the time-honoured model of justice (dharma) and regal fame and power (*ksatra*), Rama was remarkably well suited to develop into a symbol of the struggle against the forces that threatened traditional Hindu society.'[11]

Bakker feels that the *Ramcharitmanas* had a profound influence on people of different social classes and helped to propagate a more populistic form of Ram worship, which resulted in a gradual increase in pilgrims.

Even the Supreme Court's five judges, who gave the final order on the Ayodhya dispute, acknowledged Tulsidas's contribution. In its 1,024-page order, the court devoted 116 pages to an 'Addendum' which supported the belief that Lord Ram was born at the exact spot which was under the central dome of the demolished Babri Masjid. It referred to *Ramcharitmanas's* 'Bal Khand', the first section of the myth that deals with Lord Ram's childhood, which 'points to a place where he will take a human form, which is clearly depicted in the words *tinha ka grha* (in this house of Dashrath and Kausalya)'.

At this stage, it is crucial to clarify another aspect—the impact of Lord Ram and the *Ramcharitmanas*. The *Indian Express* in July 2013 went through the names of 677,459 inhabited and uninhabited villages in India listed under Census 2011 and found that 3,626 people were named after Lord Ram. They were spread across all states, except Kerala.[12]

This research is a testimony that the Ramayana was written with a cultural and geographical unity in mind. Like a national emperor, Lord Ram is known across the subcontinent and has friends and enemies tucked away in different corners.

It needs mentioning that there are many who assume that Ram is not as popular in the southern states as he is in those of north and central India, where his religious base is more expansive. Alok Kumar, international president of the VHP, says that people who have such assumptions are unaware of several facts. 'It is indeed strange that people imagine that Ram is not a popular god in south India.' He refers to one of the most beautiful temples, Ramanathaswamy Temple in Rameswaram, in the southern state of Tamil Nadu, dedicated to Lord Shiva. In this abode, it is believed that the small lingam made out of sand, which is the main deity, was created by Sita as Ram waited for Hanuman to bring the *vishwalingam* (that symbolized evidence of Lord Shiva's existence) from Mount Kailash, the abode of Shiva in the Himalayas. Alok reminds me of what Tulsidas wrote in the *Ramcharitmanas*, 'Those who visit Rameswaram Temple and worship the deity there, they will always reside in *Shivaloka* [In Shiva's abode, meaning heaven]; they will never be born again in this world and go through the sufferings of a human life.'

There are many other temples in south India associated with Lord Ram. These include Seetha Ramachandraswamy Temple in Bhadrachalam, Andhra Pradesh; Maduranthakam and Ponpadirkudam temples near Chinglepet, Tamil Nadu; and Hazar Rama Temple in Hampi, Karnataka. The Thanjavur district in Tamil Nadu can boast of several temples dedicated to the same lord.

In his book, *Land of the Seven Rivers: A Brief History of India's Geography*, Sanjeev Sanyal, while beautifully interconnecting history and geography, refers to several places mentioned in the Ramayana. He talks about two ancient highways that transported goods and people across the subcontinent and still exist today. 'The first is the Uttara Path (Northern Route), which has been continuously rebuilt in some approximation to the original. Rulers like Sher Shah Suri, Mughals, and British invested heavily in maintaining it.' In modern parlance, it is called the Grand Trunk Road and connects the north with the east.

The Dakshina Path (Southern Road), Sanyal writes, has 'drifted over time although certain nodes remained important over long periods'. According to Sanyal, 'this probably began near Allahabad (Uttar Pradesh), went into a south-westerly direction towards Nashik (Maharashtra) through central India, and down eventually to Hampi (Karnataka)'. The author believes that this was perhaps the route that Lord Ram took to the forest where he had to be in exile for fourteen years, along with Sita, and Lakshman. As mentioned in the epic, his journey is 'from the Gangetic plains to the southern tip of India and on to Sri Lanka'.

Many believe that there is a possibility that the names of the places in south India were retrofitted, since the epic has been written and rewritten. But Sanyal, who visited some of the places that the lord travelled to according to the epic and subsequent texts, does not think so.

Describing the landscape as 'evocative', Sanyal feels convinced that Valmiki had either visited it or was given detailed accounts of the place from those merchants who were often using the 'Dakshina Path'. He then lists out places like 'medieval ruins of Vijayanagara at Hampi', 'the lake of Pampa' and a sloth bear reserve close to it. His take is that it's too much of a 'coincidence' that these places seem exactly like those described in the epic. The ruins of Vijayanagara still have troops of monkey skipping and jumping all around and the locale looks so much like Kishkindha—the kingdom of the simians—and the lake of Pampa with lotuses and birds chirping situated amidst 'rocky hills' seems so much like the one where Ram meets Hanuman for the first time. In the same way the sloth bear reserve reminds the writer of 'Jambavan, Hanuman's sloth bear friend'.

'If one traces the various places that Lord Ram stayed in, and which are mentioned in the Epic, the route map comes alive.'

The author interestingly brings out the route map which was perhaps taken by Ram, Sita and Lakshman—Chitrakoot in Madhya Pradesh where the three of them spent the first eleven years of their exile. From there they moved to Panchavati in Maharashtra. This stay was most crucial as Lakshman in a state of anger had cut off Ravana's sister Surpanakha's nose, which is why Ravana decided to take revenge and abduct Sita. Further down is Lepakshi, a town in Andhra Pradesh where Jatayu (a gigantic eagle) dared to fight with Ravana to 'rescue Sita but failed. And as the injured bird breathing his last, he cited all what he had witnessed to Lord Rama. It was Jatayu who also directed him towards Ravana's kingdom—Sri Lanka'.

Sanyal also mentions places like Rameswaram, and Ashok Vatika, 'where Sita was kept by Ravan'.[13]

When I had visited the Sita Vatika in 2015, the tour guide showed a significantly large indent on a rock painted in yellow and told me that it was Hanuman's footstep that had been marked out on the huge boulder!

Hence, it is understandable why pilgrims from north, central, south and west India thronged to Ayodhya in the past few centuries. People from the east, too, were involved as Sita hailed from that region. Hence, the legacy of Ram and his life story crisscrosses the country. But this is not to say that he was the god of gods. Obviously, in stature, Lord Shiva and Lord Vishnu enjoy more following among the Hindus. Ram is considered an avatar (reincarnation) of the latter.

There were other aspects of the Ramayana that subliminally touched Hindu hearts in various parts of the country, especially in the regions above the Deccan Plateau. One of them was the story's distinction from other epics.

Among the famous mythologies in the north, east and west, the Vedas, Puranas and Upanishads are too esoteric, ritualistic and philosophical to appeal to the masses. Hence, in the popularity battle, it was a toss-up between Lord Ram and Lord Krishna, that is, the Ramayana and Mahabharata.

The Mahabharata, and its sub-text, the Bhagavad Gita, is complex. The Mahabharata is full of tales of wars, intrigues, machinations and grey areas. There are nuanced arguments between right and wrong. Lord Krishna intervenes in the various battles and moments of tensions as one who is needed to find a way out of tricky situations.

The Bhagavad Gita, as a result, is full of knowledge and introspection. It can be interpreted in several ways—the readers can reach their own conclusions. To understand the text thoroughly requires the highest level of self-realization, or an evolved guru to explain the book.

On the other hand, the Ramayana is a simple story about love and sacrifice, family-related tensions, and good and evil. The characters and stories are primarily black and white, and there is little grey to deal with. There is father–son love between King Dashrath and his favourite eldest son, Ram. The brotherly love between Ram and Lakshman, who leaves for the forest with the former, and between Ram and Bharat, who decides to rule by placing Ram's padukas on the throne, are exemplary tales.

Family differences among the queens prompt one of them to jealously manipulate events so that her son, and not the king's eldest son, Ram, takes over from King Dashrath. This sets the tone for the patriarch's dilemma when dealing with separate wives with varying personalities.

Of course, despite being knowledgeable and a Brahmin, Ravana is in the wrong because he abducts another man's wife. And Ram follows the correct path as he fights to get his wife back. As it happens in every war, different characters transparently choose sides and then extend their support and loyalty to their leaders.

Given the state of the society in those days, and even now to some extent, there is some form of male dominance in the text. This is visible when Ram sends Sita away because he is concerned about what his people may say and believe about their king accepting back a wife abducted by a demon. He also, for the same reason, takes a long time to accept his sons, Luv and Kush.

In most ways, the Ramayana is closer to the everyday lives of ordinary people. They can relate to the feelings and emotions depicted in the epic. There is no derived learning from the text, and one doesn't need to strain the brain to understand or dissect its subtleties.

When Tulsidas rewrote the text as *Ramcharitmanas* in the sixteenth century in the Awadhi language, it dovetailed beautifully and seamlessly with the expanse of the Bhakti movement. As professor Vasudha Paramasivan, from the Department of South and Southeast Asian Studies, Berkeley Research (University of California) writes in her PhD dissertation 'Between Text and Sect: Early Nineteenth Century Shifts in the Theology of Ram': 'The Ram kathā, or the legend of Ram the prince of Ayodhya, became central to the medieval devotional traditions known as bhakti.' Paramsivan further describes how 'Originating in South India, bhakti spread toward the North around the fifteenth century.'[14]

According to Paramsivan, 'The *Ramcharitmanas* is also considered the definitive text of Ram bhakti in North India, as it was the first

North Indian vernacular work to place the Ram katha within a devotional framework. The text presents a "syncretic" view of some of the key factions/positions of contention within North Indian bhakti—Shaivism and Vaishnavism, and *sagun* and *nirgun* bhakti.' The Bhakti movement diverged into *nirgun* (aniconic) and *sagun* (iconic) streams in the north. Nirgun bhakti means worshipping God without any qualities, that is a formless God, and sagun bhakti means worshipping a personal god.

Around the same time when the *Ramcharitmanas* was written, the Ramanandi sect took roots in north India. Several streams and sub-sects owe their origins to Saint Ramanand, whose biography is sketchy and incomplete. This is also because the sub-sects released several versions of his life in a bid to appropriate him.

Richard Burghart, a German anthropologist, provides an insight into these variations. In his essay, 'The Founding of the Ramanandi Sect', he writes, 'The Ramanandi sect, which is said to have been founded by Swami Ramanand in the 14th century, performed a particularly significant role in the development of both Hindu religion and Hindi literature.' He adds that some believe that Ramanand, a Ramaite ascetic (or a devotee of Lord Ram), went from Tamil Nadu to Benares around AD 1430 and taught the preaching of south Indian saint Ramanuja. Others contend that the saint was born in Prayag (Allahabad) in AD 1300 and his initiation as a Tridandi sannyasi was by Swami Raghavanand, who was the abbot of the Sri monastery in Benares.[15] Yet another narrative is that Ramanand went from the south straight to Ayodhya. A Tridandi sannyasi of the Vaishnava school accepts three rods (*tridandi*), representing the vow to engage in the service of the lord with body, mind and speech.[16]

If one takes a collective look at the various documented lifespans of the saint, he must have lived for at least 150 years! This is because his birth ranges from the fourteenth to the fifteenth century. However, he lived before Tulsidas wrote the *Ramcharitmanas*.

Over the next few centuries, and as late as the twentieth one, the Ramanandi sect evolved in a way that it could present itself as central and integral to the Hindu religion.

Ramanand was initially pitched as a spiritual descendant of the famous Ramanuja. This enabled him and his devotees, to claim the more accepted, popular and stronger Brahmanical roots. Ramanuja was a prominent saint in the Brahmin order.

Burghart expounds, 'The most interesting feature of this early Ramanandi spiritual genealogy, therefore, is its ambiguity. Ramanand is a spiritual descendant of Ramanuja thereby making Ramanand a member of the Sri sect, but Ramanuja received the mantra from Ram and Sita, not Narayan and Laksmi, thereby making Ramanuja a Ramanandi or Ramavat ascetic. The genealogy does not prove that Ramanand was, in fact, a member of the Sri sect, but it does indicate that at the time of its compilation the author of the genealogy, either Ramanand or one of his followers, found it advantageous for Ramanand to be included as a spiritual descendant of Ramanuja.'

As one can imagine, this change twisted the tale and maintained the gravitas of the Ramanandi sect. It was, as they say, a win-win for Ramanandis.

The second genealogy of the Ramanandis emerged in the sixteenth century. As per Burghart, 'Nabha Ji, who was in the fourth generation of Ramanand's descendants, compiled the Sri Bhakta Mala in the late 16th century. The Sri Bhakta Mala genealogy was compiled during the period of greatest diversity within the Ramanandi sect. The list of disciples includes a weaver (Kabir; it is not specifically mentioned that Kabir is a Muslim), a cobbler (Rai Das), a farmer

(Dhana), a barber (Sena), a woman (Padmavati), and a married couple (Sursurananda and Sursuri). No doubt Ramanand had more than twelve disciples, but twelve was a sacred number and we find that other famous ascetics who founded sects, such as Gorakhnath, were also known to have had twelve disciples. Ramanand is included within the Sri sect, but he is attributed twelve disciples as if he had founded his own sect.'

This means that out of the twelve key disciples, only half of them were Brahmins. One was a Kshatriya (an upper caste of martial people below the stature of Brahmins). However, the remaining five belonged to the lower castes, including untouchables.

Such a genealogy benefitted the Ramanandis in several ways. One, it increased their popularity by absorbing the followers of Sufi and non-Brahmin saints like Kabir and Rai Das, who amassed massive popularity in north India. It proved that the Ramanand sect was not a strictly Brahmanical order and was more inclusive. Two, the Ramanand sect still maintained its Brahmin character due to its origins from the lords and Ramanuja, besides the fact that six of Ramanand's disciples were, in fact, Brahmins. The Vaishnavite traits were established as even the Sufi saints were followers of Lord Ram and Lord Krishna, both avatars of Lord Vishnu. Three, this absorption sent a message that the Ramanand cult was different from the more established ones in south India, like the Sri sect, which excluded non-Brahmins even in north India. This showed that the Ramanandis now constituted a new sect, whose identity was both similar and separate from the older ones. Finally, this new genealogy was more acceptable to the followers of non-Brahmin saints like Kabir and Rai Das, as it enabled them to show evident Brahmin roots. Thus, they felt more like a part of the mainstream and established in the Hindu religion than outsiders.

Till the seventeenth century the ethos of the Ramanandis was not very clear for the masses. 'A number of poems written in the vernacular were attributed to Ramanand; but other important texts attributed to Ramanand were written in Sanskrit and hence were accessible only to disciples of Brahman birth.'[17]

With time the followers of Ramanand kept growing in numbers and started to influence people by and large. It was only at the turn of the eighteenth century when 'Ramanand became retrospectively and retroactively the founder of the Ramanandi sect'. The reason for this is attributed to cleansing within the order wherein 'certain impure spiritual descendants were excluded from the sect and the Sri ascetics were displaced from the *catuh sampradaya.*' Initially there were four main Vaisnavite sects based on their founders, namely, Ramanuja, Nimbarka, Madhvacarya and Visnuswami. Collectively these four sects were known as the catuh.[18]

What were the reasons for this turnabout of the Ramanand sect—from tracing its roots in south India's Ramanuja and Sri sects in the fifteenth century to inclusiveness of non-Brahmin saints in the sixteenth century to a strict and staunch Brahmanism that was distinct from the Ramanuja and Sri sects in the eighteenth century?

Experts contend that this was related to the dramatic political and allied social changes over these three centuries. In the beginning, the Ramanandis had to prove their Brahmin roots that went back to Lord Ram and Sita. However, at the same time, India witnessed a period of Islamic expanse with the Mughal empire.

In this milieu, the Hindu sects had to both preserve their Brahmin origins as well as become more inclusive. The reason was apparent—as the Muslim culture and religion expanded, especially during the Mughal reign, the Hindus, especially Brahmins, felt insecure. They had to latch on to and save their faith against this invasion.

Conversions of Hindus into Muslims, especially among the lower Hindu castes, became common. Thus, the Hindu sects, including the Ramanandis, were focused on both re-conversions, that is from Islam to Hinduism, and prevention of conversions. Hence, the critical focus during this period was preserving the original Brahmanical culture and the prevention of Hindu followers going into the Muslim fold. Socio-religious issues gained dominance over economic and political ones. This meant that it was critical for the Brahmin orders to become inclusive and expand their popularity and following among the lower castes. This explains why the appropriation of lower-caste saints like Kabir and Ravidas became an unavoidable part of this practical strategy in the sixteenth century.

In the beginning of the eighteenth century, with the death of Aurangzeb, the Mughal dynasty crumbled. And it decimated faster than anyone could have imagined. Suddenly, apart from dozens of Muslim satraps, nawabs and rulers of smaller kingdoms, the century witnessed a revival and growing power of a similar number of Hindu rulers, who established their command over small and large kingdoms.

Most Hindu sects, especially in north India, where the Mughals dominated, saw tremendous opportunities to gain political patronage from the new Hindu rulers. The Ramanandis and the other clans could quickly gain proximity to political power, which would obviously translate into socio-religious power. But most of the rulers wished to align with the cults that had strong and staunch Brahmin roots.

Political patronage obviously translated into religious and economic patronages. The Hindu kings doled out vast tracts of land and other monetary benefits to the Brahmin sects that they sponsored, respected, protected and allowed in their palaces.

Within their specific empires and kingdoms, the kings allowed the religious sects access to control over the Hindu temples and pilgrimages. Suppose a specific Hindu sect managed to gain proximity to several kings and build a social following among them, it could comfortably lay claim to the most prominent Hindu pilgrimages.

In tussles over the rights to prominent temples and pilgrimages, the kings could emerge as the adjudicators in some ways and influence the power bases of the Hindu sects. Once the British emerged as the colonial rulers, they gained similar powers and responsibilities.

According to historians, there were several such tussles between the various Hindu clans in the eighteenth century. For example, in 1760, the Dashnami (meaning ten names) sect who were establishd by Shakaracharya in the eight century took over Haridwar, and the Ramanandis were able to return to this holy city only after the British took it over.

For the Ramanandis, both political and religious patronages were crucial in the eighteenth century. In the early part of the century, they were in the doldrums vis-à-vis the power structure with the other sects. Ayodhya, the birthplace of Lord Ram and, hence, the most important centre for the Ramanand sect, was not in their grip. Routed from their most sacred place, one of the priorities was to regain control over this place of pilgrimage and expand their authority over the others.

In fact, in this century, we see the origins and evolution of the militant orders, or akharas, within the Ramanandi sect. By the time of Aurangzeb's death, Sawai Jai Singh, the ruler of Amer, turned out to be one of the popular princes of north India. A staunch Hindu, he held a conference of the Ramanandi sect at Galata, near Jaipur, during the first quarter of the eighteenth century. It is in this meet that Balananda, who was the then head of the Ramanandis, was conferred with the task of 'organizing military wings (*naga* sections) of the various Vaishnava sects.' The instructions given by Jai Singh were all well executed by the sages. 'Govindadas (of the Nirmohi Akhara) established the first akhara of the Ramanandis in Ayodhya soon after his arrival from the Conference. Around the same time, Abhayramadas founded the Nirvani akhara on Hanuman Tila.

Gradually, in the course of the century, all other Ramanandi akharas established themselves in Ayodhya.'[19]

Thus the famous three akharas—Nirvani, Nirmohi and Digambar—established headquarters and started having a considerable presence in Ayodhya during this period.

The purpose of the militant orders was to help capture the places of pilgrimages through violence and alongside gain from the growing political patronage. These akharas, along with the others, are proudly showcased at the regular annual Kumbh festivals, even today.

By the early twentieth century, the transformation was complete. The Ramanand sect emerged as a full-fledged separate sect and turned itself into becoming the most famous and established one in north India.

Burghart explains, 'According to the (fourth) spiritual genealogy of the Ramanandi sect which was approved at the Kumbh festival held at Ujjain in 1921, Lord Ram divulged his mantra which was transmitted down through twenty-one generations of gods, rishis, and saints to Ramanand. The Sri (sect) tradition and the Dravidian (south Indian) preceptors were purged from the history of the Ramanandi sect thereby affirming the sectarian independence of the Ramanandi ascetics.'

Ayodhya, as was obvious, became the spiritual centre of the Ramanandi sect, although their sub-sects were distributed in several parts of the country. Most akharas and sub-clans had their offices and headquarters in Ayodhya. The Ramanandis ruled Ayodhya.

The British carried on with their policy to divide the Hindus and Muslims. To protect the Hindus both from the British connivance and the Muslims, the Ramanandis and the Sikh Khalsas joined hands. This may be one reason why in the infighting between the bairagis and the Muslims, the Sikhs had chipped in to support the Hindus.

The constant violence between the Muslims and the Hindus in Ayodhya that carried on even after Independence and Partition also led to a conspiracy that helped install Ram Lalla's idol under the central dome of the Babri Masjid in 1949.

However, over the next few decades, mainly because of the Congress rule, several Hindu political parties and religious groups and sects felt compelled to remain at the sidelines. Until the 1970s, even as the Hindus and Muslims battled over Ayodhya, rioted in several parts across the country, the war remained within the realm of the judiciary. At the social level, the divisions were few, and the two communities continued to live in proximity in the temple town.

The scenario changed in the 1980s. The decade witnessed the political and electoral rise of the Indian People's Party, more popularly known as the Bharatiya Janata Party. The Hindu right-wing party established strong bases across north India, both at the national and state levels. As I document in other chapters, a few developments helped it foment sentiments to take advantage of the growing nationalist and patriotic fervour rooted in Hinduism.

Simultaneously, the Universal Hindu Council or Vishva Hindu Parishad, one of the RSS affiliates, fanned the feelings around Lord Ram and Ayodhya, which centred on social violence. For example, in this modernized narrative, Ayodhya became the place for yet another socio-religious battle to reclaim Hinduism.

VHP leaders claim that there were around seventy-six wars fought during the Mughal rule in which around three lakh Hindus lost their lives.

Within Ayodhya and across the country, ancient legends were revived. One of these mythologies mention that Lord Shiva cursed the River Sarayu, which the common folk believe was the reason for so much bloodshed over the centuries.

The lord of simultaneous creation and destruction was angered by the fact that the river allowed *jal-samadhi* (suicide by drowning in the water) to Lord Ram. In a rage, Lord Shiva said that any devotee, follower or saint who took a dip in this river would commit a sin. River Sarayu asked for forgiveness and the curse changed to a milder one. Lord Shiva said that the river's water would never be considered holy enough, unlike the water from several other Indian rivers, and so would not be used for religious rituals.

The seventy-seventh fight to liberate the Janmabhoomi was launched in the mid-1980s and spearheaded by the VHP. The website of Hindu Vivek Kendra, 'a resource centre for the promotion of Hindutva' specifies, 'Those who criticise the present Rama Janmabhoomi movement as a politically inspired stratagem appear to be blissfully ignorant of the fact that ever since the ancient birth-place of Sri Rama was desecrated by Babar's hordes in A.D. 1528, there has been a continual succession of struggles waged by the Hindus for recovery of the Janmasthan. As many as 76 major wars have been fought for this cause in the past. The present Rama Janmabhoomi Mukti Yajna is the 77th, and a nonviolent struggle.'[20]

The fact, however, remains that the Ram Janmabhoomi was won through the killings of thousands of people in various incidents. In October and November 1990, Mulayam Singh Yadav, chief minister, Uttar Pradesh, ordered firing on the karsevaks, killing sixteen people.

Most Muslims in Ayodhya believe that after the Babri Masjid was demolished on 6 December 1992, many karsevaks carried on a rampage for almost two days at a stretch. When I asked a few of the minorities how they were so convinced that it was the karsevaks who were targeting the local Muslims, Asif, whose house was set on fire the same evening, promptly counter-questioned, 'Who else would respond so enthusiastically to the summoning of senior right-wing leaders like L.K. Advani, Uma Bharti, Praveen Togadia and Ashok Singhal and take trouble to come from all across the country to Ayodhya for the sake of Ram?' Most of the local Hindus became a part of the Hindutva movement in these years.

Thousands of Hindus and Muslims died in national riots soon after. At the end of the day, this battle, which culminated in the 2019 Supreme Court judgment, was about a structure and not a community.

In 1994, historian Gyanendra Pandey wrote in his paper, 'Modes of History: Writing New Hindu History of Ayodhya': 'It will be clear by now, it is not a history of the region, much less the people of Ayodhya. It is not even about a spot, Ram Janam Bhoomi; it is about a building on that spot. This entire history is focused on a monument, which we can, for the moment, designate the "grand temple" built on the site of Shri Ram's "birth". Everything revolves around this monument. The narrative begins with the destruction of the monument and returns to this point again and again.'[21]

Hence, it was unlike the previous wars, when the Ramanandi sect fought with other Hindu sects for access to pilgrimages and dominance over the Hindu devotees and followers. It was also different because the seventy-seventh war, unlike some previous ones, pitted Hindus against Muslims, not Hindus against Hindus.

Since violence was an integral component of the rise of the Ramanandi sect, which was also signalled by the deliberate decision to form the akhara-army in the eighteenth century, it was not too difficult to add the ingredients of aggression and fierceness to the seventy-seventh war of religious liberation. Emotions were stirred in the spiritual cauldron, and the toxic vapours affected millions.

One could sense this in just three words, *Jai Shri Ram*, which formed a phrase that echoed with shattering tempo. It became a regular greeting, like a hello and namaste, since the 1980s. The earlier greetings in Ayodhya were the likes of *Jai Sita Ram* or *Jai*

Siya Ram, unlike the new phrase that revealed masculinity and had a more macho tone and tenor.

Stickers appeared in Ayodhya and elsewhere, which instructed people with the order: '*Hello nahin; bolo Jai Shri Ram* (Don't say hello; greet with Jai Shri Ram).' Similar stickers can be seen at the RSS headquarters in Nagpur. On new posters, the image of Lord Ram changed from a god with a beatific smile to a warlike image, ready to battle with a trident and bow and arrows.[22]

Lord Ram was used by the VHP and Bajrang Dal and their lakhs of followers more for his warrior expertise than the benevolent king who believed in spreading love and kindness wherever he went. The concept of Ram Rajya—an administration that was fair, transparent, peaceful and kind—was used, but in a different context. Ram Rajya could now only come after victory over the Ram Janmabhoomi.

The Rambhakts had selective amnesia when they tried to emulate Ram or even follow the epic. Vishwamitra, who was Ram's spiritual guide and philosopher, made it clear while awarding him with celestial weapons that attacking the weak or innocent to prove his might did not count as dharma of the brave.

Even the most benevolent and helpful, although strong and powerful, Hanuman's character was recreated in an animation form to highlight anger. In 2015, twenty-nine-year-old Kerala-based graphic designer, Karan Acharya, created an image (portrait) of an angry Hanuman for reasons that he maintained were 'playfully and for free for his friend'.

Within no time, this version of Hanuman was on T-shirts, laptop covers and windscreens of cars and buses. The image went viral and was appreciated by Prime Minister Narendra Modi. Speaking to the NDTV news channel, Karan said he was both 'shocked' and 'happy' that his work was praised by Modi at an election rally in Karnataka.[23] Speculations began within media circles as to why some cars displayed this incomplete portrait—the designer claimed he had yet to finish it. One media house said that it could possibly be an internal code, in case of violence. 'The cars with the sticker might be allowed to pass through by the security forces and rioters.' Obviously, this was not true. It was a fad, triggered by the state of consensual emotion.

Such reactions clearly indicate that people are encouraged to appreciate aggressiveness and anger and fan macho elements from the epic. The phrase Jai Shri Ram gradually became a social battle cry.

Most battle cries used by the army are of the feminine goddesses who symbolize shakti (power). The Gorkha Regiment worships Mahakali and Gorkhakali, the Jammu and Kashmir Rifle hails Durga, and Jammu and Kashmir Light Infantry calls out *Bharat Mata ki jai*. Among the male gods, Shiva is famous, along with his other name, Mahadev.

While both the Kumaon Regiment and Rajput Regiment hail Bajrang Bali (Hanuman), Ram is used by the Rajputana Regiment, whose war cry is *Raja Ram Chandra ki jai* (Hail King Ram). However, the salute to Lord Ram was used rampantly during the Kargil War in May 1999. When the martyrs were saluted for their bravery, the salutations mostly ended with 'Jai Shri Ram'.

In the last week of July 2019, forty-nine celebrities from across the country wrote to the Prime Minister about the phrase and the way it was being used. 'Regrettably, "Jai Shri Ram" has become a provocative war cry today that leads to law-and-order issues, and sadly many lynchings take place in its name.' They made a request, 'Ram is sacred for the majority community, stop defiling the name of Ram.'

The phrase Jai Shri Ram definitely lacks the softness that comes with the older versions, Jai Siya Ram or Jai Sita Ram. In his book *The Healing Power of the Human Voice*, James D'Angelo writes that the 'sound S animates, inspires, purifies, it generates warmth. The combination of AY is all about making connections, of finding the WAY through, as it were. The sound of R, which is a fiery one resonates with particular potency and, at the beginning of a word, tends to propel its sound forcefully.'[24]

However, the impact of the violent tones, phrases and sentiments that were pummelled by the VHP and other RSS wings in the hearts and souls of Hindus was aided by other social developments.

It is a typical winter evening. The sun has just set on Ayodhya. Life is at its usual pace. Everything appears calm and reticent till I step out of the parking area in Shringar Market and spot a crowd. People, as in Hindus, are standing in a semi-circle. There is no sermon or slogans rejoicing the verdict of the apex court. No Muslims are spotted here.

I hear a familiar song, '*Mangal bhavan amangal haari*', which brings back memories from decades ago. It was the jingle played as the hit Hindi TV serial, *Ramayana*, began every Sunday. I am transported to the 1980s when it was first aired by the state-owned Doordarshan.

But this is 2019. It seems that a local club set up a TV screen and decided to play clippings from Ramanand Sagar's serial to celebrate the Supreme Court's verdict.

The serial, which started on 25 January 1987, gripped the country with its mythological magnetism. Every Sunday, there would be a lull on the streets and marketplaces, as people glued to their or their neighbours' TVs.

In 1987, TV was a luxury. Those who lacked the privilege were given options—call it benevolence or soft advertising of the local business class—and several community clubs, stores and restaurants played the serial for public consumption.

The serial had lavish sets, actors with apt dresses, heart-touching dialogues and innovative flying weapons. The TRP (Television Rating Point) was never less than 80 per cent. Marketers introduced masks and maces of Hanuman, and sets of toy bows and arrows were sold both by street hawkers and plush toy-store owners. Children gave up on battery-operated cars and delicate dolls for these new toys, which ironically embodied the weapons in an ancient text. Hanuman, who flew like Batman with his mace, became the most popular and loved hero with kids.

'The decision to televise religious serials represented a considerable departure from the earlier broadcasting policy, and clearly signalled an attempt to formulate a cohesive, Hindu upper-caste-dominated cultural identity for the nation. Justifying the telecast of the Ramayana serial, the information and broadcasting secretary overseeing the decision, S.S. Gill, described the epic as cultural rather than religious, with universalist values applicable to all. There was a majoritarian premise to his argument, but clearly, the quotes were being removed from "religious" programming: a Hindu epic was now identified with Indian culture in general.' Arvind Rajagopal, a professor of media studies at New York University, analyses that it was a strange coincidence that the serial *Ramayana* which was broadcasted from January 1987 to August 1989 'covered'the most crucial phase of the Janmabhoomi movement when it changed from a relatively little-known "tala-kholo" agitation to the dominant political issue before the country—one that made and unmade prime ministers and ruling parties'.[25]

The serial reinforced Ayodhya as Ram's birthplace and thus propped up the town's significance as one of the most important pilgrimages for Hindus. Indirectly it hyped the Hindu sentiments of completely acquiring Ram's Janmabhoomi and doing away with anything that came in the way. In his book *A History of India*, historian Burton Stein wrote, 'Media-generated "Ramayana fever" soon found a wider public expression. This focused on growing agitation over the mosque, known as the Babri Masjid, built in 1528 in the reign of the Mughal emperor Babur, which was said—on the basis of disputed historical evidence—to be on the site of an earlier Hindu temple and birthplace of Rama. The VHP led demands that the mosque, in the town of Ayodhya in Uttar Pradesh, should be demolished and replaced by a new temple dedicated to the deity.'[26] Dr Surendra Jain, international joint general secretary of the VHP, does not believe that it was the serial *Ramayana* that created all such reactions. He explains, '*Hindu samaj ko Ram ke prati hamesha atoot shraddha thi aur rahegi, ye koi serial ke wajah se nahi bana sakta hai koi* (The Hindus always have had indomitable faith towards Lord Ram, no serial is capable of creating such a belief).' He does not approve of giving so much credit to one serial in comparison to the strife that the Hindus took up for Ram Janmabhoomi. His logic, 'After all, there were many similar serials before *Ramayana* that were aired.'

Yet the coincidence cannot be overlooked. The *SAGE Handbook of Media Studies* states, 'The same year saw massive protest demonstrations by Muslims, countered by rallies of Militant Hindus determined to "reclaim" the Babri Masjid site. These were followed by laying of the foundation stone for a temple at the disputed site in 1989 and culminated eventually in December 1992 with the attack on the Babri Mazjid and bloody confrontations throughout the country.'[27]

In unique ways, the serial succeeded in garnering emotional and entertaining childhood memories that several generations grew up with. Consider, for instance, the Ram Lila during the Dusshera festival. As a child, I watched Ram, Sita, Lakshman, Hanuman, Vanar Sena, Ravan and the rest of the characters from the Ramayana at the annual street-side, tent theatres. They were enacted in most northern towns, cities and villages during the ten days of the Dussehra festival.

Both kids and adults watched it in the evenings for a couple of hours. On the last day, the towering effigies of Ravan with his two brothers, Meghnad and Kumbhakarna, were burnt. As Ram appeared on stage, the crowd would cheer, hailing the characters from the epic, '*Jai Sita Ram, bolo bolo Ram Chandar ji ki jai*' and so on. The actor who played Ram became a living god for those days. I remember how I would pine to go and meet the actor 'Ram' and 'Sita' after each show. However, much to my dismay, I often discovered that a boy played Sita's role.

The charm of Ram Lila, though less now, still draws audiences. Puranand Kalra is a businessman from Rajendra Nagar in New Delhi. He has participated in the local Ram Lila staged by the Rajendra Nagar Art Club for thirty-five years. He has played Ram's role for the past twenty-five years. He says, 'People still come in huge numbers, about a thousand at least. Those who have faith and want their children to learn about the great Lord Ram make the crowd these days.'

Kalra enthusiastically shares, 'I love my role, and once every year, I feel as if I am being cleansed of every worldly sin.' There is an oath-taking ceremony two months before the staging of the Ram Lila. The participants promise to leave their personal tasks and devote themselves to the theatre group for the next eight weeks. The actor playing Ram even changes his diet to become a pure vegetarian.

There were two years when Kalra played Hanuman. Like the god he was to play, he led a celibate life and slept on the floor (Hanuman was a *brahmachari*, a celibate). The interesting part about the Ram Lila is that in several regions Urdu couplets are used along with Sanskrit *shloka*s (religious couplets) and Hindi dialogues. The percussion instruments, violin and synthesiser are mostly played by Muslim musicians.

'They are as dedicated as Hindus. It is about Ram's values that we imbibe during these months, and no thought of divisiveness ever crosses our minds,' adds Kalra. He mentions that even Bollywood star Shah Rukh Khan participated in the same Ram Lila during his teenage days. In April 2016, the superstar confessed that he lost his stage fright because of his acting in Delhi's Rajendra Nagar Ram Lila. 'I was cast as a monkey with a long tail. It was a good start and a great platform to showcase my talent. I would mimic Prithviraj Kapoor and even do *shayaris*. That's how I lost the fear of the crowd. It gave me a lot of confidence, performing live in front of thousands,' he said.[28]

4

Ram's Protégés

'Mukhmen Tulsi Ghatamen Ram, Jab Bolo Tab Sita Ram'

—FROM THE BHAJAN '*RAGHUPATI RAGHAV RAJA RAM* ...'

Probably no other Indian city can claim to be the cradle of an ancient epic as palpably as Ayodhya. And its status as the birthplace of Lord Ram granted the Ramanandi sadhus the religious licence to make this city their own.

With the sages calling the shots (until recently), the temple town remained a destination whose popularity revolved around the Hindu Vaishnava God Ram. The sadhus still believe that they have been the ones who have kept the cult of the Ramanandi sect alive for centuries. Their common guru is Ramanand, who they believe was an avatar of Ram. Over a period, these followers established their institutions, commonly called akharas.

As mentioned in the previous chapter, different akharas were founded after a conference of the Ramanandi sect was held at

Galata, near Jaipur, in the first quarter of the eighteenth century, under the auspices of Hindu King Sawai Jai Singh. It was in these sessions that a decision was taken to organize the military wings of the Vaishnava sadhus.

Apart from the Nirmohi and Nirvani akharas, the third famous akhara in Ayodhya is Digambar. All three are attached to the Akhil Bharatiya Akhara Parishad (All India Akhara Council), an apex body of Hindu sages and saints. Besides these majors, there are hundreds of smaller ashrams and temples in the town. They, too, draw the interests of the enthusiastic pilgrims.

After the 2019 Supreme Court verdict, I visited Ayodhya several times. One of my priorities was to talk to the mahants of the akharas and the heads of different other smaller ashrams, whom I had met many times earlier. This time, I was keen to understand their reactions to the decision of the apex court. I also wanted to meet those sadhus who are not under the radar of any formally established religious order, as also the regular residents whose belief in Lord Ram is possibly firmer than that of many saints.

More than that, through these Hindu religious and spiritual leaders, I wanted to re-understand the town. What had changed, and what had not? For me, it was always a town that was divided on several fronts—the constant strife between the temple and the mosque, between Hindus and Muslims, between the local Hindus and the VHP as also between some well-known mahants.

Many mahants I met over the last two decades exuded superficial spirituality. They were wracked with and influenced by jealousy, ego, power games, greed, and other such human sins. They blatantly blamed others within the religious fold for these negatives and absolved themselves in the process.

At the same time, Ayodhya was also a place that somehow unified people from various walks of life in many ways. Several

Hindus and Muslims intermingled and lived peacefully, at least till the demolition of the Babri Masjid.

Then there have also been a couple of dedicated and devoted mahants who fought for their people, that is, the Hindus, but never at the expense of Muslims. For them, a temple was a possibility, and so was a scenario when the two communities could live together.

It is an unusually foggy winter morning. The contours of the butter-yellow imposing archway defeat the smoky haze and stand out conspicuously against the dull grey backdrop. Buff-coloured granite slabs lie on top of each other on either side of a large iron gate. The arch announces: Akhil Bharatiya Sri Panch, Ramananda Nirmohi Akhada, Ram Janmabhoomi.

Waiting in queue outside is not a great experience.

Dirty yawning gutters bind both sides of the rutted road. A municipality janitor on duty passes by with an empty cart. His attention is focused on the devotees instead of the muck lying around. As time passes, more pilgrims join the queue outside the akhara.

A few locals warn us to hold on to our cellphones tightly. 'Even the monkeys have a fascination for mobiles and prefer to snatch them instead of the victuals these days,' explains one of them. People laugh and spontaneously tighten the grips on their handsets.

The ashram gives the feel of a mediocre guest house with a covered portico that opens into a garden. The only fanciful element is a white SUV, parked outside the main door. There is a tiny shabby garden patch that looks pretty despite being uncared for.

The mahant of the Nirmohi Akhara, Dinendra Nath Das, makes an appearance and welcomes me with folded hands, saying, '*Jai Sita*

Ram.' Before we step indoors, I begin the conversation by asking him about the plants cropping up randomly in the garden. He responds with a mischievous grin, 'The plant in that corner is of curry leaf gifted by a devotee from south India. And the wild shrubs are Shiva's prasad!'

The security constable lets out a chuckle and quickly adds, 'The sadhus need the prasad.'

I thought the mahant's mood would be a bit off because of the Supreme Court order. It stated that the Nirmohi Akhara does not enjoy any claim as a *shebait*—a person or entity appointed to serve a deity, maintain the property and manage it—for the Ram Janmabhoomi Temple. Hence, the mahant of this akhara is not deemed to be a pujari in this temple. Thus, the akhara has lost all rights it had enjoyed once upon a time over the then disputed property.

The order clarified that 'a stray or intermittent exercise of management rights does not confer upon a claimant the position in law of a de facto *shebait*. It cannot be said that the acts of Nirmohi Akhara satisfy the legal standard of management and charge that is exclusive, uninterrupted and continuous over a sufficient period of time. Despite their undisputed presence at the disputed site, for the reasons outlined above, Nirmohi Akhara is not a *shebait*.'

Robed in a soft shade of saffron over his small frame, the akhara head puts up an act of insouciance and appears neither flustered nor angry. On the contrary, he seems to be amused at the queries that the devotees smother him with. His replies are loaded with forged metaphors.

For example, while discussing the akharas, he distinguishes between the literal meaning of the word—a place for wrestling—and the role of his institution. 'These days, we teach the art of mind games and train sadhus how to wrestle the brains in the right direction. We are living in *ghor kaliyug* (the dark ages) where no one cares about building muscles but are ready to play tricks on one another!'

He elaborates that the akharas have to play different war games now. 'Haven't you read how we were removed from what was our right?' he asks. And soon backtracks: 'At the end of it, we are willing to accept the law of the land, as we want peace, not *paisa*.'

The idea of organizing a martial army goes back to the mythological legends from Ramayana. There were occasions when the *rakshasa*s (demons) created havoc in the affairs of the pious men. The holy men then requested the king of Ayodhya, Dashrath, for help. An army was subsequently formed to ensure the safety of the sages.

Perhaps for the same security reason, wresting became an important activity in some of these akharas (arena). However, it was not an activity in two of the most popular akharas in Ayodhya, the Nirmohi and Digambar Akharas, ever since they were formed or even early in their evolutionary phases. On the contrary, this would be a feature in the Nirvani Akhara of Hanumangarhi. When I discuss this difference with Dinendra Das, he clarifies that the Nirmohi and Nirvani akharas have always worked differently and never been in sync, 'I really do not want to comment on them; they have done me much harm.' Instead of giving any further details, he quickly changes the topic.

It is important to dwell a while on this age-old animosity, which resulted in Nirmohi Akhara's inability to produce the official 'title' papers in the apex court to prove its ownership rights over the Ram Janmabhoomi.

Sushil Jain, the lawyer for the Nirmohi Akhara, informed the Supreme Court bench that a 1982 robbery led to the loss of the records that were required to prove their claim. Soon after the theft, an FIR (first information report) was lodged at the local police station, but the case was quashed through an out-of-court settlement.

I want a one-on-one chat with Mahant Dinendra, which seems impossible on that particular day because of the enormous crowd of devotees. I get an appointment for a few days later. This worked out well as I find him in a more relaxed mood. Seated on a charpoy under the warm sun, he begins to talk nostalgically about his past, with no prompting from me.

His father was a high-school teacher in Rajapur Saraiya, a tiny hamlet in eastern Uttar Pradesh. Dinendra Nath was only eight years of age when his life took a 'holy turn'. After the 1978 local elections at the Baurababa Mutt, he was elected the new mahant. The mutt's legacy includes donation of male children by certain families, usually when the child turns five. Dinendra's family had done the same. During the elections, the kid was thus elected as the new mahant because of the earlier benefaction.

'People were envious when I was selected. Many wanted their children to grab the post. One of the reasons was probably because of the wealth the ashram generated. Thankfully, my family was well-off, had no longing for material things and were happy to give me away for the service of the Lord. They were delighted also because my new role had given the family an exalted status in society,' says the mahant.

The elected child most times continued with his usual everyday life, 'I went to school, amused myself till late evening in the open fields and, luckily, I was not even reprimanded for being mischievous or playing pranks. You see, no one dares to shout at an abbot!'

The child-mahant had no clue about religious nuances and the behaviour expected from a religious chief. He confesses that the only person he was afraid of during those early years was the head priest. 'It was a Saligram Temple, which means that there were idols of various gods and goddesses. There is a similar one in Ayodhya. Visit it when you can,' he adds. Devotees would visit the mutt to get initiated, and whenever this happened, the new child-mahant was sent for.

A quick ritual followed—he was handed out a set of fresh saffron attire and his forehead was smeared with sandalwood paste. He had to listen to each word that the head priest said, which, in turn, had to be repeated verbatim in the ears of the devotees.

Dinendra Nath Das laughs as he recollects, 'I was around eight years of age and studying in Class IV. In those years I barely knew Sanskrit. It was impossible for me to remember all the mantras. The head purohit was kind and would stay by me during all the important ceremonies and would help me recite the right lines when required. Even at that tender age, I was accepted as a profound guru and had several followers.' He is convinced that it was God's will to make him work for the Almighty from a very young age.

On my earlier trip, I had noticed teenage boys in dhotis and kurtas in the large open area within the Nirmohi Akhara. I ask about them this time, and the mahant gladly sends for them. I am informed that they are brahmacharis (celibate students with devotion and loyalty to a guru) who reside within the campus. At the time of my visit, there are a dozen of them hailing either from Bihar or eastern Uttar Pradesh. Besides them, there are also a handful of adults hanging around the premises. They are not saints but constitute a vital part of the akhara.

Durgesh Shukla is one of the most sought-after among them. He is well-versed in Hindu scriptures and appears to be the mahant's right-hand man. Tall and well-built, his demeanour stands out. Though a family man, he spends a lot of his time with his guru. He is a political activist whose heart lies with the Hindu Mahasabha.

'My guru of this yuga, Maharaj-ji, does not like me giving political statements or opinions. Despite it, I would like to affirm that the VHP, which is hand in glove with the ruling government, has a mercenary interest in the Ram Temple.'

A few students arrive after their school hours, and I chat with a couple of them. Sarvendra Nath is a resident brahmachari. The sixteen-year-old is from Siddharthnagar in Uttar Pradesh, a border town close to Nepal. He and his five mates attend the decrepit Sanskrit Sriram Mahavidyalaya, which is opposite the Nirmohi Akhara. They are fully dedicated to their institution as much as they are to Ram. One of them defends it almost angrily when I talk about the poor condition of the school building, 'So what if it looks shabby? What we learn here is far better than the other students from swanky schools.' To prove his point he tells me how well he knows the *Bhagavat Katha* (a holy text of the Hindus) which most boys of his age would not. The adolescent who is visibly dedicated to Lord Ram and aspires to spread the Sanatan Dharma.

There are around eighteen such Sanskrit institutions in Ayodhya. The most popular is the Sri Raj Gopal Sanskrit Mahavidyalaya, located on the banks of the River Sarayu. Named after the founder, it started in 1864, and, till today, the mahant of the Raj Gopal Temple remains the de-facto principal. From the Nirmohi Akhara, I leave for this reputed institute. On the way, I visit the Nageshwar (lord of the cobras, another avatar of Lord Shiva) Temple. Naval Rai, who was the prime minister and army commander of the second Nawab of Awadh, Safdarjung, had renovated this temple in 1750.

As per the legend, the temple was built by one of Lord Ram's twin sons, Kush. One day when he was bathing in the Sarayu, his armlet slipped off and was lost. One morning, Naag-Kanya (daughter of a cobra) found it and returned it to the prince. Since she was a devotee of Lord Shiva, Kush built the temple in the honour of the same god.

The temple's mahant, Sabhapat Tiwari, insists that I first anoint the *shivaling* with wood-apple leaves and milk, as is the tradition here. There is a queue of devotees, and I join them. I tiptoe ahead as the floor is slippery with a thick film of milk and water on it. One has to be extra careful, as there are bulls and cows loitering inside as well. These animals are considered auspicious as they are Shiva's and Krishna's companions, according to Hindu belief. They are happy to chew on the offerings—loads of flowers, wood-apple leaves and fruits. No one dares disturb them.

Later, I go upstairs to the mahant's office. He is busy. Commenting on the present status of the town, he shoots from his hip, which clearly projects his dislike for the ruling party. At the same time, he does not want his voice against the VHP on record. He instead plays it safe and states that it is an organization that works mainly for the development of the Hindus.

A little further down the road is the Sri Raj Gopal Sanskrit Mahavidyalaya, whose students are also mainly from eastern Uttar Pradesh and Bihar. The curriculum includes Sanskrit, Hindu philosophy, literature, astrology and teachings from the Yajur Veda (one of the four Vedas with teachings about karma or action).

Rumour has it that the students here even learn skills to defend and attack. This possibly started due to the infighting within the ashram. When I ask about these frictions, Madhusudan Das, a senior faculty member, dismisses the question. Meanwhile I wait for the principal, Mahant Kaushal Kishore, commonly referred to as Falahari (a person on a fruit diet) Baba. A tall and well-built man, he looks stately as he walks out of his room located at one end of the terrace.

It is about 2 p.m., and the teachers and pupils have just finished their lunch. Falahari Baba dons a short white kurta and *lungi* (a drape wrapped around the waist extending to the ankle) with an ochre-yellow shawl covering his upper body. Students passing by stop to bend down and touch his feet. He appears relaxed as he sits on a deck chair earmarked for him.

He begins the conversation on his own. Regarding the Supreme Court verdict, he says, 'One needs to do thorough research on our country before coming to any conclusion. You wait and watch. The construction of the Ram Mandir will widen and deepen the fracture that already exists between Hindus and Muslims.' He believes that this divide has been created solely by the saffron leaders who do nothing to bridge it.

The octogenarian seems to forget some of the past events and seeks help from Madhusudan. But he has strong views, 'Most of our leaders are biased. *Jhagra tab tak hoga jab tak buddhi aur vivek kaam nahi karegenge* (The fights will continue if intellect and wisdom don't work).'

Muslims, he believes, have never been allowed to rank up with the Hindus, which is why this judgment will make them feel even more alienated. 'Muslims in our country should be respected as equals. What an emperor did centuries ago should not be repeated by us. Why spoil the present for the misdeeds of the past?'

He laments that the spiritual ethos of Ayodhya will change in the future as everything will gradually turn commercial. '*Vikriti aa jayegi hamare sharir ki tarah aur ek din yeh Ayodhya khatam ho jayegi* (Just as the body decays and dies, Ayodhya might too [if this happens].)

It is ironic that Mahant Nritya Gopal Das, the head of the Ram Janmabhoomi Teerth Kshetra, which is entrusted with the task of constructing the new Ram Janmabhoomi Temple, besides other related tasks, is a product of this institute. In public, Nritya Gopal Das maintains that he completed his graduation from Kashi in Uttar Pradesh, never mentioning his association with Sri Raj Gopal Sanskrit Mahavidyalaya.

Mahant Nritya Gopal Das is a stalwart and the most imperious sadhu in Ayodhya. He heads Mani Ram Das ki Chhavni, popularly known as Chhoti Chhavni, meaning small cantonment; but in contrast to its name, it is the largest ashram in the town. He became the head in 1965 when he was twenty-seven years old, and old-timers remember the pomp and show of the occasion. He succeeded Mani Ram Das Maharaj (after whom this ashram has been named) as the sixth head.

His powers became national, even global, when he was appointed as the head of the Ram Janmabhoomi Nyas (RJN) in 2003. The RJN was founded a decade earlier, on 15 January 1993, to look into the religious affairs and construction of the then-proposed Ram Temple.

The mahant lives on the first floor of the ashram, from where one can easily see the Valmiki Bhavan standing bang opposite, a temple dedicated to the ancient and original writer of the Ramayana. Thousands of couplets from the epic are inscribed on the pillars of the Valmiki Bhavan, and frescoes depict scenes from the same. The bookstall within the premises sells the Ramayana, books on stories of Ayodhya and even a biography of Nritya Gopal Das.

My first attempt to meet the chief is unsuccessful. He is out on a PR exercise with some bigwigs from Delhi who are in Ayodhya. His second-in-command, Kamal Nayan Das Shastri, gives me another appointment and explains, 'After the Supreme Court's order, there are celebratory functions, and Mahant-ji is invited to each of them. He has a tight schedule.'

Kamal Nayan's gratitude and hyperboles about the judgment are unending. He feels sad that Ashok Singhal, the brain and brawn behind the VHP, is not alive to see his dream come true. 'The architect of the Ram Temple is Singhal.' From Singhal, he moves to the Prime Minister. 'We Hindus are blessed to have Modi-ji as our head, as he is not any different from us sadhus. He is endowed with all saintly qualities.'

He informs me that Modi had earlier stated that Singhal's death was a huge personal loss. He had also mentioned that the people should respect the departed's dream to construct a Bhavya Mandir (grand temple).

Once again, after a gap of almost a month, I return to Ayodhya. This time, meeting Nritya Gopal Das is one of my top priorities. 'Mahant-ji needs to relax, as he has lots of responsibilities,' explains a visitor sage. I nod and spend the waiting time looking around. Both of us are waiting for our turns to meet the head of the Shri Ram Janmabhoomi Teerth Kshetra Trust set up by the Government of India in early 2020. The trust has been entrusted with the responsibility to construct the Ram Temple.

Tall, sturdy pillars in the two adjoining prayer halls seem to hold up the high ceiling. A few of these have beautiful engravings. In the far left corner of the hall, a priest reads out non-stop from the *Ramcharitmanas* which is placed on a wooden book stand. This chanting continues through the day. Next to this small stand is a tiny marble Hanuman, like the ones sold in curio stores.

Lord Ram, Sita and Lakshman are dressed beautifully and placed conspicuously under a huge silver umbrella at the temple's extreme end, opposite the vast entrance door.

Devotees admire the statues and even hug the pillars as they wait for the prasad. Every afternoon, huge quantities of bhog is distributed among all devotees who visit the ashram. There are two *daan-peti*s (donation boxes) prominently placed on a pedestal at the entrance—one marked for the temple and the other for the 'Holy Cow'.

My summon arrives. Nritya Gopal Das is reclining on a well-stuffed bolster. His sevak massages the guru's feet non-stop. After the usual greetings, I get straight to the point, 'I see the Muslims have become quiet and distant after the judgment?' But I soon realize it was not the right way to start the conversation. 'The media reads too much into things. You are absolutely mistaken. They will surely join us in the construction of the Ram Temple,' he promptly and authoritatively replies.

I am reminded of the feelings of fear and trauma that the Muslims expressed a few weeks ago. I change the topic and ask the chief about his pre-sanyasi years. He touches his right ear, mentions his guru's name (a Hindu custom to show respect), and talks about his *diksha sanskar* (a ritual when a guru entrusts a mantra to a disciple) when he was eighteen years old.

Born into a Brahmin family on 11 June 1938 in Kerhala village, Muttura, western Uttar Pradesh, he joined the Lala Ram College in his town to study commerce. The structured curriculum did not hold his interest. On a Gandhi Jayanti day, he left for Ayodhya in search of a guru. He was fortunate to meet an enlightened sage, Ram Manohar Das, as he tells me.

'My guru encouraged people to be educated. Initially, I taught Sanskrit here and then decided to pursue higher studies. I went to Varanasi, where I enrolled in the Sanskrit University, and graduated as a "Shastri" (a title given to scholars),' he claims with pride.

I am a bit confused. Earlier, Falahari Baba had told me that Nritya Gopal Das graduated from Sri Raj Gopal Sanskrit Mahavidyalaya but Nritya Gopal Das makes no mention of those years. I let it be and leave with the large packet of prasad he gives me. About a kilometre down the street, under the long, stout and wavy hanging roots of a peepal tree, Lord Shiva resides inside a nondescript temple. The man in charge is Ram Balak Das —an architect, builder, manager and priest, all in one. Just like him there are several such enterprising sages in this holy land who shifted to Ayodhya and made the town their home. To get a feel of Ayodhya it is important to know their pursuits and views as well: Ram Balak came to Ayodhya from Madhya Pradesh four decades ago, when he was twenty-two.

He claims proudly, 'It was all Ram's will.' In the same vein he also proclaims that he knew each line of the Ramayana by heart by the time he was eight years old. 'Then why did you build a temple for Shiva and not Ram?' I ask. He quips, 'Even Lord Ram worshipped Shiva. Besides, Ram has several abodes here, so I constructed one for Shiva. And soon Ram Lalla will be living in a grand temple in the Janmabhoomi site which will be one of the best temples in the world.' He adds, 'You must not forget that Ram was an ardent devotee of Shiva.'

His small Shiva temple reminds me of my childhood. We as kids would often construct similar but smaller such structures in our garden with bricks, leftover cement from neighbourhood construction sites, sand and white paint. But Ram Balak is far from being childlike. I ask him about the demolition of Babri Masjid. 'Don't call it by that name. We dub it as a mere *dhancha* (structure). Trust me, it was Lord's Ram's plan that brought it down. Mere mortals couldn't have done it without his blessings.' Dibyesh Anand, who has done extensive research on right-wing majoritarian nationalism in India, in his essay, 'The Awakened Hindu India—Ayodhya and Gujarat' observes that, 'Hindutva leaders, especially in recent decades, deny the very existence of the mosque—they call it *dhāñca*, "structure"—while maintaining the continual existence of a Lord Ram Temple despite architectural and historical evidence to the contrary.'[1]

I need to get out of this overload of religiosity. I absorb the surrounds as I move to another destination. The town is full of narrow lanes, monkeys and cows, deep dirty ditches, trails of tourists, buzzing bikes, and loudspeakers bellowing bhajans and melodious holy chants, many based on Bollywood numbers. Ayodhya creates an exciting and unique brew for anyone, no matter which part of the town one is in.

Balaji Tea Shop in Shringar Market is my favourite break-stop. Manoj Kumar has replaced his father (who has retired) as the owner. His standard response to any question is, 'I don't look at the customers; I just give them what they ask for.' A very politically correct guy, he does not seem interested in the temple-talk. Pilgrims drop by and sit on the wooden benches; some order tea and others prefer hot milk with saffron, a delicacy especially prepared during winters.

Occasionally, sadhus pop in to buy milk, cottage cheese or curd. Some of them are on bikes and sport sunglasses even after sundown. Sadhus in Ayodhya can be grouped into two lots—those who have established lineages and those who have found spaces in an akhara or ashram to lead a rather cushy life, far away from home.

A young sadhu sits across me and orders dumplings and coffee. He places his bag and prayer beads next to his plate. The arrangement interestingly symbolizes the recent juxtaposition of the modern and ancient in this town.

He is a graduate from the Saket University in Ayodhya. He came here after completing his high school in Basti, a small town in eastern Uttar Pradesh in search of a guru.

His found his guru in Mahant Anand Das from the Haridwar Patti (section) of Hanumangarhi. He refuses to share his original name; he was named Kamal Das in his new sainthood avatar. For some pocket money, he reads out from the Bhagavat to devotees every evening at the Anjani Gufa, a temple located two hundred metres away from Hanumangarhi complex and dedicated to Hanuman.

Kamal Das explains the four 'pattis' of Hanumangarhi, which is a small bastion with a gripping history of its own. It ranks among the three prestigious temples in Ayodhya. It was built on land granted by Nawab Safdarjang of Awadh and is an important landmark.

The akhara here works on the Panchayati system. It comprises three *jamaat*s (assemblies) and four *pattis*. The temple's head is known as the *Gaddi Nashin* (Urdu phrase meaning Crown Prince). Interestingly, all the rules governing the management are also scripted in Persian, a language that was brought to India in the eleventh century when Mahmud of Ghazni conquered part of northern India and established his power. Persian for a long time was used as the official language in many parts of the country.

In his essay, 'Sites of Memory and Structures of Power in North India', William R. Pinch explains, 'The rise of the Ramanandis was also due to the patronage of the Shia Nawabs—Safdarjang, Shuja-ud-daulah and Asaf-ud-Daulah (often today generalized as "Muslims"); the "key in this process was the agency of Kayastha ministers in the nawabi court, especially the staunch Vaishnavas, Naval Ray and Tikait Ray (Hindu). Further, legend recorded in the 1960 held that prior to the construction of the Ramanandi fort-monastery in the 18th century, Muslim devotees used to visit the mound upon which the Hanumangarhi would eventually be built. The site was generally known as "Hanumat-tilla".' Pinch in his essay mentions that though the site was popularly known as 'Hanumat-tilla', the locals revered it as a shrine dedicated to the Sufi saint, Hathile Pir, one of the Panch Piriya (five Sufi holy men) immensely popular across eastern Uttar Pradesh and Bihar. He further writes, 'The historian Hans Bakker added that when he was conducting research in Ayodhya in the early 1980s, he was told that until the riots of 1948 the compound of the Hanumangarhi contained a room in which Muslims used to offer their prayers.'[2]

After bumping into the young sage, Kamal Das, I decide to visit Mahant Gyan Das, one of the most popular and oldest sadhus from Hanumangarhi, who meets his followers at 6 p.m. every day. As the head of the temple-fort since 1962, he strives to maintain secularity as far as possible. 'How can anyone forget that Hanumangarhi was gifted to us by the Muslim Nawabs?'

In 2015, 'Mahant Gyan Das, facing the allegations of misbehaviour and criminal charges, [was] removed from the post of the president of All India Akhara Parishad (AIAP) and Mahant Narendra Giri elected as its new chief.'[3] He became an eye sore among his equals and other Hindutva leaders; his central folly was that he entertained Muslims—and even invited a hundred of them to break their Eid fast, Roza Iftaar, at his house. Almost ten times the number turned up. When reminded of this incident, he smiles and states, 'I still see no logic in misbehaving with the Muslims or snatching their rights.'

According to locals sadhus within Hanumangarhi the people who side with the VHP, vehemently opposed this act. Critics alleged that the action contaminated the sanctity of a Hindu holy place. Gyan Das had to ask a Muslim friend, Sadiq Ali, who is popularly known as Babu Tailor, to organize a Hanuman Chalisa (forty quatrains in praise of Hanuman scripted by Tulsidas) recital at a mosque. 'This was just to quieten all the noises made by those who had opposed the Iftaar,' reveals an insider who has been close to the mahant for decades. Sadiq arranged a prayer meeting on his lawn where hundreds of sadhus got together to chant. When I checked with Sadiq, he said, 'The VHP intended to create a divide between the two communities. They have always been intolerant towards our friendship.'

Gyan Das's authority grew in the first half of the 1990s, when he, along with a dedicated band of young and energetic Nagas, emerged as supporters of the Congress Prime Minister P.V. Narasimha Rao. It is believed that the Congress used him to thwart attempts by the VHP to exploit the Babri Masjid–Ram Janmabhoomi issue for political gains.

In April 1993, as per Rao's request, his guru and trusted aide, Chandraswami, organized a gathering of three hundred sadhus and *dharamcharya*s in Delhi. Gyan Das played a crucial role in it. One of the resolutions adopted at the meeting was to urge Hindu religious leaders to stay away from politics. Gyan Das became the focal point for anti-VHP forces in Hanumangarhi.[4]

He was elected as the president of the AIAP in 2004 during the Simhastha Mela in Ujjain. He convinced the sadhus not to fall in line with the Sangh Parivar.

The VHP thereon maintained a safe distance from Hanumangarhi but continued its efforts backstage to remove Gyan Das. The organization propped up Dharam Das, the mahant of the Nirvani Akhara, against the more renowned saint of Hanumangarhi. Sanjay Das who looks after the aging mahant and is his most relied secretary and sadhu gives details of how the VHP has always remained disgruntled with Gyan Das, mainly due to the latter's secular temperament.

Despite this history, Gyan Das sticks to his philosophy, 'Humanity is most important. Did the gods ever ask us to fight with each other over religion?' Although he isn't in his element ever since he suffered a mild stroke in July 2019, he makes it a point to spend at least one hour each morning and evening with his devotees.

I go for another interview with Mahant Gyan Das and find him seated on an old wooden plank, in the veranda outside his room. He is dressed in a fawn-coloured woollen cap, hand-knitted white pullover, woollen socks, and a thick shawl to keep the winter chill away. There is also a room heater placed right next to him. He puns, '*Nyas hai toh lambi pyas hai* (When there is a trust, there is unquenchable thirst).' He feels that after the apex court's order, the lust for religious supremacy will increase in the future.

His anger against the VHP is palpable. He compares Nritya Gopal Das, the head of the Ram Temple trust, to Kalnemi, the demon Ravan had appointed to kill Hanuman as per the Ramayana.

'Now, don't ask me who Ravan is,' he laughs. The next second, his sainthood is back. '*Achcha hai, mandir jab banega sab sadhu bhi darshan ke liye jayenge. Hum bhi jayenge* (It is good, as once the temple is built, the sadhus will visit it. I too will).'

Gyan Das's bête noire, Dharam Das, who Mahant Dinendra Nath Das also despises, lives in the adjoining alley. Dharam Das's house is a simple run-of-the-mill building. I notice a very old man, almost skeleton-like, lying on a frugal mattress right beside the entrance door. He is breathing heavily. A plastic water jug is placed beside him, and a young brahmachari stands on duty. He is Mahant Dharam Das's elder brother. As he lies there, no one seems to notice him; the devotees are all focussed on meeting the mahant.

It is Tuesday, a busy day when pilgrims visit the temple to offer prayers to Hanuman. Dharam Das smiles at some devotees who have come to see him before returning home. They are busy taking group selfies with the mahant. After they leave, I ask Dharam Das about what he thinks of the Supreme Court verdict. The mahant, who was born in Chappra, a town in west Bihar, claims he is not educated enough to get into details. Yet, like everyone else, he seems worried about the new temple's ownership now that a trust is being appointed to build it.

Suddenly, he asks me a strange question, 'Where do you keep your gold? In a locker for sure! Let me take out my wealth and show it to you.' A sadhu pulls out two very thick bound books from inside an iron vault fixed to the ground. They have many-many files related to the Ram Janmabhoomi from 1949 onwards. 'Even the DM of Faizabad asks me for references,' he claims with a sense of self-importance.

I ask him about his involvement in the theft of Nirmohi Akhara's revenue papers on the ownership related to the Ram Janmabhoomi. '*Woh ek jhoota hai* (He is a liar),' is his take on the head of Nirmohi Akhara. He places the files on the table beside plates of laddoos. 'Have some prasad and read the contents from those papers as I don't know English,' he gently orders.

His face brightens when the Supreme Court verdict mentions him as '*chela* (disciple) to Abhiram Das', who was one of the masterminds behind Ram Lalla's idol-placing in the mosque in December 1949. 'My guru was the only mahant who dared to place the Lord in his birthplace. Only a true devotee can take such a high-risk task.'

'I was destined to find him (my guru),' says Dharam Das categorically. Dharam Das's pre-sanyas name was Dhannu Kunwar. His father was a farmer, and the family lived in Buxar in east Bihar. After his Class X examination, he left home on the sly. His destination was *Ram Lalla ki Janmasthan* (Ram Lalla's birthplace). 'The very next day, when I was walking on the banks of Sarayu, after taking a few dips in the river, I was overwhelmed looking at all the sadhus around and their dedication.'

For weeks, he stayed at different ashrams and ate prasad to deal with hunger. One day, as he was walking on the banks of the river Sarayu, he spotted '*ek mahaan sadhu jo laal wastra mein chal rahe the* (an evolved sadhu in red clothes)'. Dhannu was drawn towards this sage. 'I started following him. After about 500 metres, he turned around, noticed me and questioned my intentions.'

'I divulged that I was on the lookout for a guru. Without wasting a second, he took me under his wings.' Meanwhile, Dhannu's parents landed in Ayodhya, searching for him. 'They were aware of my love for Ayodhya and Ram. Thankfully, they were happy with my decision. My mother would visit me regularly in those early years. Guruji had no objection to this. He was very understanding,' says Dharam Das.

We move on from the past to discuss the present scenario in Ayodhya. He laments that the sadhus these days are not half as spiritual or dedicated as those of the earlier years.

Coming back to the present, he tells me that ideally, the disputed property should be handed back to the older and senior religious leaders. 'It is simple. Instead of a new trust, the charge of the temple must be given to the ones who converted the mosque back into a temple (in 1992) in the first place. The sadhus who looked after the (changed) structure since then are familiar with the rituals and need to be involved.'

Although the VHP backed him once upon a time, Dharam Das is no more enamoured by the institution. 'They are all juvenile,' he says, laughing acerbically with his stained teeth peeping through the thick mass of long, white flowing beard.

Individuals and institutions that lay claim to the Janmabhoomi, he believes, have to be kept out. '*Inn logon ne mandir ko baniye ki dukaan bana rakha hai. Becho aur paisa looto* (These claimants have made a business out of the temple. They intend to sell and loot).'

From money and religious power, the conversation veers towards physical power. 'My guruji never wanted me to indulge in spiritual discourses. He felt I was cut out for *kushti* (wrestling).' He cites an example. In 1972, he was among several others at a function in Barabanki (110 km from Ayodhya). The sadhus had assembled to read the Ramayana. 'When Guruji was in another room, I too read out a few verses. He heard me and was livid as I had diverted my attention from kushti to another activity.' In 1974–75, Dharam Das won the second position at an international wrestling meet in Shimla and received his award at the Guru Badri Akhara in Delhi.

With pride, he relates that even former Prime Minister Indira Gandhi, and her two sons, Rajiv and Sanjay, had watched him wrestle. Dharam Das began kushti when he was sixteen. 'The lessons started at 4 a.m. with two hours of jogging, followed by different technique-learning lessons. Our diet included liberal doses of almonds, home-made ghee and milk,' he explains.

He believes that physical training helped him elevate his spiritual power. 'What I learnt in kushti honed my skills in attaining spirituality. I can meditate better, sit in *padmasana* (lotus) posture for hours and even years if need be! If the human body is trained, the mind can be trained better.'

I take leave and step out. My mind is in a whirl, not because of what Dharam Das said, but because of the scene before me. Hanumangarhi is one of the busiest areas in Ayodhya, especially on Tuesdays and Saturdays. Pilgrims nudge and push as they move in a couple of endless cues towards the temple. Then there are as many devotees returning from the temple. Both take breaks in the street-side stores. Sounds of 'Jai Shri Ram' fill the air as much as their loud chatter. In this tiny narrow street, there are at least hundreds of stalls glued to one another. They sell holy touristy stuff—books and booklets on Ram's life, vermillion and prayer beads. Some display toys, besides cruddy replicas of *gada*s (a club that looks like a blunt mace that was used by Hanuman), priced between Rs 20–200, and sets of plastic bows and arrows—the weapons Ram used.

The shops that sell garments include casual wear, along with saffron stoles and dhotis. Most of these have 'Jai Shri Ram' written on them or are embossed with Hanuman's images. Others bear clumsily copied logos of Gap and Levi's.

The utensil stores have wares required for Hindu rituals. Of course, some shops showcase figurines of different gods, mainly Lord Ram and his family, along with Hanuman. Placed among them are exquisitely carved statues of Valmiki in marble. Closer to the temple are stalls and carts placed randomly. While some of them are overladen with besan laddoos, others have marigold flowers overflowing from them; both are a popular offerings for Hanuman.

One way to take a break from this crowded zone is to move towards a more peaceful locality where the chief priest of Ram Janmabhoomi, Acharya Satyendra Das, resides. He is the oldest of the three guru-bhais, brothers because of the same guru—Abhiram Das—while Dharam Das is the youngest. The second brother is Mahant Ram Vilas Vedanti. Acharya Satyendra Das and Mahant Vedanti have been more well known to the general junta as compared to Dharam Das. While Satyendra Das has been the *mukhya pujari* (chief priest) of the Ram Janmabhoomi Mandir since 1 March 1992, Mahant Ram Vilas Vedanti was a functioning politician at the Centre till 2004.

Vedanti's tutor at one time, Satyendra Das, lives almost bang opposite the Nirmohi Akhara. His house is well done up with posters of Ram, Sita and Lakshman, Hanuman and the model of the Ram Janmabhoomi Temple, and is adequately furnished. A young brahmachari leads the way to his room which is at one end of the house. There are a few young spiritual aspirants who are his students. Like in all other ashrams, here too these adolescents are attired in white clothes. They run all his errands too as is the criterion in every mutt. In his meeting room there is a divan which has two saffron bolsters. On the side of the acharya lays is a life-sized poster of Ram looking handsome as he adorns a crown, holds a bow in his left hand and hangs a quiver full of arrows from his right shoulder. On the wall against which the bed is kept is a huge poster in yellow on which is printed the wooden temple model. In front of this picture, Satyendra Das's life-sized image has been superimposed. He looks sententious and stands out in his red kurta. His flowing silver hair and beard and a mild smile together add to the aura of his priesthood.

The chief pujari is very warm and welcoming. He is in a good mood and willing to have a long chat. He chronicles one event after the another from the time he arrived in Ayodhya. 'It was February 1958. I was about nineteen years of age when I first visited Ayodhya. It was during this trip that I met Guruji. I was on my way to Hanumangarhi, and Uddharak Baba stopped to ask me how I was doing.' The acharya tells me that Abhiram Das was extremely perceptive. '*Unhone yeh dekha ki maine ek bada jhola latkaya hua tha aur yeh samajh gaye ki main bahar se aaya hoon. Unhone adesh kiya ki darshan ke baad main unse milne jaoon* (He noticed that I had a big bag hanging from my shoulder which is why he figured out that I had come from outside town. He almost ordered me to go meet him after I visited the temple).' Satyendra Das adds nostalgically, 'After the darshan I came down the stairs and headed straight to his ashram. He lived exactly where Mahant Gyan Das resides now.' The chief priest elaborates how '*mugdh*' (mesmerized) he was when he first saw Abhiram Das. '*Hum sab unko Uddharak Baba ke naam se jaante the* (We all knew him as the Liberating Saint).' He continues, 'I felt so special that he had not only noticed me but encouraged me to fulfil my wishes as a saint. He would later make it a point to announce to all that he wanted me to take charge of the Ram Temple. I owe my education and spiritual knowledge to him.'

A day later I pay a visit to the second of the guru-bhais, Mahant Vedanti, who had a role in politics as well. He was elected to the eleventh Lok Sabha in 1996 and re-elected for a second term in 1998. In 2004, he was pitched against Rahul Gandhi of the Congress party who had made his entry into active politics that year. Rahul successfully contested the general elections held that year from Amethi, a seat that was earlier held by his father, Rajiv Gandhi, while Vedanti lost. Post this election, the sage did not contest any other. It is not the norm for a sage to join politics in India. Vedanti confesses, 'I was not at all keen to join politics, but our leader Ashok Singhal-ji was very keen that saints from Ayodhya should join mainstream politics and have a role in governance. Despite my listening to all his instructions, I continuously refused this one proposal. In a few years' time when Atal-ji, Murli Manohar Joshi-ji and Advani-ji along with Singhal-ji requested me to contest the elections, I could no more refuse.'

Dr Ram Vilas Vedanti, who is a Sanskrit scholar from Sampoornanand Sanskrit Vishwa Vidyalaya, Varanasi, like Satyendra Das, met Abhiram Das on his way back from the Hanumangarhi temple. He was only fourteen years old then. '*Hum sabse pehle apne Guru-ji se Mahant Saryu Das-ji ke ashram mein miley. Yeh ashram Hanumangarhi ke parisar mein tha. Unhone shuru se hi mujhe padhne ko kaha aur Satyendra Das ko mujhe padhane ki jimmedari di* (I first met my Guru-ji in Mahant Saryu Das's ashram which used to be within the premises of Hanumangarhi. Right from the start he instructed me to put my mind to studies and entrusted Satyendra Das with the task of tutoring me).' Perhaps because of this instruction, Vedanti refers to Abhiram Das as his '*shiksha* guru'.

The politician–sage from Ayodhya then talks about his association with the 'Ram Janmabhoomi Andolan' since 1984. '*San 1984 mein Gorakhpeethadishwar Mahant Sri Avaidyanath-ji Maharaj Ayodhya aaye aur Digambar Akhada mein ek baithak hui, Paramhans Ram Chandar Das-ji ke adhyakshta mein. Isme Ashok Singhal-ji, Acharya Giriraj Kishore-ji, Acharya Dharmendra-ji, Jagat Guru Shankaracharya Swami Shantanand Saraswati-ji aur Ayodhya ke Nritya Gopal Das-ji bhi shamil the* (In 1984, Gorakhpeethadishwar Mahant Sri Avaidyanath-ji Maharaj visited Ayodhya and a meeting was then held at the Digambar Akhada which was presided by Paramhans Ram Chandar Das-ji. Many leaders and saints attended the meeting including Ashok Singhal-ji, Acharya Giriraj Kishore-ji, Acharya Dharmendra-ji, Jagat Guru Shankaracharya Swami Shantanand Saraswati-ji and Nritya Gopal Das-ji).' Vedanti mentions that there were several other sages from Ayodhya who were present. He informs that it was in this meeting that a decision was taken to build the Ram Janmabhoomi Temple for which the Ram Janam Bhoomi Mukti Samiti was formed. Ashok Singhal had wanted a senior mahant from Ayodhya to be the president of the newly formed committee but the mahants refused to take up the responsibility. The Congress party was in power in those years. At that juncture Mahant Avaidyanath-ji stepped forward, saying that he had no cause to fear and volunteered to take up the role of the president of the newly formed committee. Dau Dayal Khanna, who was then a Congress MLA, was made the general secretary. Vedanti became a member of the Ram Janam Bhoomi Mukti Samiti along with a few other mahants from Ayodhya. He proudly claims that he continued to be a part of the struggle right till the Supreme Court's decision. All the while we chatted, almost like a pause after citing an incident, Vedanti would boastfully announce that he went to jail twenty-five times for the sake of Ram's birthplace. There is no doubt that Vedanti had worn many hats for the sake of Ram! However, he did not seem too keen to discuss his pre-sanyasi days.

As I wrap up my trip, I feel a vacuum. I cannot meet the late Ram Chandra Paramhans, the former head of Digambar Akhara and one of the first litigants of the disputed site. He was one of the foremost proponents of the Ram Janmabhoomi movement. On my previous trips, I always made it a point to meet him.

Till date, he is remembered as the torchbearer of the movement. I still remember the scene when I had first reached his place in 1999—beyond the entrance door was a worn-out staircase with a sticky bannister. It was a little dark as the only light came from the tiny skylights. The paint on the walls was flaky, and the place looked rather worn out.

I landed in a room that opened out to a terrace. Seated on a charpoy was a man who looked like a sadhu from a children's book. He had hair tumbling down to his shoulders and a long beard that reached his chest. His eyes looked like tiny hazel beads shining below bushy white brows.

'*Baitho, beta*, (Sit, child),' he said in the most affectionate tone. The parent-like concern created a connect. He ordered hot brinjal fritters and chai, which became a regular treat during my subsequent visits. His heart was for Lord Ram, and he could do anything for him. But there was anger too.

Although he condemned the first Muslim Mughal emperor for building the mosque over a temple, he always spoke warmly about his Muslim friends in the city. His love for Ram's aide, Hanuman, and the *vanar sena* (army of the apes) showed when he took me to an adjoining veranda with hundreds of monkeys sitting below.

He called out to them, chatted and laughed with them as he threw bananas and peanuts. The monkeys chattered and screeched back. I had never seen anything like this before. 'They are my dear friends.' Feeding them at a fixed time was a daily exercise with the sage.

Most people know him as Phakkar Sadhu (happy-go-lucky sage). True to this nickname, Paramhans seemed least interested in the material world. The money and gifts he received from devotees, he distributed among the needy. He also spent a fair amount of money buying fruits and nuts for the monkeys and fodder for cows. The land over which the Mandir Karyashala (temple workshop) stands was donated by Paramhans long ago to the VHP to build the pillars and other structures for the Ram Temple.

Paramhans was born in a Brahmin family from Chhapra district in Bihar, sometime around 1910. At the age of twelve he left his home and wandered in the company of sadhus before himself settling down as a sadhu in Ayodhya.[5]

The popular sage had once mentioned to me that as a child he often conversed with Ram and Sita in his dreams, which is why from a very early age that he felt his purpose of life was to take care of Ram Lalla and so he landed in his birthplace.

'For Paramhans, then, the influence of his revolutionary upbringing, and his attachment to Lord Ram in particular, explain his involvement with other sadhus in broadening the Hindutva campaign around the Ram Janam Bhoomi (RJB) issue. Although unity with like-minded organizations was natural for Paramhans, he considered the RJB issue as his fight and his personal cause and believed that it had been taken up by others.'

Paramhans had his own reasons for supporting the saffron brigade. 'Because the RSS is a supporter of Hindutva, I support it and the VHP. And I support the BJP because it took up my cause of the Ram Janmabhoomi Temple and even gave up power in four states while fighting for that cause. Today when no one wants to give up a political seat, the BJP gave up chief ministers in four states for this cause (after the Congress dismissed them following the destruction of the mosque).' He added that it would be utterly unethical and ungrateful of him if he did not extend his support to the BJP and VHP. The sage confessed that his aim was not to simply build a temple 'but to create the awareness of being a Hindu among Hindus. Hindus are losing their self-respect and self-pride as Hindus.'[6]

The rumours are that Paramhans too played a role in the events of December 1949, but he gave the alibi that he was in Calcutta at that time. He preferred not to talk much about that incident.

There was this one statement that the happy-go-lucky sage would often reiterate, 'No religion teaches violence. Gods never misled people. I see no reason to fight against any community though I believe we must have a Ram Temple.' Given such views, it is not surprising that he was close to Hashim Ansari (the first Muslim litigant in the Ram Janmabhoomi title suit). The two attended the hearings together and travelled on the same rickshaw. They fought bitterly for their religions in the courtroom but shared tea during the breaks. To date, people talk about their camaraderie.

To create awareness about Ram Janmabhoomi, Paramhans published a newspaper, *Virakt* (Unattached). He soon became famous all across the country. Eminent people visited him—the first President of India, Rajendra Prasad, shared a rapport with the saint as both hailed from the same district, Chappra, in Bihar. When the first Prime Minister, Jawaharlal Nehru, went to Uttar Pradesh to propagate the removal of untouchability, he too made it a point to meet the sage.[7]

On my tour after the apex court order, I find the akhara deserted. The monkeys come for their bites, but there is no one to have fun with. Ram Chandra Paramhans passed away in July 2003. His dream to see a new temple at Ram's birth spot remained unfulfilled during his lifetime.

Apart from the struggles for political, social and economic power, the religiosity of Ayodhya has been punctured by violence—brutality from the spiritual men.

I particularly remember an incident dating back to December 1998 when I was in Ayodhya to cover an attack on the fishermen community at the Guptar Ghat. The senior cops were open about the unholy deeds of the holy men.

Senior Superintendent of Police Anil Agarwal said, 'An identification system has been introduced to track down the black sheep. But considering that every house is also a temple, it will prove to be a Herculean exercise.' He added, 'We now check people with arms in the various ashrams.'

When I reached Guptar Ghat, the residents seemed stunned and mortified. They had woken up to the sounds of gunshots early in the morning on 12 November 1998. The neighbouring sadhus charged at them with 0.12 bore guns and sharp-edged weapons. Four people were injured, and a similar number were dead.

After the looting and killings, the sadhus vroomed away on their motorbikes. Their leader, Baba Mohan Das alias Mauni Baba, the mahant of the Yagya Shala Ashram, took shelter in a nearby grove. The audacious act reached a climax when the sadhus opened fire at the police, who tried to stop them. B.B. Pathak, station in-charge of the Cantonment police station, admitted, 'This speaks of the hardcore criminal traits of the sadhus of Ayodhya.'[8]

Over the past two decades, the sadhus have turned modern in several ways and, at the same time, more violent. They do not step out without shades these days. One can spot them with smartphones in their hands, expensive watches and gold bracelets on their wrists; wooden clogs have been replaced by floaters on their feet, and smart T-shirts and pullovers have replaced the yogis' toga.

In August 2020, according to the Times Now News (Mirror Now Digital), a sadhu, Ramsevak Das, allegedly attempted to sodomize a brahmachari. The holy man lured the student to his ashram. When the fourteen-year-old resisted, the enraged sadhu tried to cut off the boy's private parts. The boy escaped and narrated the ordeal to his guardians, who filed a police case. The sadhu was arrested.[9]

Various similar reports lie with the town's police department. In yet another incident in the summer of 2016, a student was almost driven to self-immolation because of mental torture.[10] Mahesh had been a student at the Pujari Ayodhya Nath Temple for eighteen months. His crime was that he was an obstinate boy and would barely follow instructions. When Mahant Prapannacharya, the senior monk, was out of the station, visiting Ujjain, Mahesh turned even more defiant. When he heard about Mahesh's behaviour, the mahant called his guardians and asked them to take the child home. However, Mahesh was apparently abused and insulted at the ashram. One night, he went to the bathroom, poured kerosene over his body, and set himself on fire. The case was registered under a section that prescribes a jail term of up to ten years. It reads, 'If any person commits suicide, whoever abets the commission of such suicide shall be punished with imprisonment.' The ashram's officials were at fault in this case.

In early 2020, the Ayodhya police gave me copies of registered cases against the sadhus. As per Crime number 235/14 registered with the local police, a young homemaker left her door open as it was time for her children to return from school. She was on her way to the washroom when a sadhu suddenly entered her house and grabbed her from behind. He asked her to surrender to his sexual demands. When she screamed and pushed the sadhu away, he ran out but threatened to kill her family. The sadhu was identified as Mahant Awadh Ramdas of Jamwant Qila. A case was registered for assault or criminal force against a woman with an intent to outrage her modesty.

In another case registered on 23 August 2018 it was charged that Parmata Das, a chela of Ram Ji Das of the Vidya Mata Mandir, murdered Ram Charan Das, a chela of Raghuvar Das, who lived in the same temple.[11]

All is not wholly pious in this holy land!

5

Legal Trails, Travails and Trials, 1858–1950

'Hinduism would not have been much of a religion if Ram had not steeled his heart against every temptation.'

—MAHATMA GANDHI[1]

It was an early morning at the beginning of 1858. Amidst the plethora of typical sounds and colours, Prabhadevi—not a real name, but she could be any woman resident of Ayodhya from that time—a middle-aged and devout Hindu, took her daily bath in the Sarayu River that silently flowed through the kingdom that was once ruled by Lord Ram. After a few dips, she retraced her steps towards her cottage. Changing into fresh clothes, she walked up to her garden and plucked some flowers and arranged them beside a few fruits on a *thali* (plate).

With three of her neighbours, Prabhadevi then headed for the Kuber Tila, the highest mound in the Ram Janmasthan area.

It was a long walk, and what had become a daily exercise for the four women for the past couple of weeks. None of them had a clue about how things would be very different on that particular day. When they reached the destination, they were shocked to see that the tamarind tree they had worshipped for the past few weeks was no more.

The tree that had become sacred for the locals after Ameer Ali, a *maulvi,* and Baba Ramcharan Das, a Hindu mahant, were hung to death from its branches by the British army.[2]

During the First War of Independence in 1857, Ramcharan Das of Ayodhya's Hanumangarhi temple led the local troops against the colonial forces. Ameer Ali willingly joined him, along with his followers. It was a show of harmony between the two communities in their otherwise longstanding love-hate relationship.[3]

The two religious groups kept aside their communal feelings during the war; Ameer Ali convinced Muslims to give up their hold over the Ram Janmasthan and hand it over to the Hindus.

The British faced defeat in the Battle of Chinhat (a suburban town near Lucknow). It was a battle that was fought between the colonial and Indian forces on 30 June 1857, as this report states, 'Led by Barkat Ahmad, a highly trained mutineer of the Company's Army and joined by a number of Indian sepoys who defected from the army on the site, the rebels had managed to completely outflank the British.'[4]

Several sections, such as Hindus, Muslims, Sikhs, taluqdars and farmers united under Ramcharan Das and Ameer Ali's combined leadership in the mutiny. From Chinhat, the battle moved 118 km eastwards towards Faizabad. However, the British finally won this First War of Independence and recaptured Lucknow on 3 March 1858 and Faizabad on 17 March the same year.

And soon after, the two religious heads, Ramcharan and Ameer, were hanged from the tamarind tree. The tree became a symbol of unity. It turned into a spot of reverence for the local communities, so much so, that with time it had turned into a religious relic. It stood distinctively on the mound with smearings of vermillion and red, yellow and orange worship flags tied all around its hefty branches. But that morning, the ground where the tree stood was barren—there was not even a stump of the trunk or the usually scattered fruits and flowers. The tall tree, the local symbol of faith, was completely uprooted.

The symbolic show of unity, the joint participation of the Hindus and Muslims, as well as people from other religions, in the war, infuriated the British imperialists, who despised the coming together of the various Indian castes, classes and communities.

Prabhadevi and her friends knew this. What they possibly didn't know on that morning was that the offenders were the British officials themselves. Having uprooted the tree the previous night, they were guarding the spot to ensure no one dared to come back to it with the usual fervour of faith and devotion. The village women were confronted with the situation. They were shocked and went into a stupor. Meekly and silently they placed the flowers, garlands and fruits on the bare land, lit a few lamps and quietly walked back home.

The decimation of the tree seemed to symbolize what was to happen next, the end of the short-lived community camaraderie between the Hindus and Muslims. They went back to their old ways, and once again, the tensions between them grew.

The strain between the two groups stemmed from a fight for ownership over an area which the Hindus believed to be the birthplace of Lord Ram and where a mosque was built in 1528. The mosque was named after the first Mughal emperor, Zahir-ud-din

Muhammad Babur, as it is believed that he had asked his general, Mir Baqi, to construct it.

For more than 300 years, the Hindus charged that the mosque was built after the destruction of an existing Lord Ram temple that stood at the exact spot where the avatar was born.

The locals referred to the mosque by different names—Masjid-e-Janmasthan, Jami Masjid, Sita Rasoi Masjid, etc. According to the old documents of the District Gazetteer of Faizabad, 'the mosque was used as a place of worship by both the Hindus and Muslims'. However, this led to clashes between the two groups over several centuries, which manifested as skirmishes and riots from 1853 onwards.

For a brief while, the war of 1857 brought an end to these communal conflicts. But when they resumed, it was with a vengeance. The reason being none other than the famous Divide and Rule policy of the British to prevent another 1857—they thwarted any attempts by Indians to unite themselves across the country. Ayodhya was no exception, and the uprooting of the tamarind tree was a step in that direction.

The first-ever recorded document of the communal riots that took place after 1857 was written by Sheetal Dubey, *thanedar*, Oudh (Station House Officer or SHO of Ayodhya). In *Ayodhya Revisited*, Kishore Kunal writes, 'In his report dated 28 November 1858 AD Sheetal Dubey the SHO of Ayodhya reported that in the middle of the Masjid Janma Asthan Sant Nihang Singh, Faqir Khalsa of Punjab, performed *homa*. It stated that Nihang Singh, a faqir Khalsa from Punjab, performed "*homa*", worshipped Guru Govind Singh, "erected the flag of the Bhagavan" (God), which was being protected by 25 Sikhs.'[5]

These Sikhs were Nihangs, often referred to as '*guru di laadli fauj* (the Guru's loved army)'. The Nihangs were established as a military sect when the tenth Sikh guru, Gobind Singh, started the Khalsa Panth in 1699.

Etymologically, the word 'Nihang' perhaps comes from the Persian word that means 'alligator', an amphibian that symbolizes reckless courage. Another root could be the Sanskrit word, *nihsanka*, which means 'careless and fearless'.

The local Muslims were wary of these militant Sikhs. Two days after Nihang Singh performed his ceremony at the Janamsthaan, the Muslims lodged a series of complaints with the cops. On 30 November 1858, Syed Mohammad Khateeb, the muezzin of the Babri Masjid, who read the namaz every Friday and on Eid, submitted one of them to the SHO Ayodhya.

The complaint said that a '*nishan*' (symbol) was installed by the Sikhs. It added that Nihang Singh had created a riot inside the masjid. He had forcibly made a *chabootra* (a platform-like structure) inside the masjid, even placed a picture of the idol inside, lit a fire and had conducted puja. 'He had written the words "Ram Ram" with coal on the walls of the masjid. The masjid is a place of worship of Muslims and not Hindus, and if someone constructs anything forcibly inside it, he should be punished,' the complaint read.[6]

Syed Mohammad urged SHO Dubey and other police officials to visit the spot, remove the Hindu religious symbols and ensure that the Hindus leave the mosque, which was solely for Muslims.

The Sikh–Muslim tangle was possibly premeditated. According to Sikh legends, a mahant in Ayodhya, Baba Vaishno Deo, wrote a letter to Nihang Singh and asked for the latter's help. Was this because the Nihang Sikhs were known for their aggression?

Giani Gurjeet Singh, the current head of the Brahmakund Gurudwara in Ayodhya, explains, 'Everyone was familiar with the bravery of the Nihangs, especially the way they faced Emperor Aurangzeb. People identified these crusaders as saviours of the truth.' He adds, 'The *Panth Prakash* (history book on Sikhs) describes a

Nihang as an individual who has no fear of death and is ever ready to embrace martyrdom.'

SHO Dubey took immediate action and summoned the Nihangs. He ordered them, as well as their leader, to vacate the mosque. Nihang Singh, their leader, refused. He claimed that the place was used to worship the 'Bhagwan' and so belonged to the Nirankaras.

He demanded justice from the 'Saheb Bahadur'. Compelled by the defiance of the Sikh visitors, the SHO filed a report on 1 December 1858 that reiterated the audacious attitude of Nihangs. On 1 December 1858, Sheetal Dubey, thanedar, submitted a report in Case Number 884, describing that when he took the summons order dated 30 November 1858 addressed to Nihang Singh Faqir to leave the place, he received no reply. He reported what had actually transpired and sought instructions from the higher authorities.[7]

On 6 December 1858, Dubey confirmed that the mosque was still in possession of the Sikhs. His report stated that the latter inscribed 'Ram Ram' all over the walls of the mosque, and even hoisted a religious flag within the premises.[8]

On 10 December 1858, an order was passed recording that the *jhanda* (flag) was uprooted from the masjid and the faqir residing therein was ousted.[9]

These, and subsequent police records, which were reproduced in the 2019 Supreme Court order, provide an insight into the mind of the SHO, and what he felt about the controversy. The official wrote that the actions of the Nihang Sikhs 'testify to the indisputable fact that a very large section of the society regarded it (disputed property) as a sacred site of Lord Rama, and there existed a temple thereon. Or else,' added the records, 'there was no occasion for a Nihang Sikh to travel from Punjab to Ayodhya and occupy the mosque forcibly.'

On 10 December 1858, the SHO wrote that Nihang Singh was ousted from the mosque and the Hindu flag was removed by a court order. However, Nihang Singh 'did not stop his activities'.

In a bid to establish peace and harmony among the two communities, the British erected a fence in 1859. The divide defined the separate areas in which the Hindus and Muslims could carry out their respective religious activities within the larger Ram Janmabhoomi–Babri Masjid premises.

While the Muslims could use the inner court, the Hindus had access to the outer court. The Hindus were allowed to construct a raised *chabootra* in the outer area, which they could use for worship.

Author Nilanjan Mukhopadhyay writes in his book, *The Demolition: India at the Crossroads*, 'The fence that was erected by the British within the compound of the Babri Masjid in 1859 was symbolic of the divide between the Hindus and Muslims of Ayodhya—something that came about only in the first half of the century. Similar actions of the British accentuated this division among the two communities.'[10]

Matters worsened after the construction of the fence. On 5 November 1860, Mir Rajjab Ali, the Babri Masjid *khateeb*, submitted another complaint to the court of the deputy commissioner, Faizabad. He requested the removal of the chabootra that was built by Nihang Singh. In another application on 15 November 1860, the khateeb stated that the chabootra adjacent to the mosque was being expanded daily.

'Besides, when the (Muslim) Muezzin recited Azaan, the opposite party begins to blow conch (*shanqh/naqoos*). This has never happened before,' the complaint added, according to Kunal Kishore's book, *Ayodhya Revisited*.

The Muslims wanted the court to restrain the Hindus from the 'unlawful act' and order the demolition of the chabootra, 'which had never existed'. They wanted a bond to be executed so that the Hindus agreed not to 'unlawfully and illegally interfere in the Masjid property and will not blow conch at the time of Azaan'.[11]

Even today, the Muslims involved in the Ayodhya case have immense regard for Rajjab Ali, who took up their grievances. Zafaryiab Jilani, the advocate who played an essential role in the Ram Janmabhoomi case, asserts, 'In all probability, Mir Rajjab Ali belonged to the lineage of Mir Baqi. Mir Rajjab Ali claimed to be the son-in-law of the daughter of the grandson of Syed Baqi Mohammed. This also confirms that Asghar Ali, Mir Rajjab Ali's son, was related to the fourth generation of the original Mutawalli.'

Mohammed Ashgar Ali was a persistent man, and he carried on with his father's fight. The former's doggedness shows in that he would run to the local administration every now and then with complaints against the Hindus.

One such accusation was over a pair of charan paduka that were affixed on the Janmasthan platform. The installation of the Lord's charan paduka disturbed the Muslims. The reports of the Deputy Commissioner, Faizabad, also hinted that a local bairagi sadhu, Mahant Baldeo Das, was responsible for this action.

Asghar Ali added that the bairagi sadhus had expanded their hold over the mosque and, much to the horror of the Muslims, they set up a new *chulha* (hearth), beside the old one that was used to prepare *bhog* (food for the gods). As per the description in the Supreme Court order, 'On 7 November 1873, an order was passed in the case of Mohd Asghar vs Mahant Baldeo Das directing the removal of the *Charan Paduka* which was not complied with; and on 10 November 1873, Baldeo Das was directed by the Deputy Commissioner to remove an image placed on the Janmasthan platform. A report was submitted stating that an officer had gone to the house of Baldeo Das who was not found. The order was explained to other priests who said they could not carry out the order. These orders were not complied with, and the image was not removed.'[12]

Fresh controversy over the disputed land broke out in early 1877. Khem Das, mahant of the Janmasthan, insisted on the rights of the

Hindus over Lord Ram's birthplace. He demanded that the main gate on the northern side (Singh Dwar) be opened for the devotees, in addition to the existing entrance on the eastern side.

The divisional commissioner saw the logic in this request. He felt that if a separate gate was opened, the movement of the enormous throngs of devotees on special occasions like the local festivals would be easier to handle. On such occasions, the crowds were large and could be uncontrollable. *The Gazetteer of the Province of Oudh*, which was first published in 1877–78, also mentions the huge gathering during such festivals, 'Ajodhya was to the Hindus what Mecca was to the Mohammadans and Jerusalem to the Jews.' It added that the Ram Navami festival in Ayodhya to celebrate Lord Ram's birthday was as popular and famous as the Jagannath festival in Puri (Odisha), and the religious events in Haridwar. According to recent arguments in the Supreme Court by Parameshwarnath Mishra, 500,000 devotees assemble to honour Lord Ram in Ayodhya on Ram Navami.[13]

On 13 April 1877, Mahant Khem Das was granted permission to construct the new gate. Asghar Ali intervened to stop it. But to his dismay, his petition was dismissed.

A month later, on 14 May 1877, the deputy commissioner justified his decision. He maintained that if the other door was not opened, human life would be endangered as there was a great rush on festivals and fairs. He clarified that the new doorway was 'not at all in Baber's mosque, but in the wall which in front is divided from the mosque by a railing'. He added, 'I marked out the spot for the opening myself so there is no need to depute any (European) officer.'

Asghar Ali did not give up. Six months later, on 13 November 1877, he filed another petition to the deputy commissioner. This complaint was against both the mahants of Janmasthan and Nirmohi Akhara.

This time the khateeb of Babri Masjid said that four years ago, the divisional commissioner ordered the removal of the charan paduka, which was ignored by the bairagis. He claimed that the area within the mosque premises, including the boundary, belonged to the Muslims. The location of the new gate was within it.

To back up this argument, he wrote that as a 'sole evidence in support of his claim was one-word Allah that was engraved on the wall of the masjid (at the entrance)'.

Ultimately, on 13 December 1877, the appeal was dismissed on the ground that the outer door was in the interests of public safety. The order stated that the petition was merely an attempt to annoy the Hindus by making them dependent on the pleasure of the 'mosque people to open or close the second door'.[14]

According to the 2019 Supreme Court order, the issue dragged on. Asghar Ali asked Raghubar Das, mahant of Nirmohi Akhara, to pay rent for the use of the chabootra and takht (small platform) near the door of the Babri Masjid, and for organizing Kartik Mela and Ram Navami in 1878. The sub-judge, Faizabad, dismissed the suit on 18 June 1883.

Two years later, on 19 January 1885, Mahant Raghubar Das took the tussle forward. He filed a suit in the court of the sub-judge, Faizabad, to construct a temple on the chabootra. 'The sub-judge held in his favour on February 24, 1885 but declined permission because of proximity to the mosque. His appeal was dismissed by the district judge Faizbad, Col J E A Chambier, who inspected the place on March 17, 1886. In his judgement of March 26, 1886 he remarked, "It is most unfortunate that a masjid should have been built on the land specially held sacred by the Hindus. But as that occurred 356 years ago, it is too late now to remedy the grievance. All that can be done is to maintain the parties in status quo."'[15]

More than a century later, after the demolition of the Babri Masjid in December 1992, various parties gave different meanings to the 1885 attempt by Mahant Raghubar Das to construct a temple in Ayodhya. The BJP White Papers (1993) saw it as an effort by the Hindus to invoke the 'Rule of Law' that was established by the colonial empire.

In his essay, 'The Abuse of History: A Study of the White Papers on Ayodhya', published in *Social Scientist*, 1994, historian Sushil Srivastava pointed out that it was most unlikely that when Mahant Raghubar Das filed a civil suit to seek permission to construct a temple, he implied that the new structure encompassed the entire area including 'the whole of the revenue mauzas of Fyzabad and Ayodhya, Ramkot, Bagh Bijesi and part of Manjha Jamthara'. Srivastava further explains 'that it is obvious that Raghubar Das only sought permission to construct a canopy over the platform in front of the Babri Masjid. It is wrong to raise the issue that he actually demanded re-possession of the site of the mosque'. The writer further analyses that it is not correct to argue that 'the suit was dismissed because the court was anxious that if the mosque was displaced there would be communal issues and rioting'. Once again, Srivastava bases this on the fact that, 'In case the court was convinced of the alleged claims of Raghubar Das then it could have easily pulled down the structure as it had done in the case of several buildings in Faizabad. Contemporary accounts clearly state that after annexation, the government destroyed several "mazaars", mosques, temples and houses in order to broaden the roads in the city.'[16]

Starting from the end of the nineteenth century, the tensions between the Hindus and Muslims continued over the next six decades. Court documents refer to the riots of 1934 and several other complaints from the Muslims over the Hindus' attempts to build permanent structures in the areas, as also to destroy some of the Muslim graves. News of cow slaughter in Shahjahanpur had triggered the 1934 riot in which mosques had been damaged in Ayodhya (though later repaired). The Hindus maintained that a mosque could not remain in the holy place of Lord Ram's birth.

These skirmishes went on until one of the most important events occurred on the dawn of 23 December 1949.

To understand its backdrop, one needs to know the region's electoral politics just after India gained independence. Many political parties, with differing ideologies, had come together under the umbrella of the Indian National Congress during the freedom struggle. After Independence, several of the smaller parties weaned away from the latter and went their separate ways.

One of the smaller parties was the Congress Socialist Party, which Acharya Narendra Dev had founded. He represented the Faizabad–Ayodhya Legislative Assembly seat in the United Provinces (Uttar Pradesh) when India gained independence. He was familiar with the twin towns as he had spent his early years in Faizabad.

It is a known fact that Acharya developed an interest in politics when he was only ten years of age. As a freedom fighter, he was imprisoned several times by the British. It was during his tenure in Nasik Jail, where he was imprisoned in 1932, that he dabbled with the idea of pitching a political party that would focus primarily on the farmers' welfare.

He launched the Congress Socialist Party in 1934, which continued working along with the Indian National Congress but pulled away in 1948. As a consequence, Acharya Narendra Dev gave up the assembly seat, which led to a by-election in Faizabad.

He nonetheless decided to re-contest the constituency under the new banner. This angered the Congress premier of United Provinces, Govind Ballabh Pant. In retaliation, he favoured Mahant Raghav Das, whom he had personally hand-picked.

Born on 12 December 1886 in Pune, Maharashtra, in a well-to-do Brahmin family, Raghav Das was seventeen when he travelled to the holy cities of Prayagraj and Kashi in search of a guru. His desire was fulfilled in Barhaj, Deoria, where he met Yogiraj Ananta Mahaprabhu. Since then, Deoria became his home.

Hence, by default, the by-election became a battle between Acharya Dev, a socialist and secularist leader, and Mahant Raghav Das, a staunch Hindu. Premier Pant openly played the 'Hindu' card and hobnobbed with the Hindu Mahasabha, a right-wing party with a religious bent, and the mahants of Ayodhya to ensure victory for his candidate.

Call it insecurity or power hunger, Pant took it as a personal challenge to defeat Acharya Dev, who was popular among all the communities and was held in great esteem by Prime Minister Jawaharlal Nehru. The by-election was doused in communal shades, and banners blatantly broadcasted that it was a contest between Lord Ram and the demon Ravan.

Decades later, reminiscing about the age-old Hindu–Muslim conflict, Hashim Ansari, the first plaintiff from the Muslim side, told me, 'Whoever says the (Indian National) Congress has no role to play in this tangle knows nothing about the June 1948 by-elections. I was in my late twenties then. No one in Ayodhya knew Baba Raghav Das, but overnight the chief minister ensured his popularity. In those years, Raghav Das would give vitriolic speeches against Acharya-ji.'

The handpicked sage won by a small margin of 1,312 votes (Raghav Das 5,393; Narendra Dev 4,080 votes), but Faizabad–Ayodhya grabbed the nation's attention. Most leaders found it difficult to believe that Acharya Dev, the fifty-eight-year-old erudite scholar and freedom fighter who was close to the Prime Minister, lost.

'The Baba's victory was a shot in the arm for the Hindu communalists, whether inside the Congress or outside it. The Muslims of Ayodhya had overwhelmingly voted for Narendra Dev. Even before the by-election, Muslims were threatened by sadhus and Hindu Mahasabha not to offer namaz in the Babri Masjid,' wrote Asha Kiran in her book, *Ram Mandir*.

Another crucial 'person of interest' in this modern post-Independence 1949 saga was Mahant Digvijay Nath, who has been described by the Dutch academic Peter van der Veer as the 'leading light in the movement to re-capture the Babri Mosque in Ayodhya and re-convert it to a temple to Rama'.[17]

There is a very interesting and long link between Digvijay and the current Uttar Pradesh Chief Minister Yogi Adityanath. Which is why it is not a surprise that the latter has been consistently showing keen interest in the Ayodhya imbroglio ever since he assumed power on 19 March 2017. Earlier, from 1998 to 2017, Adityanath was regularly elected from Gorakhpur, believed to be one of the safest constituencies for the BJP, and won five parliamentary elections in a row.

In September 2015, Yogi Adityanath was anointed as the mahant of the Gorakhnath math, Gorakhpur. Though his religious master was Avaidhyanath, another hardcore supporter of Hindutva, Adityanath enthusiastically also carried forward the task that was taken up by his Guru Avaidhyanath's predecessor, Guru Mahant Digvijay Nath, who was the first abbot of the Gorakhnath math. Digvijay was the mahant who knew and well demonstrated how to get political mileage using religion.

It was known to all that Digvijay Nath nurtured political ambitions. Initially, he was a member of the Indian National Congress and, later, in 1937, he joined the Hindu Mahasabha. Given its crucial role in the Ram Mandir dispute, it is surprising that this organization is rarely given credit these days. This obvious side-lining of the party prompted me to call Pramod Pandit Joshi, the All India Hindu Mahasabha's spokesperson. He invariably talks turkey, and this time he ridiculed the BJP leaders, 'These men are most ungrateful. They seem to have completely forgotten the role of the Hindu Mahasabha in the history of the Ram Janmabhoomi chronicle. They lacked the basic decency of inviting many important people who worked day and night in the Ram Mandir movement.' (Joshi and other members of the Hindu Mahasabha were not called for the Ram Mandir foundation-laying ceremony held on 5 August 2020 where there were 150 invitees.)

As if to remind me of the key role taken up by his party, Pramod Pandit talks of an important meeting held on the night of 9–10 December 1949 in Delhi, where the RSS Supremo, Veer Savarkar, had summoned Digvijay Nath from Gorakhpur. It proved to be the turning point in the Ram Mandir movement. The meeting was presided over by Dr N.B. Khare, the president of the Hindu Mahasabha. One does not know what transpired between the trio, but it triggered a sequence of events that changed the country's political future.

Barely two weeks later, on the night/dawn of 22–23 December, Lord Ram Lalla's idol (God as an infant) was placed under the central dome inside the Babri Masjid. It occupied the same spot that the Hindus believed to be the Lord's birthplace.

Later, the event was presented as a miracle, the mysterious appearance of the deity. However, investigations proved that it was a well-planned, efficiently executed move, a conspiracy of sorts to regain religious control over the mosque. There are no doubts that several locals, government officials, and sadhus were involved in it.

There are several key characters in this story. It is better to introduce them before we get on with the events. The foremost among them, the chief architect, was obviously Digvijay Nath. He was a kind of an enigma for most. Interestingly he maintained a considerable gap between his public and private persona.

Despite his politico-religious public stance, the mahant was a close friend of 'Miya Sahib', the head maulvi of the Gorakhpur Imambara. Digvijay Nath would go to Miya Sahib's house daily at 4 p.m. to play tennis in which they both excelled. The former's top-spins, overhead lobs, drops, volleys and smashes were visible even in his professional actions.

Interestingly, both the Imambara complex and the Gorakhnath temple compound are located in heavily Muslim-dominated neighbourhoods. Tens of thousands of weavers from the Muslim community coexist with the math in a relatively peaceful environment.

One of India's most popular and revered Sufi poets, Kabir, was from this particular community. One can find several of Kabir's dohas (couplets) engraved on the walls of the Gorakhnath temple.

While the mahant was later involved in the takeover of the Babri Masjid in Ayodhya, there was no conflict between the chiefs of the Imambara and Gorakhnath temple either in those years or in the following decades. The two compounds in Gorakhpur were—and still are—next to each other, separated by just 500 metres. Never did Digvijay disturb the Muslims in his native town.[18]

Even now, the two communities, living in the adjoining localities, co-exist peacefully. Dr Sarvesh Kumar, professor, department of geography, Deen Dayal University, Gorakhpur, agrees, 'The Muslims are duteous towards the temple, and Hindus reciprocate the feelings. It's an old tradition that has been around since time immemorial.' He adds, 'Whenever the Muslims have problems, they approach the temple authorities. Even Yogi Adityanath, as the member of Parliament from Gorakhpur (1998–2017), had been extremely compassionate towards the Muslims in his hometown.'

During our conversations when this *esprit de corps* was brought up with Hindu Mahasabha's Pramod Joshi, he chuckled and said, 'That's because Gorakhnath peeth is not the Janmsthan of any bhagwan!'

Among the top British India officials, district magistrate (DM), Faizabad–Ayodhya, Kadangalathil Karuna Karan Nayyar (K.K.K. Nayyar), played a leading role. His Hindu sentiments and a personal bias towards the Ram Mandir were known to all and sundry. These have been well fleshed out in the book, *Ayodhya: The Dark Night* by Krishna Jha and Dhirendra K. Jha. As per the book, a few months after Independence, when Nayyar was the DM of Gonda, he met Maharaja Pateshwari Prasad Singh, head of the princely state of Balrampur, at a religious function organized by the latter. The Balrampur state was within the Gonda district.[19]

Perhaps in his desperation to talk to a like-minded person, the Maharaj revealed his secret dream-plan to Nayyar. The former wanted to re-convert the Ayodhya Babri Masjid into a temple. However, the conversation ended there as national events with global implications ensued.

Mahatma Gandhi was assassinated in January 1948; the RSS, Hindu Mahasabha and other Hindu organizations were banned; and there was turmoil in the country. The political situation was in flux.

Apart from the religious beliefs, Nayyar shared another passion with the Maharaja—tennis, a sport that brought the duo close to Digvijay over the next two years.

Another critical link in the British India Faizabad district administration was Thakur Guru Datt Singh, who became the Faizabad city magistrate in 1948. On one of my several trips to Ayodhya, I spent time with Shakti Singh, Guru Datt's grandson and a local BJP leader.

Over chai and cookies on his patio, the third-generation family member gave insights about his grandfather's role in the events in December 1949 and after that. 'I believe that my Dada-ji worked whole-heartedly on the task and pursued it till it fructified,' he says.

Thakur Guru Datt hailed from Balia district in eastern Uttar Pradesh and was a devout Hindu: a teetotaller and vegetarian. He continued to wear his saffron turban despite the angst of his British seniors. A zealous Rambhakt, he would visit the Ram Janmabhoomi almost daily.

During these visits, he observed that though the namaz was not read in the Babri Mosque for years, the Muslims controlled the premises considered sacred by the Hindus. 'This attitude of the Muslims worried my Dada-ji,' explains Shakti Singh. As per the Supreme Court, 'Though, the case of the plaintiffs in Suit 4 is that the mosque was constructed in 1528 by or at the behest of Babur, there is no account by them of possession, use or offer of namaz in the mosque between the date of construction and 1856-7.'

The city magistrate, Guru Datt Singh, had two close friends, Captain Kripal Singh, SP, Faizabad, and Veer Singh, district judge, Faizabad. Kripal Singh felt that the Muslims asserted their right over the masjid complex only to provoke the Hindus, who were deprived of the opportunity to build a temple at the spot where their God was born.

'I heard stories from my father, Guru Basant Singh, on how these three officials held clandestine meetings for hours in our house to perhaps discuss these issues,' admits Shakti Singh.

Now, it is time to introduce the implementer of what transpired in December 1949, the man who carried the Ram Lalla idol and physically placed it inside the mosque—Abhiram Das, a mahant from the local Hanumangarhi temple. He stood six feet tall, was dark and well-built and had an authoritative persona.

Abhiram Das's reverence for Lord Ram was described by his disciple, Dharam Das, whom I met several times. Since I became friendly with Dharam Das over the last two decades, after the 2019 Supreme Court verdict I tell him at one of our meetings, 'Now, you are the hero—the main lineage to Abhiram Das.' This fuels Dharam Das's memory.

'My guru was called Uddharak Baba. Devotion for Lord Ram ran in his veins, and he was obsessed with Ram. Therefore, he had the strength and courage to help the Lord reach his appropriate abode (inside the mosque),' he proclaims with pride.

On another day, I sit in Dharam Das's room in Hanumangarhi. It is around 11 a.m., and there are devotees to meet him. Dharam Das appears oblivious to the waiting crowd, gets up, takes long strides towards a table and pulls out a 'Hindu Calendar' hanging on the wall. He shows a few dates in December that were encircled with a red sketch pen.

He explains that a true Hindu follows an auspicious day and time for any ceremony. 'Being a religious man, my guru chose an opportune date to fulfil his dream task.' To date, Hindu organizations, including the VHP, celebrate the December 1949 event as Ram Prakatotsava (appearance of Lord Ram) in Ayodhya with joy and fervour.

Given that he was a popular sadhu and had a commanding personality, Abhiram Das, the main actor of 1949, was also rather friendly with the local officials. We also know that his mentor, Digvijay Nath of Gorakhpur, was close to Nayyar and others. Nath possibly shared the plan de rêve with Guru Datt, the city magistrate, in mid-1949.

'Yes, I heard that he did, and I was told that my grandfather was jubilant to have a sage (Digvijay Nath) in the plan. There was no turning back,' says Guru Datt's grandson. Such connections perhaps gave Abhiram Das courage, and he became more resolute in carrying out his mission. His confidence grew in leaps and bounds, for he was sure that the administration was on his side.

Abhiram Das, as it turns out, was an immaculate planner. According to Shakti Singh, 'On 20 December 1949, the mahant ensured that his *chela*s (followers) spread a message, "*Chalo Ayodhya* (Let us go to Ayodhya)" in the adjoining districts of Gonda, Basti and Sultanpur. It was just the summon with no details. This increased the people's curiosity, and soon there was a buzz that "*Hanumangarhi se bulawa aaya hai* (we have received invitation from Hanumangarhi)". People had no idea of what lay ahead ... A well-planned scene was systematically being executed back in Ayodhya. Direct contacts were possibly made with the Hindu guard who was on duty during the day at the mosque. The night guard was a Muslim, Barkat Ali, and one does not know whether he knew about the operation or not.'

In those years, explains Shakti Singh, a lone sage, Ram Das, made his home in a tiny open space outside the mosque's boundary. He was neither attached to any akhara, nor did he have a guru. He kept to himself. But no visitor could escape his presence, although all that he did during the day was perform non-stop *parikrama*s (circling of the structure) with ceaseless chants of 'Sita Ram, Sita Ram'. He rested only after darkness set in.

The Muslims, the story goes, threatened Ram Das several times and asked him to leave the site. But the latter stayed on adamantly. The town legends speak of Abhiram Das looping in Ram Das in his Ram Lalla scheme. In total, about four dozen sadhus were roped in to fulfil the long-cherished ambition.

Yet another bairagi sadhu played a key role in the stealth act, explains the narrative in *Ayodhya: The Dark Night*. Vrindavan Das from the Ramanandi sect belonged to the Nirvani Akhara. He lived in a mud hut outside the mosque's gate. Abhiram Das entrusted him with the task to carry the Lord Ram Lalla's idol from the chabootra, situated outside the mosque boundary, to the masjid wall.

It was late in the night; the date was 22 December 1949. A thick sheath of haze liberally wrapped the trees, mounds and buildings—the universe seemed to be an ally in the conspiracy. On that fateful night, Vrindavan picked up the idols (Lord Ram Lalla and Sita) and ran towards Abhiram Das, who waited next to the railing built by the British almost a century ago to separate the inner and outer courtyards. Abhiram Das grabbed the idols and did not exchange a word. He ran towards the masjid's boundary.

Shakti Singh explains what could have possibly happened that night. 'At the stroke of midnight, when Abhiram Das jumped across the railing, Barkat Ali, the Muslim guard, was at his post. Though utterly careful, the mahant accidentally hit a brass bell hanging from atop. The sound alerted the guard who, within seconds, found himself in a scuffle with the six-feet-tall mahant. The guard soon gave up, and Abhiram Das darted into the mosque.'

Dharam Das, Abhiram Das's disciple, adds more nuggets to the episode. 'That night, it was Guru-ji who shifted the idols of Lord Ram Lalla and his wife, Sita, from the chabootra to the spot under the dome. He held both tightly against his lap as he jumped inside the railing.'

He adds, 'Orders had already been given to the assisting sadhus to carry holy water from the Sarayu, along with a woven mat and camphor. Guru-ji wanted to perform the religious rites, even at the risk of his life. So, he placed Ram Lalla in his exact birthplace and completed the requisite rituals and ceremonies.'

At about 3 a.m., Abhiram Das placed the idols in the mosque and, by 4 a.m., he finished the *sthapna puja* (installation ceremony). Finally, says Dharam Das with a wide grin, '*Aur masjid ko mandir bana diya* (And he transformed the mosque into a temple).' Shakti Singh adds, 'Once he lit the camphor in front of the idols, Abhiram Das shouted in a frenzy, "*Bhagwan Ramprakat ho gaye* (Lord Ram has appeared)".'

Ayodhya witnessed a new dawn.

The message of Lord Ram Lalla's miraculous appearance inside the Babri Masjid spread like wildfire. The lamp-light flickering from within and the camphor smell cast a spell on the bystanders. Thousands of devotees swayed as if intoxicated by the fragrance of religion. They sang Tulsidas's popular bhajan, *Bhaye prakat kripala, deendayala* (The merciful has appeared in light).

Nowadays, the older adults in the town have deconstructed why it was deliberately called a miracle. 'Devotees get more emotional when they hear about miracles. Religion is not science. Calling it a miraculous act went down well with the believers. By the afternoon of 23 December 1949, there were around five thousand people outside the mosque.'

Rajinder Singh, a retired bank officer, Gopal Singh Visharad's son, gives me more details. Visharad was the man who was named as the first litigant in the final Supreme Court order in 2019. It can be easily said that he was the one who carried forward the Ram Mandir legal legacy in independent India.

The events of 23 December 1949 are etched in Rajinder Singh's memory. 'In the wee hours, there was a rumour that people had sighted a flash of light inside the Babri Masjid. Devotees were caught in a strange state of frenzy. They shouted out in absolute glee, "*Ram Lalla prakat hue* (Ram Lalla has appeared)." From the crowd came a loud response, "*Ram Lalla bhookey hai, unko bhog charahiye* (Ram Lalla is hungry, please offer him food)." Within no time, both mahants and devotees made the required arrangement. Like other Rambhakts my father too was euphoric with the "appearance of Ram Lalla".'

Soon the action shifted to the corridors of power in Faizabad, Lucknow (capital of the United Provinces) and New Delhi. First, let us examine the immediate reactions of the police. 'No one knows till today why the authorities were not informed right away, but Ramdeo Dubey, the SHO of Ayodhya police, hardly a kilometre away from the site station, reached the site by 7 a.m. the following morning, probably on a routine inspection.'[20]

At around 7 a.m., when he reached the scene as per his daily routine, he lodged an FIR. 'At about 7 am when I reached Janam Bhoomi, I came to know from Constable (no. 7) Mata Prasad, who was on duty, that 50–60 persons in the night have entered into the mosque by breaking the lock and scaling the wall and installed an idol of Sri Ramchandraji there. They have also written on the wall inside and outside, the words "Sita Ram" etc. by *geru* (saffron) and yellow colour. Constable Hans Raj, who was on duty at that time, told them not to act in this manner but they did not listen to him. The PAC which was posted there was also called but by that time they had already entered into the mosque,' Dubey wrote in the FIR.[21]

A radio message was sent at 10.30 a.m. on 23 December 1949 by District Magistrate K.K. Nayyar to Chief Minister Pandit Govind Ballabh Pant, the chief secretary and the home secretary. It read thus: 'A few Hindus entered Babari Masjid at night when the Masjid was deserted and installed a deity there. DM and SP and force at spot. Situation under control. Police picket of 15 persons was on duty at night but did not apparently act.'[22]

Guru Datt, the city magistrate, imposed Section 144 of the Indian Penal Code (IPC), a ban against people's gathering. This ban brought an end to the festivities that included prayers and visits by the Hindu followers to the shrine, where Lord Ram Lalla had miraculously appeared.

DM Nayyar was dutiful enough to reach the spot at dawn to take stock of the situation, but did not take any action to remove the idols. '*Arrey hum ne toh yeh bhi suna hai ki Nayyar-ji par bhi prabhu ki kripa chha gayi thi* (We even heard that God's grace enveloped and mesmerized Nayyar-ji as well),' says Dharam Das, as he looks skywards and folds his hands dramatically.

In their book, *Ayodhya: The Dark Night*, Krishna Jha and Dhirendra K. Jha write, 'The district magistrate (DM) of Faizabad was among the first to reach the spot once Abhiram Das finished the operation successfully in the dead of the night. At that time the masjid only had a handful of people and Ayodhya was asleep.' The authors further mention that if the DM wanted 'he could have easily restored the mosque's status quo ante without creating any fuss among Hindu believers. That was also expected from any district magistrate anywhere in the country. But it was not a normal situation and the district magistrate of Faizabad was not acting innocently; he was more interested in complicating the problem than resolving it.'

In retrospect, one can assume that the DM stood at the spot in the wee hours like a mute spectator as described by Dharam Das. Besides, it is known to all that he took around six hours to report the incident to his seniors in Lucknow.

Over the next few days, despite repeated directions from the state government to immediately remove the idol, Nayyar refused. In one of the letters dated 27 December 1949, sent to Bhagwan Sahai, chief secretary, United Provinces, he mentions the slogans that the commoners chanted, '*Nyay anyay karna chhor do, Nayyar bhagwan ka phatak khol do* (Leave being just and unjust, just open the door to the God).' He ended the same letter stating very clearly what his intention was, 'I would, if the government decided to remove the idol at any cost, request that I be relieved and replaced by any officer who may be able to see in that solution a merit which I cannot discern. For my part, I cannot, in my discretion which is the only legal sanction as I am fully aware of the widespread sufferings which it will entail to many innocent lives.'[23]

Ironically, he castigated the state government for showing such interest in a local affair. Nayyar gave the ultimate threat a bureaucrat could. On 27 December 1949, he wrote, 'If Government still insisted that removal should be carried out ... I would request to replace me by another officer.'

This was after altercations had ensued between New Delhi and Lucknow. When the news reached Prime Minister Jawaharlal Nehru, he was shocked. A self-proclaimed atheist and a propagator of secularism, he realized that the communal balance that he was hoping for had already been disturbed and tampered with the night the idol of Lord Ram was placed inside the mosque.

Nehru sent a telegram to Gobind Ballabh Pant on 26 December 1949, in which he expressed his feelings, 'I am disturbed at developments at Ayodhya. Earnestly hope you will personally interest yourself in this matter. Dangerous example being set there which will have bad consequences.'[24]

After a few exchanges with the PM, the CM had to tell the local administration in Ayodhya to remove the idols immediately. As mentioned earlier, instead of obeying this order, Nayyar wrote that the removal was 'fraught with the gravest danger to public peace' and this could lead to a 'conflagration of horror'.

Shakti Singh agrees that his grandfather, Guru Datt, the city magistrate, took on the chief minister. 'When Pant-ji decided to visit Ayodhya on 25 December, my grandfather stopped him at the border explaining that it would not be safe even to make the slightest attempt at removing the idols.' At this, the chief minister retorted angrily, 'What kind of an administrator are you if you cannot provide security when needed?' Throwing caution to the winds, Guru Datt publicly told the chief minister, '*Main kisi ko Ram Lalla ko haath nahi lagane doonga* (I shall not allow anyone to touch Ram Lalla).'

After deliberations with Nayyar, Guru Datt resigned a few days later. 'My dada-ji had eight years of service left at that time, but it didn't matter to him. He felt that he had completed his mission in Ayodhya. When he resigned, he simply said, "My task is done,"' says the grandson with some pride.

An order was issued to seize the mosque. A receiver was appointed to take care of the premises, and the masjid was locked up. However, a provision was made to allow Hindus to continue with the prayers and offering of bhog, besides other rituals required to be carried out in the new 'Ram Lalla' temple.

In a couple of years, Nayyar and his family joined the Jan Sangh (the former avatar of the BJP). Three years later, in 1952, Shakuntala, his wife, contested elections and became a state assembly member. Ten years later, the couple became members of the fourth Lok Sabha; their driver also won the assembly election from Faizabad.

Thakur Guru Datt Singh, the city magistrate, joined the Jan Sangh and, in 1953, was appointed as chairman, City Municipality Board, Ayodhya.

Once the Ram Lalla idol found its place within the mosque's premises, the stage was set for a bigger, longer legal war between the Hindus and Muslims. As mentioned earlier, Visharad was the first one to approach the courts after the December 1949 events.

The best person who can talk about Visharad's life is Rajinder Singh, his son. I call him and, without any reluctance, he narrates his father's legal journey. Each word he speaks is tinged with nostalgia, pride and relief.

We have several telephonic conversations after the apex court's final order. He is delirious that what his father aspired for half a century ago was fulfilled. He remembers that his father's love for Lord Ram prompted the family to shift from its ancestral home in Jhansi, Bundelkhand, to Ayodhya.

'My father was a pious man who visited holy places at least twice a year. He wanted to make a *teerth sthan* (pilgrimage) his home. In fact, his wish was to settle in a religious town where there would be a temple in each house.' Ayodhya seemed the perfect destination, and Visharad shifted lock, stock and barrel in 1941. He set up a grocery store, Bundelkhand General Store, and lived in a rented house close to the banks of the Sarayu.

Every day, after a bath in the river, Visharad visited the Hanumangarhi temple and Ram Janmasthan. From there, he went to his store, which he opened diligently at 10 a.m. In the evenings, he met his bosom pals and sadhus, Ram Das and Ram Chandra Paramhans, at Ganga Surmawalla's shop in the Janmasthan locality.

Rajinder Singh, Visharad's son, remembers visits to the Ram Janmabhoomi Temple, sometimes with his father and on other occasions with friends. 'It was pretty far from where we lived, so

Pita-ji would often take a rickshaw. During those years, Ram Lalla was seated on the chabootra under a temporary roof. Devotees offered prayers and circled around the holy place.'

On 16 January 1950, Rajinder's father, Visharad, changed the legal course of the Mandir–Masjid conflict. Over the next seven decades, this legal tangle continued through extreme twists and turns, ups and downs.

Rajinder explains why his father was compelled to go to the courts. 'In those days, Zaroor Miya, a staunch Muslim, was the manager who would also be there as a guard at the mosque. On the morning of 14 January 1950, during his regular visit to the Janmabhoomi, he was stopped by Zaroor. The police arrived and prevented my father from visiting the mosque-cum-temple.'

Visharad lost his patience and the matter escalated. Soon, the news of the altercation spread across the town. Visharad was asked to meet DM Nayyar in his office. 'When he returned that evening, he was visibly excited,' remembers Rajinder. Two days later, Gopal Singh Visharad filed a civil suit in the court of Faizabad, which demanded that he and other Hindus be permitted to worship the Ram Lalla deity inside the mosque.

He requested a 'temporary injunction' to stop the government officials from removing the idols. The judge granted the injunction but did not rule on the question of his right to worship.

Decades later, this plea was considered as Suit No. 1 in the combined Ram Janmabhoomi cases. In its final verdict, the Supreme Court stated, 'The right of the plaintiff in Suit No. 1 to worship at the disputed property is affirmed subject to any restrictions imposed by the relevant authorities concerning the maintenance of peace and order and the performance of orderly worship.' Visharad won after seven decades!

There seems to be a link between Suit No. 1, DM Nayyar and many players who participated in Lord Ram Lalla's installation.

Rajinder Singh confirms, 'One evening, my father was summoned by the district magistrate. That was the beginning of the many meetings that were to take place almost every day, either with Nayyar or Guru Datt Singh.'

At some of the meetings, even Mahant Digvijay Nath, the architect of Ram Lalla's appearance, was present. Since Nayyar, Datt and Digvijay were from the Hindu Mahasabha, I ask Rajinder about his father's political allegiance. 'As much as I remember, my father's loyalty was always with the Hindu Mahasabha, though he joined it officially in 1942, a year after he shifted to Ayodhya. It is possible that the state party leaders noticed his dedication. He was made the head of the party unit in Faizabad district in 1949.'

6

Legal Trails, Travails and Trials, 1950–2019

'No religion taught man to kill fellowmen because he held different opinions or was of another religion.'

—MAHATMA GANDHI[1]

Acts such as the installation of Hindu idols inside a mosque, followed by Gopal Singh Visharad's legal complaint, were not expected to be endured quietly by the Muslims in Ayodhya.

It was much after 9 a.m. on 16 January 1950, an unusually late hour, that Anisur Rahman woke up. He had not been able to sleep a wink the night before. He plodded to the entrance of his house with his morning glass of chai. There he stood silently with a faraway gaze. He barely blinked as his eyes settled on the Babri Masjid where he had spent innumerable days since his childhood.

It looked as beautiful as ever; it appeared strong despite the blasphemous incidents that had occurred inside it three weeks ago.

Not being able to carry the burden of religious intolerance any further, he decided to slug it out in the court for the rights of his community. Later in the day, the thirty-year-old got on his bicycle, left for Faizabad, filed a petition in the local court and became the first Muslim in independent India to tread the legal path to keep the Babri Masjid in control of his brethren.

Maybe it was more than a coincidence that Visharad and Rahman made their respective moves in quick succession. There is a possibility that the Muslims heard rumours about the earlier meeting between DM Nayyar and Visharad. Or was it the other way around? The Hindus knew that the Muslims were up to something. In a letter dated 26 December 1949, K.K.K. Nayyar, addressing Bhagwan Sahay, mentioned that one of the deputationists, Anisur Rehman, said that on the evening of 21 December, there were a few Hindus who had planned to install an idol in the mosque 'and also prevent Muslims from praying Friday prayer (23rd was a Friday)'. The letter further elaborated, 'When I asked Anisur Rehman why he did not promptly bring the matter to my notice, he said that he had not considered it necessary to do so since a CID officer himself was present. To me also it appears that Anisur Rehman himself could never have believed that this mischief was likely to happen for otherwise he would straightaway have rushed to the local authorities and informed them.'[2]

However, if one talks to Haji Mehboob, a well-known Muslim landowner in Ayodhya who took up the legal cudgels later, you get to understand that Rehman was not guided by any malice or revenge. The latter was an individual whose religious faith was as strong as Visharad's.

Haji Mehboob gave me details about Anisur Rehman. Rehman ran a workshop where he made and sold tin boxes. In January 1950, the constant buzz of the possible conflicts between Hindus and Muslims, which took off after Lord Ram Lalla's appearance within the mosque, affected his business. The entire incident also agitated him, bringing up disturbing memories from his childhood. In 1934, when he was eighteen, a riot had broken out in Ayodhya, even though its epicentre was in Shahjahanpur, where violence had erupted over cow slaughter. The news had spread like wildfire and had its ramifications 300 km away in Ayodhya.

Every time communal strife took place, both the Hindus and Muslims of Ayodhya sought revenge and targeted the opponent's places of worship, mainly Hanumangarhi or the Babri Masjid. In the 1934 incident, as a perceptive trailer to what happened fifty-eight years later, the Hindus brought down one of the three domes of the mosque. British officials instructed the Hindus to repair the damage. On the night of 15 January 1950, as he tossed and turned in his bed, Rehman thought about the discussions he had had with his father in 1934.

The son had questioned his father about the rights of the different communities in the context of mandir and masjid. His father had assured him that the situation would change once India gained independence, as 'it was the British who had created a divide between Hindus and us'. Thirteen years later, these comforting words seemed like a mockery.

According to Haji Mehboob, the thought in Rahman's mind perhaps was: 'If there was a Visharad, who missed out on visiting his God, were the Muslims not expected to feel the same?' The Muslims felt that the mosque was tarnished by those who had placed a Hindu idol inside it and worshipped it there. Advocate M.R. Shamshad, who appeared in the Supreme Court on the Muslim side, explains why: 'This placing of the idol definitely desacralized the mosque, but it is important to note that the nature of the mosque still remained the same.'

Haji Mehboob says that 1950 wasn't the first time that Anisur Rehman intervened in the issue. 'He had earlier cycled to Faizabad to tell the British administration about sadhus who loitered around the mosque at odd hours. The warnings fell on deaf ears. Disillusioned and heartbroken with the way things were turning out in his hometown, Rehman soon gave up the legal fight as well. He built huge metal boxes, this time for himself, packed them to the brim with his family's belongings and moved to Pakistan. Thus, his Ayodhya story ended.'

However, Visharad and Rehman started a new trend. On 5 December 1950, almost a year after the Ram Lalla idol event, the irrepressible sage from Digambar Akhara, Ram Chandra Paramhans, approached the court in Faizabad and filed a suit. He demanded an embargo to stop Muslims from creating disturbances or obstructions in Lord Ram's worship at the Janmabhoomi.

The case was admitted on the same day by the civil judge. This was typically referred to as Suit No. 2 in this legal saga. But the civil judge of Faizabad combined both the petitions on 1 February 1951, as they were similar in nature. In the final Supreme Court judgment, they were referred to in a combined manner.

Together, both Visharad and Ram Chandra Paramhans named five local Muslims as the defendants. They charged that these Muslims put pressure on the local administration to remove the Hindu idols. One of the named offenders was the famous and wealthy landlord Haji Phenku (Haji Mehboob's father). Haji Sahab was a religious philanthropic who donated massive amounts for the upkeep of the Babri Masjid, where he sometimes took up the muezzin's role.

Along with the other accused, Phenku refuted the Hindu allegations. He reiterated that the Babri Masjid was a sacred place for Muslims, and no temple was brought down to build it.

'My father would come home from the court, tired and crestfallen. He would be flustered that the Faizabad Court would often adjourn the hearings. We were not used to him [being] so angry and would leave Abba Jaan to himself on such days,' remembers Haji Mehboob.

He adds, 'Now I understand what my father had been through. I feel equally harassed, betrayed and resentful—we were given no consideration, even by the apex court. Look at how the Supreme Court doled out space for a mosque for us, far away from the main site. Are we beggars?'

Mohammad Hashim Ansari was another old litigant in the Babri Masjid case. He passed away in 2016 at the age of ninety-six. Whenever I had met him as a journalist, he had many stories to share from years ago. He once told me how, in 1954, along with a hundred-odd Muslims, he had sought permission from the administration to offer prayers at the site. It was denied. 'Consequently, Muslims angrily reacted and forced themselves into the mosque. They were arrested and jailed for two months.'

After the events of 22–23 December 1949, subsequent litigations and separate meetings among the two communities on the Mandir–Masjid issue along with the love-hate relationship between the two communities continued. On the brighter side, there were not too many riots. Amidst the religious and legal tensions, the two groups from all strata of society visited each other, sat together, chatted, shared *beedi*s and chai, and played cards almost as a daily routine.

For example, a friendship flourished between Haji Phenku, who was respected by both the communities, and the Hindu Raja of Ayodhya. The two would often visit each other in their *baggi*s (horse-drawn carriages) which were highly fashionable and a luxury that the rich and powerful loved flaunting in that era.

However, the court cases continued, and more litigations were added to them. On 17 December 1959, the Nirmohi Akhara decided to voice its demands. The akhara's mahant and his chelas were upset that their management rights over the temple (on the chabootra) were taken over by the local administration on 5 January 1950. This was admitted as Suit No. 3.

The akhara said that before 22–23 December 1949, the same idol of Ram Lalla that was now inside the mosque used to be seated on a wooden platform on the chabootra. Devotees would thus gather for prayers in the outer courtyard and not inside the mosque. The Nirmohi sadhus maintained the deity and even took care of all the religious rituals.

The akhara reminded the district court that its mahant, Raghunath Das, was the first to initiate legal proceedings in 1885. This proved that the akhara was the oldest litigant in the Mandir–Masjid dispute.

Its petition stated that it had served the deity, managed the affairs and received the devotees' offerings. Since 1934, no Muslim had entered the temple premises. Mahant Jagat Das, who was the brain behind the 1959 case, had claimed that the akhara should get 'absolute right' to manage the affairs of the Janamsthaan.

As per the 2019 Supreme Court verdict, Mahant Jagat Das added that the akhara's role was crushed by the order, which declared that the property should be under the supervision of the administration-appointed receiver. The mahant had demanded that the receiver be removed and the temple be handed back to the Nirmohi Akhara—the suit was instituted on 17 December 1959 by the Nirmohi Akhara through Mahant Jagat Das seeking a decree for the removal of the receiver from the management and charge of the Janmabhoomi temple and for delivering it to the plaintiff.[3]

While the Mandir–Masjid conflict slowly aggravated, it was an irony of sorts that around the same time, in 1961, a Bollywood film, *Dharmputra*, directed Yash Chopra, was released. Based on bigotry, fanaticism and communalism, the reel-life story that ended on a happy note became a success at the box office. Contrary to this, in real life, far away from the tinsel town in Ayodhya, the conflict between the Hindus and Muslims turned even more severe and at that time no one could even guess what the ending of this saga would look like.

It was in the same year, 1961, that the Sunni Central Waqf Board, led by the forty-year-old Hashim Ansari, filed a suit in Faizabad. It staked claim to the Babri Masjid and the adjoining graveyard. It argued that if the structure was not a mosque, the suit of 1885 should have mentioned it.

According to this petition, the Hindus did not challenge the 1936 report of the commissioner of the Waqf Board, which stated that the Babri property was a mosque. It clarified that the Muslims had owned the Babri Masjid premises till 23 December 1949.

Even if a temple existed before the mosque was built—and this was hypothetical, and not an admission—the possession over centuries strengthened the Muslims' claims. It 'perfected their title by adverse possession and the right, title or interest of the temple and or Hindu public, if any, extinguished'.[4]

As per the Muslim narratives, the city magistrate Guru Datt Singh's decision to attach the masjid in 1950 deprived the Muslims of their legal rights. The Waqf Board demanded that the property belonged to the Muslim Waqf and, therefore, it should be released to the real owner. It wanted the removal of the Hindu idols from Babri Masjid.

On 8 August 1962, the Sunni Board stated that the disputed property was dedicated to Almighty God and was a mosque for the use of the Muslim community. On 28 August 1963, it added that even if Hindus had any right in the property, it stood extinguished due to lapse of time, and the board had acquired the title by adverse possession.

Decades later, Zafaryiab Jilani, who headed the Babri Masjid Action Committee (BMAC) during the 1990s, maintained that the statement of 8 August 1962 reiterated the Muslim stance that the mosque, graveyard and other structures were Waqf properties. More importantly, the points raised again on 28 August 1963 established the right of possession as per the laws of limitation. Even if there was a temple before 1528, the rights of the Hindus stood extinguished as the Muslims possessed the site for more than 400 years.

In India, the law of adverse possession, said Jilani, was that if someone was in possession of any property for more than twelve years and no suit was filed to reclaim its title, then the one with possession was treated to have perfected the rights.

However, political developments, rather than nuanced legal arguments like Jilani's, shaped the destiny of Ram Janmabhoomi during the 1970s. It marked the rise of the BJP (the Jana Sangh in the 1970s), Akhil Bharatiya Vidyarthi Parishad (ABVP)—the party's student wing, and RSS and its affiliates. These trends accelerated the events related to the Ram Mandir in the 1980s.

In March 1971, Indira Gandhi of the Congress won a landslide victory in the national election with 352 out of 518 seats in the Lok Sabha. On 16 December 1971, her popularity peaked when the Pakistan Army surrendered to India, and Bangladesh was liberated.

But soon, the economy crumbled. To make things worse, the Prime Minister turned arrogant. Doubts regarding her capability to solve the country's socio-economic problems were raised by several parties, political gurus and even Congress insiders. Direct action to overthrow the government was widely discussed.[5]

In December 1973, a students' agitation took off in LD College of Engineering, Ahmedabad, Gujarat. It began with in-campus problems like the hike in canteen food charges. The police used force, despite which the turmoil extended to other campuses and spread across the city by early 1974. Arson, looting and strikes ensued against the state government, and students brazenly targeted the Congress leaders. The army was called to handle the situation.

Inspired by the success of the Gujarat agitation, a similar movement came alive in Patna, Bihar. It was here that the ABVP picketed the Bihar State Assembly on 18 March 1974. The crowd set fire to government buildings, warehouses and a couple of newspaper offices.

On 6 April, the president of the Patna University Students' Union, along with others from the ABVP, requested popular leader and freedom fighter Jayaprakash Narayan (JP) to assume leadership. The students assured him that they would abide by his guidance. JP was sympathetic. He felt that he could not remain a silent spectator to Indira's misgovernance and corruption. He urged the students to give up their studies for a year to 'save democracy', or else democracy would prove to be a failure.[6]

When he addressed a crowd of 500,000–1,000,000 at Gandhi Maidan in Patna on 5 June 1974 for two hours, the seventy-one-year-old JP, who shunned political and government offices, called for *sampoorna kranti* (total revolution) along the lines of Gandhian principles.[7]

Several young members of the RSS shakhas joined this call. Political analysts believe that had JP not welcomed and integrated the RSS leaders and members within his movement, the BJP (Jana Sangh) would have remained irrelevant in India's political history.

According to author Robert Graeme Salter, 'In particular, the well-organised forces of the Right—the Jana Sangh, the ABVP and the RSS—gained respectability from their participation in the (JP) Movement and were able to go about the serious business of recruiting thousands of new members and supporters.'[8]

In his book, *My Take*, Lal Krishna Advani, former deputy prime minister, writes, 'When I look back at the last sixty years of my political life and try to assess what can be regarded as the second most important contribution JS (Jana Sangh) and BJP have made to Indian politics, I would say that assisting Loknayak Jayaprakash Narayan to bring together all non-Congress parties, fighting the traumatic Emergency and saving democracy is the second major contribution. In this matter the BJP played a pivotal role.'[9]

Students from across the country enrolled in the Chhatra Yuva Sangharsh Vahini (students' wing of the JP movement). Kameshwar Chaupal, now a senior BJP member, who became famous in the Ram Janmabhoomi chronicle when he laid the temple's first foundation stone on 9 November 1989, was no exception.

Talking to me thirty years later, he recollects, 'There were a couple of highly active social workers in my village, Kamrail (in the state of Bihar). They inspired us to join the agitation. Even now, I still get goosebumps when I remember a couple of JP's speeches that I got to hear in those years.'

Chaupal is a fervent Rambhakt who prefers to underplay his importance in the movement. The enthusiasm and excitement in his voice, however, are giveaways. He loves to revisit the 'historic' role that was handed out to him then and, much to my delight, takes me through his journey during the 1970s and '80s.

On the midnight of 25 June 1975, Emergency was declared by Indira Gandhi—the reason given was internal security threat. She stressed JP's incitement to urge the public armed forces and police to rebel against the ruling regime. JP was arrested the next morning and was in prison till 12 November. In jail, he was seriously ill with kidney failure.

Indira banned twenty-seven organizations that opposed her regime, which included the RSS. The key members of these outfits were thrown in prison for six to eighteen months. Out of the 1,356 RSS pracharaks, 189 were arrested. Among the 30,000 who were arrested under MISA, more than 25,000 were Sangh's *swayamsevak*s (volunteers).[10]

RSS *sarsanghchalak* (head of the RSS) Balasaheb Deoras was arrested on 30 June from the Nagpur railway station. Before his arrest, he told the members, 'In this extraordinary situation, the swayamsevaks have the responsibility to not lose their composure. They should continue to be engaged in Sangh work as per the instructions of Sarkaryavaha (the deputy) Madhavrao Mulay and those appointed by him and continue to be in contact with common people, make them aware and educate them and thus fulfil your national duty to build a capable and aware society.'[11]

Chaupal tells me that he learnt about the RSS history and most of its leaders during this phase. 'Though I had completed graduation, I was allowed, rather encouraged, to stay back in the college hostel. It was a comfortable stay as our food and lodging were taken care of by our leaders. Most of us would find time enough to read the books recommended by the Sangh. The local leaders even made arrangements with the college library to help us issue the books.'

He adds, '*Sangh ke varisht log bhi hume kitaab dete the* (the Sangh's senior leaders would also give us books). We familiarized ourselves with the ethos of the Sangh, and its vision.' Interestingly, when Emergency was withdrawn on 21 March 1977, 'The number of RSS shakhas jumped from 8,500 in 1975 to 11,000 in 1977. After the Emergency, it further increased to 13,000 in 1979, 17,000 by 1981, and 20,000 by 1982.' Parallelly, the ABVP's membership increased from 170,000 in 1977 to 250,000 in 1982. Yet, of the only thirty-one Janata Party MPs who won the national election in January 1980, when Indira Gandhi romped back to power, a mere sixteen belonged to the Jana Sangh. It was a steep fall from the ninety-three MPs it had in the previous Lok Sabha. The RSS realized the perils of associating with a political coalition of differing ideologies. On 5–6 April 1980, the Jana Sangh announced the creation of a new party, the BJP, at a convention in New Delhi. It was formally launched at its first plenary held in Bombay on 28–30 December 1980.[12]

In less than two months of pitching the new party, an incident occurred in south India that somewhat toppled the apple cart for the BJP. But instead of losing heart, the self-appointed saviours of Hindutva began marching more aggressively towards their goals; this time with a new-found and compelling reason. On 19 February 1981, 200 Dalit families from Meenakshipuram, a remote village in Tamil Nadu, willingly converted to Islam at a public function. 'This mass conversion to Islam set in motion a vigorous process by the Hindu right-wing party such as the RSS, BJP and VHP for reclaiming them back to Hinduism. The next two decades witnessed violence against the Muslims and, in some instances, also against Christians.'[13]

In his book *India since Independence*, author V. Krishna Ananth explains, 'The fact that the Dalits, this time, embraced Islam and not Buddhism perturbed the saffron organisations. The RSS demanded a law banning conversions and unleashed the VHP, founded in 1964, with a specific brief of propagating the virtues of Hindu religion and to check the advance of Islamic and Christian missionaries among the tribal population.'

VHP volunteers were sent to villages with tribal pockets. Chaupal claims, 'I was assigned to take care of the Adivasis in the Chotanagpur belt, which was then in erstwhile Bihar. We were expected to educate the tribals and look after their welfare. We were also entrusted with the job of building Hindu temples. This was not a very challenging task for our team as Adivasis in these localities were devotees of Lord Hanuman. Later we realized that's because most tribal people have faith in gods that they can associate with nature and their own surrounds.'

In his book, *Religion, Power and Violence*, author Ram Puniyani writes, 'The existence of minority communities as distinct entities forming an integral part of India is what the Sangh Parivar is averse to.' He further adds, 'In other words pluralism does not fit into the worldview of the Sangh Parivar. In Ashok Singhal's words, "Islam has a future in this country only if it completely submerges among the hundreds of sects that already exists in India." And again. "The interpretation of the Quran in this country must be set right. It [the Quran] should be adapted according to the great traditions of India."These statements make it clear that giving up the community identity is the demand which the Parivar makes of the minority communities.' The minorities have always felt that the VHP has little tolerance towards them because of such statements made by its leadership.[14]

The Meenakshipuram conversions allowed the Sangh leaders to justify their future moves. Wasting no time, they proclaimed themselves as the saviours and guardians of Hindu religion, traditions and culture. Conscious of the en-masse conversions, they mobilized the Hindus, irrespective of castes and regions.

The VHP leaders simultaneously held conferences. On 18 October 1981, the Virat Hindu Sammelan was held at Delhi's Boat Club. A Vedic scholar and scion of the Suryavanshi family of Jammu and Kashmir, Karan Singh, presided at the rally.[15]

In media reports (*The Illustrated Weekly of India*, 1984: Volume 26), Karan Singh described it as 'a watershed event in the history of modern Hinduism' in which Hindu religious leaders argued that 'untouchability was in no way an essential adjunct of Hinduism and would have to be eradicated root and branch if Hindu society was to be strengthened and its solidarity ensured'.[16]

'In 1982, the VHP formed a Hindu ecclesiastical body, Sadhu Sansad, and invited spiritual leaders from different sects of Hinduism. They were given the task to "direct and guide the religious ceremonies, moral and ethics of Hindu Society",' wrote Prema Kurien.[17]

Vinay Katiyar, the founder-president of the Bajrang Dal, the youth wing of the VHP, launched the Hindu Jagran Manch (HJM) the same year. 'I deeply felt such an organization was the need of the hour if we were to bring back the glory of the Hindus. The HJM was created predominantly to focus on activism against religious conversion and, at that time, its primary function was to work for the reconversion of Muslims and Christians to Hinduism,' he explains as we discuss his contribution apropos the Ram Janmabhoomi narrative.

Katiyar tells me that he was overjoyed when, in April 1983, two senior Congress leaders, Dau Dayal Khanna and Gulzari Lal Nanda, attended a conference organized by the HJM in Muzaffarnagar in western Uttar Pradesh. While Khanna was a former minister in the Uttar Pradesh government and a five-time MLA from Moradabad, Nanda had been a former interim Prime Minister.

At the meeting, Khanna and Nanda proposed the idea of liberating three temples—Sri Ram Janmabhoomi in Ayodhya, Sri Krishna Janmasthaan in Mathura and Sri Kashi Vishwanath in Varanasi. 'We deliberately chose these three temples because they symbolized challenges thrown to Hindus by the inconsiderate and fanatic Muslim rulers. We intended to bring together Hindus despite regional or caste differences and rebuild their waning self-esteem,' adds Katiyar.

Chaupal, who also attended this meeting, remembers how the two ace Congress leaders almost ordered, 'You youngsters should now take up the issues as we are ageing and lack the energy required for such a mammoth task.'

Charged with passion, within a few months these leaders, along with many young and old Hindus from varied social strata, began their movement with rath yatras across the Hindi heartland stopping at different pilgrim towns.

In the Hindu religion, yatras imply pilgrimages to places considered to be replete with spiritual and religious vibrations, special powers, knowledge and miraculous capacities. In India, places with the confluence of sacred rivers and those linked to Puranic stories like the *Samudra Manthan* (Churning of the Ocean) and Hindu legends like Mahabharata and Ramayana, became the most-visited pilgrimages.[18]

The first rath was flagged off in November 1983. It was called Ekatmata (one soul) Yatra, which signified that despite all superficial or other differences, all Hindus have the same soul and are united in their hearts and minds with the same purpose. The leitmotif chosen was the River Ganga, which flows through eleven states. According to Hindu mythology, it originates from Shiva's dreadlocks, the Creator and Destroyer God who resides in Mount Kailash (part of the Himalayas).

Three important religious origins and destinations were identified for the main cavalcades. The three routes were: from the Pashupati Temple in Kathmandu (north) to Rameswaram in the south, from Gangasagar in West Bengal (east) to Somnath Temple in Gujarat (west), and from Haridwar (north) to Kanyakumari, the southernmost tip where the Indian Ocean, Andaman Sea and Arabian Sea merge.

Huge trucks were painstakingly designed like mythological raths with towering cut-outs of Ganga Mata and Bharat Mata (Mother India). The processions were accompanied by huge crowds, from energetic young followers to mellowed leaders, besides many sadhus, from all over the country.

The participants in this event still remember that wherever the vehicles halted, people ran out of their homes and offices, schools and colleges, shops and clinics to offer prayers to the carriers of divinity. The leaders and sadhus gave religious speeches, which were liberally spiced with political rhetoric. To round off this holy theatre, sadhus with long tidal dreadlocks and flowing beards, ash or sandalwood smeared on their grave faces, blessed the devotees and purified them with a sprinkle of holy water.

Huge *kalash*es (urns) filled with water from the Ganga and its tributaries were placed on these truck-turned-raths. These were never empty. Wherever the convoy stopped, the urns were refilled with 'divine water'. People who wished to carry back some item of faith could buy plastic cans filled with 500 ml of holy water for Rs 10 each. The theme song *'Har Har Gange'* resonated everywhere as the carriages moved.[19]

The raths converged in Nagpur, the command post of the RSS and the geographic centre of India. Political analyst Christophe Jaffrelot remarked, 'The Ekatmata Yatra inaugurated a new ethno-religious engineering called to become more and more political over time.'[20]

After the unexpected and massive success of the Ekatmata Yatra, the VHP held a first-of-its-kind conference, a Dharam Sansad, an improvised version of the Sadhu Sansad, on 7–8 April 1984 at New Delhi's Vigyan Bhavan. It roped in 500 sadhus and mahants who helped the organizers coat their political intentions with a saffron casing.

The speakers reiterated the agenda of removing the three mosques built by 'Muslim marauders' at Ayodhya, Mathura and Kashi.[21]

The future tasks that were discussed focussed on annihilating the edifices that personified the so-called Muslim tyranny and stood in the form of structures (mosques) over the erstwhile temples.

With Ayodhya topping the list of priorities, a special Sri Ram Janam Bhoomi Mukti Yajna Samiti was set up. The Ram–Janki Rath Yatra was conceptualized, which, unlike the Ekatmata Yatra, focussed completely on Ayodhya. It rolled out from Sitamarhi, the mythological birthplace of Sita, in Bihar, on 25 September 1984, the auspicious occasion of Sharadiya Navaratra.

The procession was 'marked by the Hindu Nationalist slogans. Saints and Sadhus from all parts of the country came to take part in the Liberation Movement. Mahant Avaidyanath preached that the people should vote only to those parties which explicitly promised to give the Hindus their sacred places back.'[22]

Chaupal, who was with this procession, explains, 'We had to convey that while Hindus enjoyed freedom, Lord Ram was behind locks. Therefore, Ram-ji and Sita Mayya were shown within a jail in the procession. For Ram's sake, we needed to get Rambhakts together. Though the tableaux were around Ram, cut-outs of Bharat Mata were displayed as well.'

He adds, 'On the evening of 6 October 1984, we reached Ayodhya and took a *sankalp* (oath) on the banks of River Sarayu—*Ram Lalla hum ayenge, mandir yahin banayenge* (Ram Lalla, we promise to come back, and build a temple here).'

I speak to local journalists who clearly remember the events of that evening: The Ram–Janaki Rath reached Ayodhya in 1984. The Sarayu looked like a bright saffron ribbon that evening, matching its colour with the hundreds of sadhus who were standing on its bridge to welcome the Rath Yatra pilgrims. However, that day the crowd was not as large as expected. The stage was a wooden platform raised on barren land close to the river. It was adorned by the torchbearers of the movement and included both *neta*s (politicians) and sadhus. Among the prominent speakers were Mahant Avaidyanath, Dau Dayal Khanna and the popular abbot of Digambar Akhara, Ram Chandra Paramhans. They spoke to the devotees about how Hindus were still not independent as their Lord was behind a locked door.

From Ayodhya, the rath moved to Lucknow and then towards Delhi. 'When we reached Ghaziabad, which is about 40 kilometres from the capital, we heard about Indira Gandhi's assassination. The sadhus advised us, *"Desh sankat mein hai, ab jab tak sab theek na ho, hume apna karyakarm sthagit karna chahiye* (The country is in danger, and till things normalize, we have to postpone this programme)",' adds Chaupal.

The next key event in this politico-legal saga came in 1986 with the opening of the locks of Babri Masjid. The locks had been on since the 1949 Ram Lalla incident. I call Umesh Chandra Pandey, who played a vital role in facilitating the opening of the locks.

With Indira Gandhi's assassination, her son, Rajiv Gandhi, became the new PM. Though he lacked the political acumen and experience his mother had in matters of the state, he tried hard to rev up the party image between 1984 and 1989. He also took the initial steps to liberalize the economy.

Rajiv Gandhi, however, faltered in meeting the demands of different religious communities. The Shah Bano order put the new PM in a quandary. Shah Bano, a sixty-two-year-old Muslim lady, filed a petition in the court of Indore in April 1978 and demanded maintenance from her divorced husband, Mohammed Ahmad Khan, a renowned lawyer.

On 3 February 1981, the Supreme Court held that Section 125(3) of the Criminal Code applied to Indian citizens, including Muslims, without discrimination. The specific section dealt with a remedy to people who were unable to maintain themselves. As per its provisions, the court ruled that Shah Bano was entitled to receive an amount 'to maintain herself and her five children'.

The decision inflamed the conservative groups within the Muslim community. They concluded that it was taken by a bench of five Hindu judges and was blasphemous. It overruled the verses of the Holy Quran and the principles of Islam.

Flummoxed by the Muslim outrage, Rajiv Gandhi spearheaded the Muslim Women (Protection on Divorce) Act, 1986. 'The Act, in effect, overturned the decision in Shah Bano's case,' said a piece on feminismindia.com. The act was received particularly well by the conservative Muslim fundamentalists.

This government's volte-face appeared to be a biased decision that denied divorced Muslim women the right to essential maintenance, which women of other faiths enjoyed. In her recently published book *Ideology and Organization in Indian Politics: Growing Polarization and the Decline of the Congress Party (2009–19)*, author and academician Zoya Hasan analyses these moves. 'Prime Minister Rajiv Gandhi, concerned about losing Muslim support, decided to enact the Muslim Women's (Protection of Rights on Divorce) Act (MWA) of 1986. This was done to revoke the landmark Supreme Court judgment, which granted a maintenance allowance to Shah Bano, a 73-year-old Muslim divorcee, to be paid by her husband under the Criminal Procedure Code (CrPC). This controversy sparked off a huge political uproar, demanding exclusion of Muslim women from the purview of the CrPC, to which otherwise all citizens have recourse.'

She adds that the government had taken this decision to invalidate the 'court's verdict and enact the MWA, declaring that Muslim women would not have recourse to the provisions of the CrPC in regard to maintenance in the event of divorce. Rajiv Gandhi had clearly succumbed to the pressure from the clergy and Muslim leaders in his own party to pass this statute.'

In an attempt to appease a section of Muslims, Rajiv Gandhi created a basis for sectarian politics. And this chaos gave the saffron leaders the chance to reinforce Hindutva and revive the Ram Janmabhoomi crusade.

In 1985, the BJP, RSS and other affiliates started the Tala Kholo Abhiyan (the operation to open the lock on Babri Masjid). The tala kholo movement had other objectives, like raising Rs 2.5 crore to construct a Hindu temple in Ayodhya. The VHP involved the Bajrang Dal, the volunteer youth corps, to assist with this project. The Bajrang Dal, organized around Lord Hanuman, adopted the slogan, 'Rest not before Rama's work is done'.[23]

Vinay Katiyar tells me how he concentrated exclusively on the Ram Temple, 'While the Dharam Sansad focussed primarily on the mahants and sadhus, I wanted to bring the Hindu youth under one umbrella.' How did he hit upon the name Bajrang Dal? 'Elementary,' he tells me. 'Hanuman-ji was the most ardent follower of Lord Ram, *aur sari zindagi unhone Ram-ji ki sewa mein laga diye the* (and he spent his life in serving his Lord). *Bajrang Dal ka naam unhi ki prateek ki haisiyat se rakha gaya tha* (The name of Bajrang Dal was coined on that basis).'

By 1985, the RSS and its affiliates were virulently blaming the Congress for playing appeasement politics. Around the same time, the young advocate, Umesh Chandra Pandey, prepared grounds to ensure that the lock on Babri Masjid where Lord Ram Lalla's idol was present was opened. A young Umesh's curiosity in the Ram Janmabhoomi movement heightened after he attended the *sants*' and VHP leaders' meeting during the 1984 Ram–Janaki Rath Yatra in Ayodhya.

'I heard the VHP leaders state that there were never any legal order to lock the Ram Temple (the makeshift one built inside the mosque in 1949), and this prompted me to look into the past cases. I spent time in the district court of Faizabad. I realized that there was indeed no court order to put a padlock. It was an administrative instruction by the district magistrate in January 1950. I instituted an appeal in the Faizabad District Lower Court (*Munsif Sadar*) on 25 January 1986.'

Umesh urged the administration to open the locks. He also questioned why the VVIPs were allowed a darshan inside, and the masses could only pray from outside the locked door. The town *munsif* (judge) rejected the plea. A determined Umesh moved the appeal before the district and sessions judge Krishna Mohan Pandey. As we discuss his role, Umesh adds, 'By the time I instituted the plea, the papers of the previous cases were sent to the Lucknow High Court. I was told that there could be no hearing until a *patravali* (formal letter) was received from the high court. Five days later, the case was taken up on an "urgency" basis.'

At 4.40 p.m. on 1 February 1986, the district and sessions judge of Faizabad stated that the lock on the temple–mosque should be opened with immediate effect. The same evening, within an hour, the rusty stubborn lock was broken. Even Doordarshan captured the event with crowds teeming to enter the shrine. With pride, Umesh adds, 'Later, I was informed that a copy of my petition was sent both to the official agency in charge of internal security and the Prime Minister's Office.'

Apart from the judiciary, politicians played a part. Under pressure from the Hindu lobbies, and as a counter to the Shah Bano controversy, Rajiv Gandhi favoured the gates to be opened. It marked the beginning of a dramatic series of violent events.

Within the Muslim community, the combination of the Shah Bano case, the subsequent divorce act, and the opening up of the lock at Babri Masjid after almost four decades led to multiple fractures and remarkable changes in public posturing.

Among the conservative and slightly radical sections of the Muslims, the divorce act led to jubilation, as it was considered a significant victory for their religion, faith and beliefs. The lock-related decision on the other hand angered them, as they felt that the government had bent to the Hindus' pressures. It was seen as evidence of the majority road-rolling the minority.

Both the joy and rage helped the extremist Muslims to exercise more power within their community and influence the masses. The sober voices within the community were muted, as they could neither justify the aftermath of the Shah Bano case nor the opening of the masjid lock. As a consequence, over the next few years, the conservatives gained control over their community.

Henceforth, the newly formed Babri Masjid Action Committee (BMAC), which was launched days after the opening of the lock, would sway the public towards strident, even violent, actions.

This was evident on 30 March 1987, when a vast congregation gathered at Delhi's Boat Club and demanded that the Babri Masjid should be wholly handed over to the Muslims. It was a massive show of strength, which rattled the corridors of power. The 15 June 1987 issue of the *India Today* magazine describes the gathering: 'For the first time in the nation's independent history, more than three lakh Muslims from all over the country had lined up on that stretch, shoulder to shoulder, to demand justice and an end to organised discrimination against their community.'

For the right-wing Hindus, the twin events of Shah Bano and lock led to mixed feelings of fury and joy. They were appalled by the Centre's impulse to appease minorities in civil marriage matters. For long, they had wanted uniform laws. The government's imperative to change an apex court order through a new act horrified them.

It was clear that the Rajiv Gandhi regime, like the previous Congress ones, believed in supporting the so-called rights of the minorities, which acted against the grain of a majoritarian rule. In no other nation was the majority treated in such a shabby fashion, felt the saffron band of the Hindus.

Of course, the opening of the lock made the saffron brigade ecstatic, even if the feeling was to stay for a brief while. They now realized that if they took up the cudgels and stuck to their guns, there was enough public support to force the government to rebuild a Ram Mandir in Ayodhya. The lock event was a shot in the arm of the conservative Hindus, who felt encouraged that they could achieve what seemed an impossible task two decades ago.

In April 1987, the Hindus showed their strength and reiterated their demand in Ayodhya. *India Today* reported on 15 June 1987, 'In this dusty town, over one lakh Hindus had gathered to vow to "protect" the birthplace of Rama. They too gave vent to rabble-rousing perorations and took a mass pledge that those present would go forth and liberate the birthplaces of all the Hindu gods.' The RSS affiliates simultaneously insisted on the liberation of Ram Janmabhoomi. This was followed up with a demand at the June 1989 BJP executive committee meeting, which endorsed the decision to build a Ram Temple at the claimed original birthplace site.

Yet again, in 1989, politics determined the course of the Ayodhya dispute. It was an election year. The BJP was on the front foot; the Congress organization was in tatters, especially when V.P. Singh floated his own political party and hurled charges of corruption against Rajiv Gandhi.

In the same year, the VHP announced that it would perform a *shilanayas* (foundation stone ceremony) for a new Ram Temple on 10 November 1989. Donations poured in, not just from India but even from wealthy and middle-class Hindus who were settled in Europe and North America.

'It is during this period that Swami Paramhans stated, "As far as the RJB issue is concerned, the only dispute among Hindu organizations is over who should build the temple. It is the VHP that has done all the work and sacrificed a lot. It collected more than 18 crore rupees (180 million) and must pay interest on many funds."'[24]

The Income Tax Department felt that the figure was perhaps higher and, more importantly, the VHP needed to pay tax on it. It questioned whether VHP, whose primary objective was to build a temple, was a charitable organization. Such investigations only made the Parishad more popular, as some sections of the Hindus felt that it was deliberately targeted.

Soon after, the VHP urged the Hindus across the country and those who lived abroad to donate bricks for the shilanayas. Soil from the holy land of Ayodhya was dispatched to key locations to be mixed along with the local clay in the respective brick kilns. All of these 'sacred bricks', or *shilas*, had to have 'Sri Ram' inscribed on them in Hindi.

Based on media reports, 200,000–300,000 villages and 50–100 million people participated in constructing the holy bricks. Soon, it rained bricks, which were wrapped in saffron cloth, in Ram's land.

With the prospect of electoral defeat looming over the horizon, thanks to the Bofors scam, diplomatic setbacks in the neighbourhood, and general unrest and unease among the voters, the Congress decided to play the soft Hindu card. The aim was to consolidate a few Hindu votes and also dent the rise of the BJP.

The Congress(I) had announced that it would go by the orders of the Lucknow bench of the Allahabad High Court on the matter. On 14 August 1989, the five cases dealing with the Mandir–Masjid legal battle were clubbed together, and the high court gave an interim order to maintain the status quo. It said: 'The parties to suits shall not change the nature of property in question.'

In September 1989, the government allowed the VHP shilanayas on one condition. The participants had to follow the Allahabad High Court order, which stated that the parties (Hindus, Muslims and others) in the Ayodhya dispute would 'not change the nature of the property in question (Babri Masjid) and ensure that the peace and communal harmony are maintained'.[25] The VHP agreed.

The next month, as PM Rajiv Gandhi kicked off the Congress's election campaign, he went off-script during his first public speech. In a bid to please the Hindus, he mentioned the coming of 'Ram Rajya'. For the voters, it seemed like an act of desperation. A party that had invariably played the minority card wished to change track. In his memoirs, *My Years with Rajiv: Triumph and Tragedy*, Wajahat Habibullah[26] writes, 'The Vishwa Hindu Parishad (VHP) began giving calls for the "liberation" of a temple at the "exact spot" where Lord Ram was born, but the issue of Ram Janmabhoomi acquired a life of its own only after the BJP decided to support the demand in its Palampur resolution in June 1989.'

Later in the book the author says, 'Together with the VHP, the BJP had, in a step replete with symbolism, appointed a Dalit … to perform the shilanyas. This was scheduled for 9 November 1989. But before the BJP made its move, a week ahead of the shilanyas, Rajiv Gandhi launched his election campaign for the forthcoming Lok Sabha elections from Ayodhya, promising to usher in Ram Rajya in his next term.'

As the shilanayas neared, thousands of workers, karsevaks, began to arrive in Ayodhya. The centre felt that the estimated crowd could go out of control. It wasn't sure if the VHP would adhere to the pact to maintain peace and harmony. Hence, it asked the shilanayas to be performed not at the exact spot believed to be Lord Ram's birthplace but at an adjacent plot. Again, the VHP agreed.

Once the shilanayas was done, both parties claimed success. The government maintained that it was performed at an adjoining plot and, hence, was not akin to laying of the foundation stone. It was a superficial exercise, which meant nothing. The VHP claimed to have performed its task despite the political opposition.

Rajiv Gandhi lost the 1989 election, and V.P. Singh came to power. However, thanks partly to Shah Bano, the opening of the lock and the shilanayas, the BJP won eighty-five Lok Sabha seats, up from two in the previous elections in 1984. The graph would only go up from here.

V.P. Singh's government was never a stable one. The RSS and the BJP found opportunities to up the ante. They believed that the Ram Janmabhoomi campaign worked, and it was a path not just to build a temple but to attain political success as well. Sometime in early September 1990, Advani spent an evening with Pramod Mahajan, the master political strategist in the party, who was billed as a future Prime Minister before his untimely death in May 2006.

At Mahajan's condolence meeting at the Maharashtra BJP Working Committee in Mumbai in 2006, Advani revealed the significance of his discussion with the former, which led to the organization of a new massive rath yatra from Somnath Temple in Gujarat to Ayodhya in Uttar Pradesh. The initial plan was Gandhian in nature.

'My idea was that of a *padyatra* (a journey on foot) between Somnath and Ayodhya, but it was Mahajan who told me that it would take a lot of time and suggested that we use a vehicle for the yatra,' said Advani. He added, 'He (Mahajan) was head and shoulders above the rest in terms of political IQ and imbibed rare qualities in politics.'[27]

Mahajan knew that for Advani's journey to be compelling, it had to pass through at least half-a-dozen states, which was impossible since his senior wished to reach Ayodhya by 30 October 1990. The date was necessary; the VHP planned to start the construction of the temple on that day. Hence, the schedule was crucial.

The two discussed how the idea could become feasible and practical. They talked about using a jeep. And then Mahajan came up with the idea of a minibus disguised as a chariot. The chariot, as we know, wasn't a new concept. It had been successfully tried and tested before.

Somnath was a carefully thought-out place to start a politico-religious journey. Centuries ago, the Muslim invaders and rulers repeatedly destroyed the temple there, and it was rebuilt due to the initiatives of Sardar Vallabhbhai Patel in 1950.

According to the BJP website, 'It was at Somnath that the assault on Hindu temples and shrines … by Islamic invaders began.' Its re-construction marked the 'first chapter in a journey to preserve the old symbols of unity, communal amity, and cultural oneness. The (Advani) yatra was scheduled to conclude at Ayodhya because the liberation of Ram Janam Bhoomi would be second'.[28]

In the 2006 condolence meeting for Mahajan, Advani also revealed that it was his departed colleague's idea to include the states in the North-east, which had historical links with freedom fighter Subhash Chandra Bose and spiritual leader Swami Vivekananda, both of whom are considered as nationalist icons by the BJP and RSS.

Within five weeks, the Advani chariot crisscrossed 10,000 km through nine states across the country. V.P. Singh tried to nip it in the political bud; most of the state governments took a back seat. However, in Bihar, Chief Minister Lalu Prasad Yadav seized the bull by the horns, stopped the chariot and arrested Advani. But he couldn't put a stop to the political mileage that ensued for the BJP.

The BJP's tally in the Lower House jumped to 120 seats in the 1991 national elections. It was predicted to be higher, but for the sympathy wave the Congress enjoyed in the second phase of the elections after the assassination of the former PM, Rajiv Gandhi, on 21 May 1991.

Obviously, it was once again time for another political voyage to further consolidate Hindu votes. In December 1991, Murli Manohar Joshi, another BJP stalwart, embarked upon the Ekta Yatra (Unity Expedition) to travel from Kanyakumari, India's southern-most tip, to Srinagar in the far north.

The tour had two chariots, one white for peace and the other saffron for Hindutva, and it reached Delhi safely. On its way through Punjab, the rally was halted due to an attack by Sikh militants. Hence, Joshi, who wanted to hoist the national flag in Srinagar at the culmination of the journey, flew down to the city to do so.

The events of 1992 are so dramatic and divisive that they deserve a chapter of their own. They are fleshed out at the end of this book. Here, it is enough to note that they ended with the demolition of the Babri Masjid. It was razed to the ground after 464 years. The Hindus considered it as the end of an era and the beginning of a new one in which a Hindu temple would be built in Ayodhya.

Although one does not analyse the demolition in this manner, it was a win-win situation for the right-wing Hindus. There are two possibilities of how it happened. The first is that it was due to mob frenzy, and the situation just got out of control. The politicians, civil servants, police and security forces, both at the Centre and in the state, only contributed to the chaos and confusion.

The second is that it was possibly a plot hatched by the Hindutva forces. This has been explained well by Dibyesh Anand in his essay, 'Appropriating Ayodhya on Valor Day': 'In interviews with Hindutva activists, I found that this reaction was repeatedly described as a "volcanic eruption," echoing a rhetorical phrase commonly used in Hindutva literature. This is, of course, in denial of the well-documented fact that the movement was elaborately organized through the active collaboration of the various sanghs or Hindutva organizations including the VHP, BJP, and Bajrang Dal. The emphasis is put instead on a universal calling to a pan-Indian body of Hindus from different regions, castes, and social groups who spontaneously came to offer their service for the Ram Janmbhumi [sic] as kar sevaks, often euphemistically translated as "volunteers."'

Dibyesh Anand further quotes a few leaders to show how they had resorted to the blame-shifting pattern: 'A senior BJP leader, Kewalram Ratanmal Malkani, alleged that the actual vandalism was committed by intelligence operatives backed by the Congress government (Malkani 2002, 164–167).' He then writes that the RSS leader Rajendra Singh believed 'that circumstances suddenly demolished the structure (Singh 1993, 72)'. Singh averred further that the violence was a blameless product of the Hindu awakening and had an ideal outcome—the obliteration of the mosque: 'Although unexpected and never planned by the organisers of *kar seva*, nevertheless it resulted in the removal of the disputed structure—that blot of foreign slavery on that holy spot" (Hartung, Hawkes, and Bhattacharjee 2003, 13)'.[29]

In fact, in 2020, the CBI Court, which took up the criminal cases against high-profile politician-ministers and leaders, concluded that there was no conspiracy, and it was not pre-planned. All the accused were found 'not guilty'.

Considering the overall scheme of things, and particularly the why of it—why was the mosque demolished—it does not matter whether it was pre-designed or happened on the spur of the moment. The fact remains that minus the mosque, the political and legal odds shifted towards the Hindu conservatives and temple construction.

Without the Babri Masjid in place, it became more difficult for the Centre and Uttar Pradesh's political set-ups to deny the Hindu right to build a temple. If there was only empty land, the Hindus, who thought of the spot as their God's birthplace, had the right because their claims went back much farther in time—more than 2,000 years compared to less than 500 in the case of the Muslims.

Significantly, it became more comfortable for the judiciary to think along the same lines. As long as the masjid stood, no judge would order its demolition and construction of a new place of worship. Of course, the judge could, and many did, order the removal of illegal holy places, but they were not replaced by another structure. Instead, they were used to build infrastructure.

As it happened, the final Supreme Court verdict on Ram Janmabhoomi rested on the premise that the Hindus had an older and more continuous claim to their beliefs and faith compared to the Muslims. If the mosque had stood intact, such a legal decision would not be implementable, as it implied a demolition and reconstruction. Minus the mosque, these legal arguments seemed logical and rational.

However, in December 1992, there were other legal issues to worry about—the criminalization of the act. The Centre pinned the guilt on the state; the President dissolved the BJP-ruled Uttar Pradesh Assembly, which the BJP accepted as a badge of honour. The Centre acquired the 70 acres of land in the disputed area, which included the 2.77 acres within which the mosque and Hindu structures existed.

Most of the affected parties contested the takeover of the property, including the adjoining land. It was left to the Supreme Court to decide this matter, along with another question that was referred to it by the President. On the latter, the court was unequivocal. It simply refused to comment on or answer whether a temple existed at the exact spot where the mosque had earlier stood.

On the legality of the acquisition of the property, the court upheld the right of the government to be the receiver of the 70 acres and assume the responsibilities for its administration. Remember, the government had done the same with the specific mosque property after the December 1949 events, when Lord Ram Lalla was placed inside it.

However, there was a vast difference and, in retrospect, a subtle and dangerous twist. At the same time while it upheld the government's decision, the apex court negated and dismissed a crucial corollary which would have ended the dispute, once and for all.

In its acquisition order, the government stated that the pending cases related to the title and ownership of the main disputed area, that is 2.77 acre and not 70 acres, were unconstitutional and invalid and, hence, completely irrelevant. This implied that no one could ever claim to be the original possessor of the contested land.

In the *Dr M. Ismail Farooqi* case (1994), the apex court struck down this clause, Section 4(3), of the Acquisition Act. It revived and reopened the various title suits filed over the decades by the Hindus and Muslims that claimed ownership over the Babri Masjid–Ram Janmahoomi property. The court specified that these cases related to the 2.77 acres included the mosque and specific Hindu structures, but not the more expansive adjoining areas that incorporate structures like the 'alleged graveyards' of the Muslims.[30]

Hence, it was established that once the relevant court(s) gave its verdict(s), the government, which was the 'statutory receiver' as per its act, would hand over the disputed 2.77 acres to whichever party, or parties, finally won the title suit. The judiciary, and not the legislative, would decide the property's fate.

Despite the government's acquisition, the focus shifted to the courts once again. In theory, the future of the dispute was taken out of the political realm and the ball was back in the legal arena. In practice, it implied that a combination of politics and law would be crucial to decide what structure would be built over the property.

Logically, if a pro-temple government assumed power, and the judiciary too was similarly inclined, the temple would become a reality. If the opposite were true, the land would be equally divided among the Hindus and Muslims. A third option was for a secular structure, which imbibed the cultural, not the religious, aspects.

The court's decision rejuvenated the Hindus' desire to push for a temple. The BJP rode this wave of expectations, which translated into larger electoral victories. When Atal Bihari Vajpayee became the PM for the third time in quick succession in the late 1990s and seemed confident of ruling for a full five-year term in 1999, hopes soared.

However, Vajpayee wanted to be seen as a secular nationalist and not a right-wing one. The court decisions were kept in abeyance for various legal reasons. 'In 2010, the Allahabad HC ruled in favour of a three-way division of the disputed area with a 2:1 majority. The land was to be divided between the Sunni Waqf Board, the Nirmohi Akhara and Ram Lalla petitioners.'[31]

Immediately, the Hindus hailed it as a huge victory, which would pave the way for the construction of the Ram Temple. This was due to two reasons. The first was that they got a significant portion of the property and, hence, enough area to build a grander structure.

The second was that the ownership of the area directly beneath the razed mosque's central dome, where the idol of Lord Ram Lalla was placed in December 1949, would rest with the two Hindu parties. Hence, when the temple was built, the deity could be placed at an exact spot believed to be the sacred birthplace of Lord Ram.

'A Bench of Justices Aftab Alam and R.M. Lodha, admitting a batch of appeals from both Hindu and Muslim organisations, stayed the September 30, 2010, judgment of the Lucknow Bench of the High Court and directed the parties to maintain the status quo at the site in May 2011. Justice Lodha told the counsel, that "The High Court's judgment is something strange."' He further questioned: "How can a decree for partition be passed when none of the parties had prayed for it? It's strange. Such kind of decrees cannot be allowed to be in operation." His logic was that it would definitely create "a difficult situation". He also stated that "the High Court verdict has created a litany of litigation".[32]

What he implied was that the Hindu and Muslim petitioners claimed to be the sole owner of the disputed area. They wanted the courts to adjudicate who was the rightful one. None of them urged for the property to be divided in any proportion between them.

It was like a dispute over a house between two claimants who each said they possessed the right ownership papers. Instead of establishing which set of documents was genuine and thus revealed the real owner, the court partitioned the house into portions and handed it over to both parties.

After staying the judgment of the Allahabad High Court on the Babri Masjid–Ram Janmabhoomi case, the 2011 Supreme Court stay order made it clear that any court will have to hand over the land to one party. The disputed property would either go to the

Hindus or Muslims. This became evident as the two communities, after being urged to do so, failed to reach an out-of-court settlement or consensus. After a series of legal tangles, a larger bench of the Supreme Court would need to give the final verdict.

The final verdict was pronounced by the apex court on 9 November 2019. After considering all the evidence presented, the Supreme Court determined that the disputed land should be given entirely to the Hindus for a temple dedicated to Lord Ram. It decided to give land to the Muslims elsewhere to construct a mosque.

7

Machine on a Mission

> 'Hypocrisy and distortion are passing currently under the name of religion.'
>
> —MAHATMA GANDHI[1]

The road leading to Karsevakpuram in Ayodhya is possibly the most well maintained in the town. It is 6.30 on a winter evening in November 2019. The township, spread over five acres, is brightly lit with sodium lamps. The well-maintained brick gate is tall with an arched top. On top of the arch are three saffron flags while right under the arch, in the centre, is an image of Lord Ganesh, a Hindu god who is worshipped at the beginning of all auspicious ceremonies. On both pillars that hold the arch, the name of the gateway—Ashok Singhal Dwar—is embossed very prominently in Devanagari script. There are two red-coloured gates on either side for pedestrians to walk through. On two pillars inside the main gate are two larger-than-life pictures of the VHP stalwart of the

Ram Janmabhoomi movement, Ashok Singhal, standing with his hands folded. Right under his feet is inscribed, '*Shradheye Ashok Singhal*', meaning respected Ashok Singhal. A little ahead is a tiny house which exhibits the Ram Janmabhoomi temple structure. A kilometre inside the gate, and one cannot miss the 'holy' dwelling of the cows—Shri Ram Gaushala Samiti. It is a long shed large enough to house sixty animals, but sadly the barn looks bare. I learn that several cows were sold a few years back to get extra funds to maintain a few buildings owned by the VHP. The holy bovines too chip in when the organization faces a financial crisis!

I walk into the shed. A worker explains his special status. 'Do you know that Lord Krishna was a keeper of cows? In fact, he was their friend. It makes me happy to work for *gaumata*s.' He pats a cow to prove his love for them. The cows look cosy in their newly bought warm jute coats. The calves too have been covered with a similar wrap but theirs have a soft flannel lining under the rough fibre topping.

Small sections are cordoned off with iron railings and are meant for bonfires to keep the bovines warm. Large stone bowls filled with water and trenches with hay are visible. There are ten-odd men to take care of the Shri Ram Gaushala.

A little ahead, near the main building of Karsevakpuram, I see a few students sauntering about in the field. They belong to the Sanskrit Vidyapeeth, an educational institute located within the premises and established in 1985. The students are well versed in the Vedas. Their holy threads—signs of being Brahmins—pop out, maybe deliberately. 'Hindutva has to be saved by hook or crook,' asserts a student, Ravi Jha, who belongs to Madhubani, a small town in the state of Jharkhand. He announces that his schoolmates, about fifty of them, share the same opinion.

His friend chips in, 'Hopefully, we too shall play a vital role in getting rid of those people who have no respect for our religion. We hope to become priests, either in India or abroad.'

Among the four Vedas, which are a part of the curriculum here, special attention is given to the Sam Veda, consisting of Brahmanical chants, and the Yajur Veda, which contains prose and mantras used for Hindu rituals. The school is affiliated with the ancient Ujjaini Vidyalaya, a renowned institute in Madhya Pradesh.

Far away, I spot an elderly man treading languidly, leaning on his walking stick. He takes each step cautiously. Dressed in a white kurta-pyjama, a sweater loosely hangs over his upper body. He greets me with the salutation that is used by all here, 'Jai Shri Ram! All okay with you?' I return his greeting and check on his well-being. 'Yes, just that I am a little cautious about my health. I have to take care as I want to live to see the magnificent Ram Temple,' replies Purushottam Narayan Singh, who at one time was the central secretary of the VHP in Ayodhya.

We amble towards his room, which is at one end of a long corridor. Despite the physical slowness, he talks with energy about the struggle to construct a 'magnificent Ram Temple'. He does not attempt to hide his hatred and anger for Muslim rulers like Babur, Aurangzeb, Muhammad Ghori and Mahmud of Ghazni.

For Purushottam, they were invaders who ravaged Hindu temples and possessions. His words reflect those of Madhav Sadhashiv Golwalkar, the man who conceived and created the VHP and nurtured the supreme aspiration to create a Hindu Rashtra.

Guruji, as Golwalkar is referred to, despised the space that Muslims had created for themselves though he had no severe animosity for them. In his book *Bunch of Thoughts*, he states, 'In fact, all over the country wherever there is a masjid or a Muslim mohalla, the Muslims feel that it is their own independent territory.' He adds, 'Such "pockets" have verily become centres of a widespread network of pro-Pakistani elements in this land.'[2]

As we sit in Purushottam's room, a student walks in with tea and biscuits. He hands over a glass of water to the senior VHP leader, who pops in a few medicines. Once again, he expresses happiness over the Supreme Court's decision and hails the ruling party. 'Had it been some other political party or Prime Minister, the Ram Janmabhoomi issue would still have remained in the cold storage. We are blessed to have Modi-ji. All is Ram's will.'

His views remind me of what Mahant Kamal Nayan Das Shastri, secretary to Nritya Gopal Das, chief of the Ram Janmabhoomi Nyas, told me earlier in the day, 'Modi-ji is no different from sadhus. He has regard for our wishes, and he fulfilled them. No one else could have done this, save a true Rambhakt.'

On the wall in Purushottam's room is a huge portrait of Ashok Singhal, the heart, soul and brain of the VHP in modern India. 'He had extreme faith in Modi-ji,' confirms Purushottam. 'I met Ashok-ji in 1988 at a VHP conference in Kanpur, and we travelled to Jhansi. Since then, he was my mentor. We worked in solidarity for twelve years. He is no less than a God to us. A fearless man, he knew how to take a stand and stick to it. He motivated Hindus across the world to demand a Ram Temple, besides educating them on other religious and cultural issues.'

According to Purushottam, as the joint general secretary of the Parishad, Singhal took on the onus of the Ram Temple in 1984, a few years after the controversial conversion of Dalits in Meenakshipuram. He got to the bottom of issues and left no stone unturned. After speaking to the VHP leaders who met the Dalits in the village, Singhal took all possible decisions to save Hinduism. 'He discovered that the main angst was that the lower castes were not allowed inside the Hindu temples. Ashok-ji wasted no time and ensured that 200 temples were constructed for the Scheduled Castes in Meenakshipuram, besides others in different states. Conversions stopped. He was indeed a far-sighted leader,' fawns Purushottam.

From my early years in journalism, I remember how Singhal's visit to Ayodhya was always big news. He was regularly seen with

Ram Chandra Paramhans, the mahant of Digambar Akhara. The last time I met Singhal was in 2003. In those years he had a withered face with deep furrows between his brows. His more-salt-less-pepper hair went well with his persona. A *rudraksha* mala (prayer-bead necklace) hung around his neck, and a saffron stole with Ram printed all over was draped around his shoulders.

Singhal and Paramhans were the firebrand leaders of the Ram Mandir movement. The former was known for his socio-political stunts and verbal bytes that would invariably make media headlines and spice up journalists' articles. I remember one of such acts in 2003.

'By high noon on 17 October, the VHP had lived up to its promise that "no power on earth" would stop it from reaching Ayodhya. Despite security personnel outnumbering karsevaks (ten to one) highly motivated VHP cadres managed to slip into the temple town through the Faizabad–Ayodhya railway track. VHP president Ashok Singhal, who had "gone underground" for the past three days, also lived up to the belief of the faithful that *"woh Ayodhya mein prakat honge"* (he will appear in Ayodhya). But as soon as Singhal, all dressed in saffron, made an appearance in Karsevakpuram, he was arrested along with 2,000 VHP-Bajrang Dal members.'[3] That afternoon, perhaps, Singhal relented only to create some ripples.

Paramhans and Singhal would speak in one voice to the media. Most outsiders assumed that they were friends mainly because the VHP always flaunted this bonding. The locals of the temple town disagree. The president of the Vyapar Mandal (Trade Board), Ayodhya, Nand Kumar Gupta, the mahant's neighbour, explains that Paramhans was on good terms with both Hindus and Muslims. 'He was used by Ashok Singhal for political reasons. They could never be friends, as they were wired differently.'

As my mind veers back to Purushottam sitting in front of me, I realize that he is engrossed in a conversation with a teacher about a special assembly to be held the following week to celebrate the

Supreme Court's verdict. The plan is to familiarize students with the two exemplary leaders of VHP—Madhavrao Sadashivrao Golwalkar and Ashok Singhal. Golwalkar was the second sarsanghchalak of the RSS, popularly referred to as Guru-ji.

I picture them side-by-side. They had commonalities. They both shared the vision to create a Hindu Rashtra. Both joined the RSS while studying at BHU. Golwalkar remained an inspiring leader for thirty-three years—until his death on 5 June 1973. Singhal remained in the VHP for almost a similar time, 1981–2011. Guru-ji took the RSS to great institutional strength after Independence, and his ideologies are still etched in the minds of the sanghis. He later played a very important role in the formation of the VHP in 1964. Singhal, on his part, spearheaded the Ram Janmabhoomi movement. Briefly explaining the reason behind the school assembly, Purushottam expounds, 'It is important that the next generation follows the VHP ideologies as assiduously as we do.'

Even Prime Minister Narendra Modi acknowledged Golwalkar's role in his book *Jyotipunj* (Beams of Light). Of the sixteen biographies in it, the chapter on Guru-ji is the longest one and is titled 'Pujniya Shri Guru-ji', meaning 'guru worthy of worship'. Describing Golwalkar, Modi writes, 'His entire life was filled with diversity. Explaining his life is like solving a riddle. When he touched the inner self of an individual, he would feel as if he were a spiritual being. But he was not like other spiritual people the world has seen. He lived among thousands of people and awakened in them social sense and nationalism.'[4]

Singhal had a similar effect on his followers but his way was different. He was an activist, a man of the world, who wanted to construct a temple to put a stamp on the spirituality and religiosity of the Hindus. However, the fact remains that like Golwalkar, he too awakened the hearts and minds of Hindus, albeit in an aggressive manner.

Ironic as it is, I do not spot photographs or cut-outs of Golwalkar in Karsevakpuram. Singhal's portraits are spread across this mini township. Born in Agra, Uttar Pradesh, on 2 October 1926, he belonged to an affluent family. He joined BHU to pursue engineering, met the RSS chief Balasaheb Deoras and joined the RSS in 1942. In seven years, he became a pracharak and, three decades later, in 1980, he was deputed to the VHP. In 1984, he became the VHP's general secretary.

Hindus have always been disjointed and different from each other. They have been divided by territory, rituals, culture and language. In the decades after Independence, one of the main challenges, the RSS felt, was to overcome this divisiveness and bring some unity of thought among them. In 1964, Golwalkar invited religious leaders to Bombay to discuss how the Hindus could work with each other. At the meeting, the delegates established the VHP and Shivram Shankar Apte, an RSS pracharak, was elected general secretary.

'During the early seventies, the organization started investing in several social welfare projects like schools, orphanages, clinics, temples, etc. This development sanctioned by the RSS leadership may have been intended to make the ecclesiastical establishment more sensitive to the social needs of many Indians and to involve itself more closely with social welfare work. At the same time, this step gave the RSS *pracharaks* working in the VHP an enhanced moral standing as they dealt with the religious leadership,'[5] opine authors Walter K. Andersen and Shridhar D. Damle.

However, the politics played out differently. Just a year before the Meenakshipuram conversions, the Jana Sangh became the BJP. At that time, it needed political allies urgently. The BJP's first president, Atal Bihari Vajpayee, decided to take a moderate approach.

Some experts contend that this was due to a backlash; others say that this was a deliberate strategy to present two different faces. In his essay 'Invention of an Ethnic Nationalism', Christophe Jaffrelot accepts the former version: 'The BJP which had Atal Behari [sic] Vajpayee as its first president, diluted the original ideology of the Jan Sangh in order to become more acceptable in the Indian party system and to find allies in this arena. The more moderate approach to politics was very much resented by the rest of the Sangh Parivar. The RSS, in irritation, adopted some distance and made greater use of the VHP to rekindle its military strategy. This strategy found its main expression in the launching of the Ayodhya movement in the mid-1980s.'[6]

The Meenakshipuram episode prompted the VHP to come to the foreground and take charge of the situation. To comprehend and iron out this much unexpected event at the ground level, senior VHP leaders reached Meenakshipuram to conduct informal investigations and interviews. After deliberations, a little more than a year later, the influential heads met in June 1982 in Delhi. The VHP created its final organizational structure. It decided to work at two levels—Dharam Sansad (an assembly of religious heads) as a central authority and Margdarshak Mandals (Advisory Committees) with representatives from different sects and communities.

In April 1984, the VHP called for a Religious Parliament at New Delhi's Vigyan Bhavan. Leaders from different religions under the broad banner of Hinduism, such as Jains, Buddhists and Sikhs, apart from the Hindus, attended it. Singhal became the commander of a vast *bhagwa* (saffron) army. The VHP henceforth resorted to mass contact using the rath as a messaging metaphor.

In October 2020, I spoke to Alok Kumar, international working president of the organization. He specified, 'It was decided both by the RSS leaders and VHP that decisions regarding the Ram Mandir will be taken mainly by the sants, or the Kendriya Margdarshak Mandal (Central Advisory Committee).'

While the Dharam Sansad met twice a year, the sages met at the annual Kumbh Melas held annually at four locations—Haridwar (on the banks of the Ganga), Ujjain (banks of the Shipra), Nasik (banks of the Godavari) and Prayag (at the Sangam, or confluence of Ganga, Yamuna and the mythical River Saraswati). He adds, 'In 1984, we decided to concentrate on the Ram Janmabhoomi movement and to facilitate it with a committee, Ram Janmabhoomi Mukti Yagya Samiti.'

One of the first experiments was conducted in 1983, even before the decision, through the Ekatmata Yatra. There were three main yatras taken out from and wheeled up to renowned places of Hindu pilgrimages—Pashupati Rath from Kathmandu to Rameswaram; Mahadeo Rath from Haridwar to Kanyakumari; and Kapil Rath from Gangasagar in the east to Somnath in the west.

According to the VHP website, there were 312 *upa-rath*s (smaller processions). The trucks-turned-raths carried huge urns filled with 'holy water' from the Ganga and Bharat Mata's idols. The number of programmes held during the yatras was 4,323, while the number of kalashes brought for *pujan* (prayers) was 77,440. The chariots moved for over 1,000 days across different states.

The Ekatmata Yatra reproduced the modus operandi of a pilgrimage. For instance, its main halts were sacred spaces of the country. As the political scientist Christophe Jaffrelot comments, recalling our definition of myth as ideology in narrative form, the 'religious geography of the Indian space was … harnessed for the ends of an ideological mobilisation'.[7]

It was a shot in the arm for the VHP, as its website too admits, 'The success in achieving its aims and objects were beyond its normal expectations.'

Another Dharma Yatra, handled mainly by dharmacharyas, traversed fourteen districts in twenty-five days. The uniqueness of this yatra was that the stopovers and destinations focussed on south India. Was this because the VHP felt that Lord Ram was more of a north Indian deity and they needed to make in-roads in south India?

No, says Alok Kumar. 'These are misnomers. People in south India hold Lord Ram in high esteem. The Shiva temple at the Rameswaram complex proves it. Lord Ram said that those who worship Shiva are automatically my followers. Hindus across India and those settled abroad gave their support to the Ram Janmabhoomi movement.'

Two years after the Ram Janki Rath Yatra was flagged off, a new chapter opened in the Ram Janmabhoomi saga, which propelled the saffron brigade to go on an overdrive with their agendas, both political and religious. It is still believed by many that in 1986, Ayodhya's disputed property was unlocked by the Rajiv Gandhi government. VHP President Alok Kumar clarifies, 'It is incorrect to state that Rajiv Gandhi opened the locks as the initiative was taken by a local Faizabad advocate. The Faizabad District Court Magistrate decided to open the premises after thirty-six years.'

In a piece in *The Hindu* (6 August 2020), Mani Shankar Aiyar wrote, 'We now (after the 2019 Supreme Court order) have Congress leaders boasting that Rajiv Gandhi opened the locks of the Masjid at Ayodhya. He did not. This was done by sleight of hand without his knowledge by leaning on the local judiciary to pass an order that was implemented with undue haste within half-an-hour of the order being passed. The Prime Minister was informed only when it was already a judicially ordained fait accompli. His main concern was to put a status quo in place and ensure that the monument was protected from vandalism.'[8]

In his book, *My Years with Rajiv: Triumph and Tragedy*, Wajahat Habibullah gives us a direct answer from Rajiv Gandhi himself. The author writes, 'So my question to Rajiv was, "Since the removal of the locks was not going to change the status quo in any way, but would earn the support of sections of the Hindu community for your party, was it not realised that such a benefit could only be limited? Afterall, with the core of the Congress remaining secular, the development could not be exploited to its maximum, and the right wing would hijack the outcome, which it could trumpet as its triumph." That is what had happened.

'Rajiv's answer was direct and instant: "No government has any business to meddle in matters like determination of the functioning of places of worship. I knew nothing of this development until I was told of it after the orders had been passed and executed."'[9]

Soon after the lock was opened, not wasting any time, the Sompuras came up with the design and plan for the new Ram Mandir. The VHP published coupons, which were sent to more than 2,00,000 villages. People could buy these coupons for a minimum sum of Rs 1.25 to donate to the temple's construction. The Ram Sheelan Pujan (worship of consecrated construction bricks) went on full throttle from September 1989.

By then, the VHP had received Rs 18 crore as donations. In August 2020, when I spoke to Sharad Sharma, an active VHP member and ex-spokesperson, he gave more details, 'Truckloads of bricks reached Ayodhya from the VHP district headquarters. The VHP sent the casts for the bricks to those brick kilns which were given certain specifications and assigned with the task across the country. The bricks were then moulded with the right inscriptions. Each truck would carry around 10,000 bricks with "Ram" inscribed on them in mainly three different ways—Jai Sri Ram, Sri Ram and Sita Ram.'

Alok Kumar described the scene, 'Each village would pile up bricks in palanquins, apply vermillion on them, decorate the sanctified bricks with flowers and sing songs hailing Ram and Sita before the shilas (bricks) were transported to Ayodhya. The VHP was surprised at the religious frenzy demonstrated by people of all rungs.'

I ask if the people were influenced. 'No doubt the leaders made efforts to inform the people, but it is incorrect to say that they manipulated or managed people's religious sentiments,' states Alok rather firmly.

From then on, plans moved faster. Hindus were under the religious spell that was continuously cast by the self-proclaimed custodians of the new Ram cult. It was then the turn of L.K. Advani's Rath Yatra, which started from Somnath in Gujarat on 25 September 1990. It was a rousing success.

'Women brought coconut, incense sticks and sandalwood paste and worshipped the motorised rath in traditional ways. Youngsters met the Rath Yatra armed with bows and arrows, swords and *trishuls* (tridents). Sadhus applied tilaks of blood on Advani and other "holy warriors" ... A torch lit in Ayodhya was multiplied and carried to remote villages, where local people were encouraged to light their Diwali lamps with this "consecrated fire" emanating from Ayodhya. On the whole the Rath Yatra was designed, however, primarily, as a drama which, through careful facilitation of extensive media coverage, was staged on the national arena,' describes Thomas Blom Hansen in the book *The Saffron Wave: Democracy and Hindu Nationalism in Modern India*.[10]

On 14 August 1990, *The Indian Express* reported Advani as saying: 'If Hindu sentiment is not going to be respected in India where else in the world can it command respect?'[11] On 12 September 1990, Advani told *The Hindu* newspaper that the temple belonged to the Hindus. The campaign would 'affect the basis of nationalism in India'. He felt that the mantle of reviving the culture and tradition of Hinduism, which was suppressed by centuries of exploitation by foreign forces and ruling parties after Independence, had fallen on the BJP. 'By undertaking this yatra, I am only reviving the spirit of nationalism that had lain dormant all these years.'[12]

Ayodhya has changed over the three decades since the Religious Parliament in 1984. In my recent trips after the 2019 Supreme Court judgment, I notice anger towards the VHP among the locals, sadhus and in akharas. The only akhara that appears hand-in-glove with the VHP is Chhoti Chhavni Akhara, headed by Mahant Nritya Gopal Das. On their part, most of the VHP leaders in Ayodhya brazenly do not take the opinions of the other akharas into any consideration. In November 2019 when I met Triloki Nath Pandey, who represented Lord Ram as his closest aide in the legal cases, he stated, 'Nirmohi Akhara behaved strangely. It supported us till the high court verdict but washed its hands off when the case went to the Supreme Court. Perhaps because the mahant of Nirmohi Akhara thought he was the only one who had the rights to singularly claim the Ram Janmabhoomi Mandir's ownership. He never wanted to join us.'

During the same trip, I tell Nirmohi Akhara's Mahant Dinendra Nath about this. He counters, 'Let them say what they want to, I really do not want to comment on this.' Durgesh Shukla who is very close to the mahant, while on his own, says, 'The VHP should give a new name to the Ram Mandir. They should call it Lakshmi (Goddess of Wealth) Mandir. It intends to loot the devotees and the public. For the common people it may appear like the Ram Janmabhoomi temple but politically it is becoming another RSS head office.' He asserts, 'The sadhus here have no greed like the VHP or RSS.' The akhara apparently sold huge acres of land to pay for the various cases over the past sixty-nine years. Lately, though, the mahant's approach has taken a different turn. In August 2020, when the mahant participated in the Bhoomi Puja ceremony, I asked one of his close supporters about this change of heart. Taking assurance that I would not disclose his name, he said, 'That's because some of mahant-ji's family members nurture political ambitions.'

Mahant Dharam Das of Nirvani Akhara, too, takes on VHP, 'The VHP has nothing to do with religion. They misuse religion.' Talking about the vice president of VHP, Champat Rai, '*Yeh dharam virodhi hain aur Vishwa Hindu Parishad jaise lootere company ke chairman hai* (He is against religion and is the chairman of an exploitative company called Vishwa Hindu Parishad).'

Suddenly, his decibel levels go up, '*Yeh toh Ayodhya ko jakar liye hain aur ab iss shahar ko ek baniye ka dukan ki tarah bana liye hain* (They have taken hold over Ayodhya and converted it into a merchant's trading centre).' When asked what he means, Dharam Das says, '*Yeh sab dakait hain, angrezon ke chamche hain* (They are all dacoits, they have taken a leaf out of British colonizing tactics).' During the first lockdown due to the Covid-19 pandemic, in one of our many telephone conversations, he analysed, 'We are all in trouble because of the sins committed by these people.' The mahant gave a chronological proof, '*Yeh log swayam Corona hai, jab se yeh log Trust banaye (2019), turant 2020 se lockdown ho gaya* (These people are themselves Corona; lockdown was declared in 2020 soon after the formation of the Trust).'

Nand Kumar Gupta, a local merchant from Shringar Market and president of Ayodhya Udyog Vyapar Mandal Trust (Industry Trade Board Trust), Ayodhya, says, 'The town may (now) progress, as it will become a pilgrim and tourist destination, but we will lose our identities. The VHP has sidelined people like us and many sadhus who have lived here for generations. In the name of Ram, the organization asks for donations, shows concern for our town, but it has huge vested interests, and we are fully aware of it.'

According to Gupta, the VHP has not only alienated the Muslims of Ayodhya, but also the Hindus. In fact, the locals think that the demolition of the mosque intensified the fissures.

On their part, the leaders have no regrets. Dr Surendra Jain, joint general secretary of the VHP, is clear that there is no need to apologize to Muslims or have regrets for the demolition. His logic, '*Woh dhancha toh hamari gulami ka pratik tha. Hindustan ke Musalmano ko khush hona chahiye ki hum ne usko tod diya* (The structure symbolized our slavery; the Muslims should be happy that we destroyed it).' He adds that those who criticize the efforts of the karsevaks in the demolition should ask for forgiveness.

In the past, Singhal had tried to unite the akharas. Alok Kumar explains, 'One of the main reasons for creating the Ram Janmabhoomi Nyas was to bring the various sects of Ramanandi sadhus under one umbrella.' However, the fact remains that when Paramhans became its head, it was not taken well by the other sects as the he was perceived to be close to the VHP and Singhal.

Early in 2001, I met Mahant Baba Biram Das, the chief of All-India Akhara Parishad, a conglomeration of the aggressive and independent Naga sadhus and ashrams across India. He was critical of, and angry with, the VHP. He disliked the fact that the VHP spoke about Ram Mandir at the sacred Kumbh Melas. 'It is yet another political stunt of the VHP. It is sad that these people try to gain mileage out of the religious sentiments of the masses. All this noise is aimed at expanding and consolidating the vote bank.'[13]

It is January 2020. I am back at my favourite tea shop in Ayodhya's Shringar Bazaar. Here, one can here enjoy French fries and noodles along with chai. I tell the owner of the neighbouring restaurant, Marwari Bhojanalay, about the strange combinations that these eateries offer; momos and laddus share plate space, just as poories and a heap of noodles! He fails to understand the humour.

'You joke about these dishes but wait till the three- and five-star hotels crop up shortly. They will have more variety of dishes to cater to the visitors' tastes. Be rest assured the changes will happen as there will be thousands of foreign tourists for sure. No one laughs at these big hotels when they come up with "fusion food" concepts!'

Most local businessmen are agitated with the idea that their town will become such a mega pilgrim city, that the old residents will eventually lose their present importance and identity.

Ramsevak, who owns a utensil shop in the vicinity, says, 'There will be a time when we will feel like strangers in our hometown. As it is, the VHP has begun to wield its power. You see its members in huge groups everywhere in our town. They own large tracts of land and seem to be planning all the time, but they never involve us in their discussions.'

The next morning, I visit the Karyashala (workshop), which has almost half of the temple beautifully carved out and ready to be assembled at the site. One hundred and twelve pillars were completed before the Supreme Court's order. They are stacked on top of each other; the taller ones are made to stand in a straight row. They are systemically numbered and can be easily assembled when construction begins. Between 1990 and late 2018, work went on non-stop, except for five years between 2006 and 2011. However, soon after the Allahabad High Court verdict in 2010, work resumed.

There is no work on Sundays and Amavasya (new moon) days, as the latter is not considered auspicious. When work is in full swing, 200 men are carving and chiselling eight hours a day. Anu Bhai Sompura, who hails from Gujarat and oversees the artistry, is a severe taskmaster and is extremely meticulous. 'Thankfully, most are skilled artists from Gujarat and Rajasthan, and they cannot afford to make mistakes while chiselling. It will lead to a crack or hole and make the slab redundant,' he says.

Most pillars have intricate lace edges with traditional Hindu motifs carved within. Earlier, the white marble beams were cut at Makrana in Rajasthan. But a cutting machine was installed here five years ago to expedite work. The red sandstone columns are made at Pindwara in the Sirohi district of Rajasthan. A few weeks after the Supreme Court's judgment, experts from Varanasi were hired to clean the grime, which had settled over the last decades, with a particular chemical that would not affect the original colour or texture of the stone.

The carving is all set to begin at full throttle after the new Trust—Shri Ram Janam Bhoomi Teerth Kshetra—gives the green signal and decides on the construction date. The Karyashala, spread across 10 acres, is advertised as a must-see place for pilgrims.

As I walk through the gate, I spot Sharad Sharma, a VHP member, who was earlier the undisputed hero of the prefabricated temple. '*Musalmano ne sadiyon tak Ram Lalla ka apmaan kiya hai, par ab Bhagwan-ji poore roop se azaad ho gaye hain* (The Muslims insulted Ram Lalla for centuries, but now our God is liberated),' he says. He credits the movement to Singhal and Paramhans. 'Had they not inspired and guided us, we would have never seen these joyful times.'

Sharad's dress code has not changed for years: a kurta–pyjama and khadi jacket. There is his trademark saffron tika on the forehead. A resident of Ayodhya, he is the oldest of the three siblings. He was sixteen when he joined the Bajrang Dal in 1989. Good at studies, the teenager excelled in the training camp and was noticed by senior VHP leaders. Sharad remembers how he became a favourite of Singhal soon after they met in the summer of 1992.

They spoke regularly; Singhal often called him from Delhi or Prayag to inform him about his travel plans to Ayodhya. 'I would eagerly wait to meet him. I wanted to follow in his footsteps. He was our greatest inspiration,' says Sharad with reverence and nostalgia. In 1990, Sharad was given the charge of the Karyashala.

His passion and commitment to the workshop and the VHP is as visible as his vanity. As we are in deep conversation, he moves ahead to meet two visitors. I hear him shout at them. The pilgrims, a husband–wife duo, have arrived from a suburban village near Allahabad, Uttar Pradesh. They hold two bricks each. They are appropriately dressed for their journey—the man is in his mid-forties and wears a beige kurta–pyjama with a saffron shawl, and the woman is in a yellow sari and red cardigan. A travel guide told them to begin the day with a darshan of the Karyashala mainly because they had taken the trouble to carefully carry four bricks from their village to donate them here.

Sharad sternly asks, 'What have you got these bricks for? We prefer bricks or stones of higher quality with "Jai Sri Ram" etched on them. First, learn the rules and then show your faith.' The couple looks ashamed and lost. And as soon as Sharad walks away, the guard of the premises, ironically named Hanuman, takes the offerings from the couple.

The trio walks towards the 'wall of faith' built by the consecrated bricks offered over the years. It stands tall and gigantic, announcing the faith of millions of Hindus, and is a popular selfie spot for most visitors. A pilgrim from Chennai explains in laboured Hindi, '*Yeh hamari mandir ke liye daan ka pratik hai. Isko hamesha saath rakhunga* (This will remind us of the small contribution we made towards Ram's abode; I will always keep this photograph).'

The huge wall, extending in length and breadth, has 150,000 bricks with the Lord's name inscribed on each. Besides devotees from India, these bricks have come from forty-four nations—the US, China, Korea, Germany, Africa, the UK, Japan, Myanmar and Holland, to name a few. The office has a logbook with the names of the devotees.

The announcement for *shiladaan* (brick donation) was made in 1988. Sharad explains that some of these bricks will be used to create a wall at the temple site. It will be a memoir to exhibit the immense devotion of the people for Ram Lalla.

Somewhere in the centre of this wall is a niche where a lamp is lit along with incense sticks. Hanuman, the guard, has been allotted the task of lighting these sticks every morning.

Hanuman's living quarter is frugal—water is stored in three used mineral water bottles; there is a kerosene stove, basic pots and pans, and a steel plate and glass. On the wall above his wooden-plank-turned-bed are three iron hooks that substitute as a wardrobe. There are two canisters, one filled with wheat flour and the other with rice. Some spice packets are stacked neatly in a corner, along with plastic jars containing lentils, salt and sugar. There is a knife with a packet of seasonal vegetables placed close to the stove.

Hanuman's morning rituals begin with an early shower, prayers at the Karyashala temple, where he reads the Hanuman Chalisa (hymns to Hanuman) and lights a lamp. The temple houses idols of Ram, Lakshman, Sita and Hanuman, which were earlier used by Paramhans in his mutt. There is a massive portrait of the sant along with that of Singhal. Once the guard is done with purifying and sanctifying the workshop, he returns to the shack to cook.

'In 1992, I was posted at the Karyashala because the VHP felt I was one of the best security guards. I was at the disputed site before the demolition,' he states proudly. And then folding his hands and looking towards the Janmabhoomi, he dramatically adds, 'It is only Lord Ram who gave the strength to the karsevaks (to bring down the mosque).'

When his morning chores are done, guard Hanuman walks to his favourite faded red plastic chair near a wooden plank in front of the gate. The plank is covered with an old bedsheet, under which are fifty-odd books on Lord Ram and Ayodhya for sale. He takes out a feather duster to remove the stone dust that has collected over the evening and night.

Apart from these stops, there is another hyped site for the visitors in the Karyashala premise. It is a tube-well named after the two Kothari brothers, Ram and Sharad, from Burrabazar, Kolkata. This locality in north-central Kolkata is India's largest wholesale market. It is crowded, and shops and residences are almost stuck to each other. The locality is dominated by the Baniya/Marwari community, who are mostly pro-BJP. The two boys were trained for almost two years at the local RSS shakha in their vicinity.

Like lakhs of others, the Kothari brothers heard about Advani's rath yatra from Somnath to Ayodhya in 1990 by word of mouth. The rath was to reach Ayodhya on 30 October. The VHP had earmarked the date for karseva at the disputed site. Mulayam Singh Yadav, the former head of Samajwadi Party, was the state's chief minister. 'Let them try and enter Ayodhya. We will teach them the meaning of law. No masjid will be broken.' Yadav, in an attempt to please the Muslim vote bank, had declared in October 1990, opposing the rath yatra of L.K. Advani.

Though Advani was arrested in Bihar by the Lalu Prasad government, the karsevaks braved it to Ayodhya. So did the Kothari brothers—they left Howrah for their destination via Varanasi. From there, they hired a cab for part of the way and then had to walk the last 200 km. They finally reached Ayodhya in the wee hours of 30 October.

Mulayam Singh Yadav took action as per his forewarning, '*Wahan parinda bhi par nahin maar sakta* (Even a bird will not be able to stir a feather there).' He alerted the security forces posted in the temple town.

Ram and Sharad Kothari did not heed the warnings, as was the case with other karsevaks. The former, along with others, climbed atop the Babri Masjid to sway a saffron flag. That was their moment of triumph and little did they know what was to follow. On 2 November, the karsevaks gathered again at Hanumangarhi to move towards the disputed area. The police opened fire and killed sixteen of them, which included both the brothers, as per the official reports then. The street's crossroad, where they were killed, is renamed Shaheed Chowraha (Martyr's Crossing).

Anu Bhai Sompura is an interesting person. He says he has to leave for Lucknow in the next couple of hours and asks me to join him for an early lunch. This was in January 2020. His makeshift house is within the premises of the Karyashala. It is neat with all essential requisites that include a twin bed, three plastic chairs, TV and refrigerator. Today is the day for Gujarati food. The starters begin with palak pakoris (spinach fritters with gram flour coating).

Between hors d'oeuvres and main course, we chat about the temple. He tells me that he has designed several temples like the Birla Temple in Renukoot (Uttar Pradesh), one in Kalyan in Mumbai and the Nagda in Madhya Pradesh. The Birla temples he has worked on were made from sandstone and marble, and each pillar and roof has exquisite carvings that include floral motifs and images of many gods and goddesses.

The temple-designer feels that the Ram Janmabhoomi Temple will take four years to complete. 'The foundation will take time as the land is uneven with steep slopes and deep ditches dug by the Archaeological Survey. We are ready with the basics for the ground floor here, but it will take time to complete the entire temple.'

I then call on the architect, Chandrakant Sompura. He has worked on designing the Ram Temple according to the wishes of the VHP leaders like Singhal and Praveen Togadia. Besides the usual features like a Singh Dwar (the main entrance) with statues of royal Indian animals like lions and elephants, there will be an exquisitely carved throne made of marble for Lord Ram in the Garb Griha (sanctum sanctorum).

Plans have already been finalized for a Rang Mandap for cultural events, and a Sitarasoi, where *langar*s (free meals) will be organized. There is a provision for a dharamshala and a school. Cows will be housed in a gaushala.

Chandrakant was a child when his father built the Somnath Temple. Later, he was involved in the making of several temples like the Akshardham in Delhi and Swaminarayan Temple in London. 'There is so much to say. Why don't you log on to my website and get the details about our family trade,' he suggests.

The website, sompuracb.com, says, 'In Northern India, the Sompuras are involved in designing and building mostly Nagar style of Temples. Amongst the Sompura families involved in temple architecture, the family of Padmashree Prabhashankarbhai Oghadbhai has been one of the leading practitioners of Nagar *shaily* (style) of temple building and designing. The post independent era of India has witnessed the most reputed and esteemed project of redesigning of Somnath Temple known as Somnath Maha Meru Prasad, carried out and executed by him.'

In Ayodhya, Chandrakant feels that pilgrims can pay a visit if the Trust decides to open the temple for them once the ground floor is ready. Work can simultaneously be carried out on the first floor. He cites the example of the Ambaji Temple in Gujarat, where work on the first floor continued even as the ground floor was opened to devotees. 'We may do the same in the Ram Janmabhoomi Temple. But to have the entire temple ready, it will take another three to four years,' he explains.

No story about aspects and perspectives of Ayodhya can be complete without bringing in the Dalit angle. It is almost as crucial as the Muslim narrative.

The Ram Janmabhoomi saga contains the story of a young Dalit from a remote village in Bihar who experienced worldwide attention as the saffron leaders chose to prop him up. No wonder the day is still etched in his mind in a detailed sequence. Kameshwar Chaupal loves to relate the events. The date was 8 November 1989, when he reached Ayodhya. He oversaw the Lohardanga unit as in those years he was the VHP joint general secretary in charge of tribal-dominated districts in Bihar. His group was put on twenty-four-hour duty.

The decision for the Shilan Puja was taken at the Kumbh Mela early that year in a meeting of the sants, which was agreed upon by the RSS as well.

On 9 November, there were meetings near the *vivadeet dhancha* (controversial structure) from early morning. One of the VHP members, Meghnath Oram, from the same district as Chaupal's, had been behaving in a very restless and desperate manner. As his post demanded of him, Chaupal decided to stay back in the camp with Oram to keep a close watch on his movements. Suddenly, Rameshwar, who was Singhal's personal secretary, reached their camp and addressing Chaupal, he shouted out, 'I have been looking for you. Ashok-ji wants you to reach him immediately.'

Chaupal left everything and ran to the meeting point. By the time he reached, the speeches of the leaders had almost ended. Rajmata Vijaya Raje Scindia gently called out his name. She made him sit next to her. As he sat down, somewhat nervous, he saw Swami Chinmayanand taking the mike and informing all, 'Attention, please. I am going to make the most important announcement of the day. We have with us *bhagyashali* (lucky) Kameshwar Chaupal.

He is truly blessed as he will lay the first brick of the Ram Mandir.' Chaupal went into a stupor. 'Rajmata kept caressing my head as a mother would, and I gradually woke up from my trance.'

He gives more details—it was a six-foot-deep trench, and Chaupal, with others, went inside with the bricks. Puja and havan took place above and next to it. A few senior sages climbed down with the help of a ladder. For days after this event, Chaupal remained in a state of suspended animation. 'I could not even talk sensibly to the media. The international journalists crowded around me, and often I stood bewildered and lost.'

Chaupal shares a personal feeling with me. 'Till the announcement of the Supreme Court's verdict, I would spend sleepless nights praying that the mandir would be built. I felt responsible as I was chosen for the shilanyas for the proposed grand temple at Ayodhya on 9 November 1989. Imagine, the verdict was announced on the same date after thirty long years. Isn't that a divine coincidence?'

As a child, Kameshwar Chaupal went to a small non-descript school, Sri Laleshwar Nath Ucch Vidyala, in Marauna. He later shifted to the District High School in Supaul, in Bihar. It was in these formative years that he was drawn to the RSS. The science teacher, Hriday Narayan Jadav, was an RSS member who initiated Chaupal into the Sangh Parivar.

Chaupal adds, 'Interestingly, Jadav Sir was our Physical Training (PT) master. He was a good planner and, at the same time, a discreet person. On the field during our PT classes, he would surreptitiously discuss the RSS with us. Maybe he had figured out which of us would be interested in joining the Sangh.'

Another Dalit, Bhanwar Meghwanshi from Rajasthan, has similar memories of being initiated into the Ram Janmabhoomi movement. Besides the initial days at the shakha, his story stands in contrast to Chaupal's.

'I was thirteen when I joined the local RSS unit in my village. I went to a small school in my village, Sirdiyas. Banshilal Sen, the geography teacher, would take up sports activities after school hours. He would sing bhajans and chant mantras and explain the significance of Bharat Mata, Surya Devta and Ganga Maiyya. Those explanations were replete with mythology but in contrast to what he taught in geography. I was left wondering which one I should believe. He would narrate stories that would glorify Lord Ram and reveal to us the power of Hanuman and tell us several tales woven around other characters of the epic.'

Bhanwar joined the RSS camp despite his father's annoyance. The teacher at the shakha never treated him and other Dalits like untouchables. This made him feel important, which was in stark contrast to how he was treated in his village. He relates that he had participated in the local Shilan Pujas that took place in different villages in Bhilwara.

'I anointed many bricks, wrapped them in saffron cloths, applied sindoor and adorned them with malas and even worshipped them before they were transported to Ayodhya. I booked myself to be present for the karseva that was held in Ayodhya in 1991. But due to some political chaos, I had to curtail my journey. I was sad that my dream remained unfulfilled.'

Inspired by the local Sangh leaders, Bhanwar put two stickers on his door, *Garv se kaho hum Hindu hain* and *Bade bhagya se hum Hindu hain* (With pride claim that you are a Hindu; and Fortunately, you are a Hindu).

And then there was the disillusionment. The Arthi Kalash Yatra, a procession carrying the ashes of those who died in Ram Mandir's cause, took place in his locality, like in several towns and villages in the country. Bhanwar remembers that for the first time there was a festive mood in his village. The main street was decorated with mango leaves and seasonal flowers of different kinds, and the procession was welcomed with the sound of conches, bells and drumbeats. The Sangh leaders spoke about the atrocities inflicted upon the karsevaks and gave sermons on equality among Hindus.

'Their speeches enamoured me; they were my Gods on earth. I so much wanted to invite them to dinner and coaxed my mother to cook for them. She conceded and prepared poori and kheer. As usual, my father objected but succumbed to my convictions about Sangh Parivar's beliefs in equality and how they had shared several meals with me. My father said, "They are hypocrites, they have a different face in public and a different one in private."' Bhanwar adds, 'Till date these people haven't changed—their speeches lead the common people to believe that as leaders they are concerned about the Dalits, the women, etc. but this is far from the truth. In practice the Sangh leaders have never kept their word and revealed a different side.'

The family waited endlessly for the guests. No one came. Nandlal, an officeholder in the Sangh for twenty-five years, told Bhanwar that it would be improper to ask the sadhus and sants to have a meal at a Dalit's home. He said that it would be better if the food could be packed and handed over to everyone at a more appropriate place.

'The next day was worse. My friend Purushottam said that the food we had sent for the sadhus was thrown away. I wouldn't believe him till he took me to the spot where I saw all the food lying on the streets. I was devastated. I fell flat on my face, and the world around me darkened. But gradually, I found my feet, shook off the burden of RSS and got over with my infatuation with it. All I could do was to detach myself from being a Hindu and remain a Dalit.'

Bhanwar discusses the atrocities against the Dalits in his village, Sirdiyas. 'Nothing has changed. We learn how we should not come in the way of people from the other castes, and we avoid such situations.' He remembers a childhood incident. He would sometimes visit a Jat (caste higher than a Dalit) schoolmate and was comfortable in their house as no bias was revealed till one afternoon. 'That day, my friend's mother saw me sitting on the *khat* (bed) and screamed that the bed had been polluted. She had never earlier disapproved of me sitting on the bed but that particular day relatives were at the doorstep, and she could not let them down.' He adds rather stoically, 'But Dalits are used to such treatment till date.'

Kameshwar Chaupal has had similar experiences. His father was a poor farmer and they lived from hand to mouth. '*Hume din-raat apman sahna parta tha, saare feelings jaise mar gaye the, hum logon ke liye toh apmaan ek aam baat ho gayi thi. Khoon jaise paani ban chukka tha, apmaan sunne ki ek aadat si ho gayi thi* (We had to endure insults day and night; our feelings seemed to have died. We were used to abuses. Our blood had turned to water, we were so habituated to discriminations and insults).'

His father, despite the measly earnings, was compelled to dole out *chanda* (donation) for festivals at the local temple but was never allowed inside. When Chaupal passed his matriculation, the family was thrilled. His mother had promised to make an offering to the village deity, Lord Dihwa, if her son made it through his high school. Chaupal explains, 'It was customary to offer either a clay or wooden horse to our Lord, especially on special occasions.'

Hours before sunrise, the mother and son had reached the temple, swept it clean and placed the clay horse at the feet of Lord Dihwa. He adds, '*Mut puchhiye, uss din kya sehna para. Pore gaon mein hulchul mach gayi, logon ne andaj laga liya ki woh ghoda hum logon ne rakha tha* (Don't even ask what we faced that day. There was chaos in the entire village, people guessed that it was our family that had placed the clay horse).'

The family was ill-treated for months. But Chaupal was determined to stand up against the discrimination. 'I would never let an opportunity go without acting for my people,' he says.

Lord Ram blessed both Kameshwar Chaupal and Bhanwar Meghvanshi in different ways. The former is proud to be a VHP and a BJP MLA from his constituency. The latter found his calling in writing and publishing books. The first worships Lord Ram, and the other despises any form of worship. He is proud to be an atheist.

8
Demolition Day

> 'A religious act cannot be performed with the aid of the bayonet or the bomb.'
>
> —MAHATMA GANDHI[1]

It was a day of triumph; it was a day of disaster. It was a day that brought hope to the Hindus. It was a day filled with despair for the Muslims. There were tridents, and there were torches. There were netas and there were chelas. It was the season of frenzy; it was the winter of gloom. The fearful hid, the brazen bellowed.

Sanity lost its way, and ignorance ruled. It was the call of the leaders; it was the task of the followers. It was the sixth day of the last month of the year 1992. A socio-religious eclipse cast a dark shadow over Articles 25–28 of the Indian Constitution. Secularism was battered; the Constitution was bruised.

In five hours of that fateful day, the four constitutional articles lay shredded. Article 25 is on freedom of conscience and free profession, practice and propagation of religion. Article 26 is on the freedom to manage religious affairs. Article 27 is about the freedom of payment of taxes for the promotion of a religion. Article 28 allows attendance at religious instruction or religious worship in educational institutions.

On 6 December 1992, fanatic fumes consumed every dreg of secularism. Bedlam was let loose. A mosque was literally hammered into tiny pieces and turned into rubble. A militant Hindutva force took control over Ayodhya. Their chieftains managed to bring most of the Hindu priests and sadhus under their overpowering colossal saffron banner.

Since the mid-1980s, the Dharam Sansads were craftily organized to feed this high—what Karl Marx referred to as 'opium of the masses'. Since then, the voices from sadhus, mutts and ashrams grew louder, and their tones turned fiercer. Orders were proclaimed in the name of religion, which the God-fearing masses conceded to. Most sadhus spoke the language of the BJP and its confederates—the VHP and Bajrang Dal.

Together, they created a blinding dust storm of wrath and aimed to claim the disputed site in Ayodhya, where the Babri Masjid stood. The leadership concretized the belief among Hindus that Lord Ram was born at a particular spot in the contested area.

The sole objective, it became apparent, was to demolish the mosque and build a temple. Since the 1980s, there were processions, congregations and ceremonies to lay the foundation stone of the temple as well as collect bricks for the purpose. The run-up to 6 December 1992 looked no different, at least until the task was finished.

To be fair to the Hindus, the nation was charged. People had waited long enough. They had done much—donated bricks and money, given their time and effort—all for a grand temple dedicated to Ram Lalla.

Their relentless hard work paid off as the RSS–BJP–VHP succeeded in slowly and meticulously creating a regiment of crusaders from the commoners. This brigade spread across the country and intoxicated people's lives with an intense love for Lord Ram. 'We feel that we have contributed to building our Lord's home,' was the common refrain from those who participated in the demolition of the Babri Masjid.

Before the event, the ruling regime, the Congress, made the right noises about peace and harmony. On 27 November 1992, the Centre organized a National Integration Meeting 'to discuss issues relating to National Integration and Communal Harmony in the context of Kashmir and Punjab problems and the dispute over Janam Bhoomi-Babri Masjid, the problem of Regionalism and Communalism, etc.'[2]

The ruling party and its allies were commonly known for their secular temperament. The government assured that it would take precautions, including security-related ones, to ensure that there was no construction or damage to the Babri Masjid.

Although the BJP boycotted this meeting, its state government in Uttar Pradesh gave affidavits and assurances that nothing untoward would happen at the karseva organized on 6 December. The Supreme Court wanted the Centre to deploy security. The state regime, headed by Kalyan Singh, refused and confirmed that it had things under control: As the chief minister, he repeatedly guaranteed that the karseva would be a symbolic act. He added that no construction materials or equipment would be allowed in the disputed area in Ayodhya. At one of the the Liberhan Commission's examinations, conducted by Anupam Gupta, counsel for the commission, Advani stated, 'It is only when the Supreme Court rejected the demand for a ban and agreed instead for symbolic karseva, and the VHP also agreed to it, that we decided to go to Ayodhya. And all our speeches during that period made it clear that it would be symbolic karseva which would be carried out.'

Mark Tully tells me about his discussion with Advani a few days before 6 December, 'I was concerned about the huge crowd getting into Ayodhya for the slotted symbolic karseva. Advani guaranteed that there was no need to worry. He believed that since the RSS was involved in the karseva, nothing could ever go out of control. The BJP senior leader's logic was that RSS believes in maintaining discipline and is extremely organized.'

Mahant Dharam Das, head of the Nirvani Akhara, says the same thing when I meet him in early 2020. 'Local mahants and the VHP leaders had specified to the BJP stalwarts that the symbolic karseva would involve each volunteer taking a fistful of sand from the banks of the Sarayu and placing it at the site, where the temple was to be constructed. We had assured the netas that we would not violate any court orders.'

To ensure that legalities were maintained, the regional VHP heads across the country were entrusted with the task of spreading the planned details of the karseva that was decided after the Supreme Court's orders to the Rambhakts in their respective territories. But later, it was discovered that the karsevaks had no clue about the court orders.

The destruction of the mosque on 6 December 1992 clearly implied that approximately 15 per cent of India's population of Muslims, who barely have any relation with Emperor Babur, or other Mughal emperors, paid the price for the latter's past acts.

In the foreword to the BJP's White Paper on Ayodhya and the Rama Temple Movement published in April 1993, L.K. Advani, describing the motive behind the construction of the Babri Masjid, wrote, 'On the other hand, the structure which Mir Baqi put up on the orders of Babur never had any special significance from a religious point of view. It was purely and simply a symbol not of devotion and of religion but of conquest. Correspondingly, quite apart from its being an obstacle, preventing Hindus from worshipping the birthplace of their idol, Sri Rama, it was for the country the symbol of its subjugation.'

'In what Harke (1993) called a "mythical" concept of history, little or no separation exists between the past and the present.' Taking this perception forward, Reinhard Bernbeck and Susan Pollock explain that 'it is just such a manipulation of time that is at work in the case of Ayodhya. Only by employing a mythical conception of history can the Muslims of India today be held responsible for the alleged injuries wrought by their ancestors (Gandhi 1992:29). The 1992 destruction of the mosque becomes a direct response to a perceived wrong of 500 years ago; bringing the past very near to the present helps to legitimate revenge for past injuries.'[3]

Interestingly, the White Paper on Ayodhya also admits how the BJP 'had always affirmed that the Ayodhya movement was not just a plea for a temple for Sri Rama, that instead it reflected a far deeper quest for recapturing our national identity'.

It further brings to notice 'the post-independence political creed of the Congress and of most other political parties had come to regard everything that inspired this nation in the past as less than secular—in fact, communal and even anti-national. The movement for restoration of the Temple at the birthplace of Sri Rama evolved as a corrective to this distortion.'

In 1992, I was not a journalist. Later, when I joined the media, out of curiosity, I would intently listen to colleagues who discussed their experiences prior to and during the demolition of the Babri Masjid. On the recent trips I made to Ayodhya I spoke to dozens of locals to gather their personal takes. Though it's been close to three decades, the locals haven't forgotten a thing about the incidents that took place prior to that day, that day itself and soon after.

My ex-colleague from *Outlook*, Prashant Panjiar, a renowned photojournalist, who was with *India Today* in 1992, shared his experiences with me. 'In the lead-up to that day which would change India for ever, BJP's three senior leaders, L.K. Advani, Atal Bihari Vajpayee and Murli Manohar Joshi all set out on different Rath Yatras converging for a rally in Lucknow on 5 December, from where they were to proceed to Ayodhya next morning. *India Today* sent out three teams to follow each of these leaders. I was assigned to be with Advani.' He then told me what had caught his attention a day before, 'On the night of 5 December, I was in Lucknow, where Advani, Vajpayee and Joshi held a rally. We were informed that they would leave for Ayodhya around 6 a.m. the next morning. Most of the outstation journalists had returned to the hotel. Out of intuition, I decided to go along with these leaders, who went to Kalyan Singh's house post the public assemblage. They got into a closed-door meeting that lasted for hours, after which I was told that the plans had changed and Vajpayee would return to Delhi while the others would leave for Ayodhya in the next couple of hours. Something seemed amiss as they changed their original plans. The next morning, I left for Ayodhya with my team.' The White Papers on Ayodhya also mentions that a week before, on 29 November 1992, L.K. Advani and Murli Manohar Joshi had announced that they would both reach Ayodhya to participate in the karseva, but would take different routes—Advani would move from Varanasi and Murli Manohar Joshi from Mathura. Besides attending the event, the two had also taken upon themselves the task of mobilizing the karsevaks.

What followed is known to most. Advani reached the temple town around midnight or perhaps shortly after that. With him was

BJP leader, Pramod Mahajan. Joshi, who was present at the public meeting in Lucknow, left separately for Ayodhya. When Advani reached Barabanki, a small town about 107 km from Ayodhya, a few police officials received him. At Ayodhya, he stayed at Janaki Mahal, a place he invariably chose to reside in when visiting the pilgrim town.

From Prashant's book, *That Which Is Unseen*, we learn that Advani had long clandestine meetings with the Vishwa Hindu Parishad, Bajrang Dal and other religious leaders, who were all leading the 'movement'. He further exponds, 'While waiting outside we learned that the militant Kar Sevaks who had gathered in Ayodhya by the thousands were furious with their political leaders for announcing another symbolic event instead of giving the go-ahead for razing the Babri Masjid to the ground. Advani was in a bind as assurances had been given to the Supreme Court that the disputed structure would be safeguarded and there would be only singing of hymns. So now negotiations were on to salvage the situation.'[4]

Prashant was the only photojournalist who got the shots of the three domes of the Babri Masjid as they fell. The reason is well-delineated in his book, 'I stuck with him (Advani) since that was my brief. We finally landed up on the terrace of the Ram Katha Kunj which was a little away from where a stage had been set up. Leaders like H.V. Seshadri of the RSS, Rajmata Vijaya Raje Scindia, Uma Bharti, Sadhvi Rithambra and many others were already there. As time moved on, the speeches became more and more fiery. From where we were standing, I could not see the platform where the Kar Seva was to take place. But I did have a distant view of the domes of the Babri Masjid. I was the only press photographer there.'

He was lucky as, unlike other photographers and camerapersons, he was spared the subsequent violence faced by the media persons.

Journalists present that morning maintain that within an hour or so after the meeting was commenced by the top leaders, the latter appeared visibly helpless as the mob went out of control. The announcements made from the stage at Ram Katha Kunj to hold them back made no difference to the frenzied gathering.

Still, there are insiders and even karsevaks who are convinced that there was a conspiracy, which was hatched at the highest levels, to decimate the mosque. However, a lower court exonerated the BJP leaders, which included Advani and Joshi, of criminal intent and acts. Now, the conspiracy resides in the realm of theory.

For those who are still interested, listen to some of the comments made in the days before the destructive event. At the Lucknow meeting on the night of 5 December, Vajpayee let loose his emotions and spoke dramatically about Hindus and their rights over Ayodhya.

He encouraged the building of a temple, as revealed by a comment he made on the evening of 5 December at Jhandewalan Park in Aminabad, Lucknow. 'Sharp stones are emerging from the ground. The ground has to be levelled (*zameen ko samtal karna padega*). If a *yagya* begins, there will have to be some construction.'[5]

The same evening Vajpayee shared his own interpretation of the court's instructions. 'I will tell you the *arth* (meaning) of the Supreme Court verdict. It does not mean we have to stop karseva. Actually, the Supreme Court has given us the right to continue karseva. *Rokne ka to sawal hi nahin hai* (There is no question of stopping us). Tomorrow we will not be violating any court order if we perform kar seva. It is however true that the Supreme Court has ruled that till the Lucknow bench announces its decision, you people cannot do mandir nirman (construction).'[6]

While reviewing P.V. Narasimha Rao's book *Ayodhya: 6 December 1992*, A.G. Noorani points out that the White Paper on Ayodhya which was published by Narasimha Rao's government in April 1993 summarized explicit threats of demolition by the highest leaders of the BJP (pages 90–92).[7] BJP President Murli Manohar Joshi, on 1 December at Mathura: 'He appealed to the gathering to assemble at Ayodhya in large numbers for karseva and to demolish the so-called Babri Masjid.' Vice president Vijaya Raje Scindia in Patna on 23 November: 'She said that the Babri Masjid will have to be demolished.' Vishwa Hindu Parishad President V.H. Dalmia in Delhi on 9 November: 'Declared that "the RJB [Ram Janmabhoomi] temple would be constructed in the same way it was demolished by Babar". Karsevaks, he said, were pressurizing the leadership that they should be called not to construct the RJB temple but to demolish the masjid.' RSS leader Rajendra Singh publicly said that he had warned Narasimha Rao on 3 December that anything could happen in Ayodhya on 6 December. Narasimha Rao chose to ignore all this because he had arrived at a 'tacit understanding' with the Sangh Parivar behind the back of the Cabinet.[8]

At regular intervals, Mahant Ram Chandra Paramhans would goad enthusiastic Rambhakts, '*Iss bar mita hi do kalank ko* (This time remove the dark stain).' Much later, when he was asked about it, he said that he had no regrets that the mosque was demolished.

According to the locals who participated in the karseva, there were frequent meetings held in the months before December 1992. The locals were repeatedly told that they should not allow any hurdles to come in the way of building a Ram Temple. They should be prepared for whatever sacrifice would be required to 'Liberate Ram'.

As the day earmarked for karseva drew closer, several volunteers from the town were given responsibilities to guide the karsevaks who came from other parts of the country. The town offered these visitors food and shelter. Karsevakpuram, the VHP headquarters at Ayodhya, made special arrangements for them—meals were served thrice a day, and camps set up as temporary living spaces.

There were karsevaks from Bihar in the east, Maharashtra in the west, Punjab and Haryana in the north, and Andhra Pradesh and

Tamil Nadu in the south. Daily *bhandara*s (places to distribute food) were held even in the local temples, where the staple diet consisted of rice, dal and vegetables for lunch and poori–sabji for dinner. Those who could not stay at Karsevakpuram found other options. The VHP had camps in the town. The residents also extended food and lodging for these visitors.

I meet Avadesh Mishra, an English teacher in a state-run junior school in Ayodhya. He was seventeen in 1992 and was excited to become a karsevak. 'I loved the idea that I was doing something for Ram Lalla, the lord of our town. The most exciting part was that I could leave home and come back late [in the night]. My parents, who would always keep a tab on me, did not ask questions during that period.' Devout Hindus that they were, his parents were proud that their son was working for their *Ishta Devata* (Supreme God). Mishra adds with an impish grin, 'For my friends and me, the campaign was like a new adventure.'

There were at least 70,000–80,000 local volunteers. The Liberhan Commission's report puts the number of karsevaks present in and around Ayodhya during the Babri Masjid demolition at 75,000 to 1.5 lakh.[9]

Eyewitnesses, photographs and police reports stated that prior to the karseva, the town was not its usual calm and contented self. It was angry and ferocious. The colours of fiery red and obstinate orange overpowered the panorama. Loud slogans dimmed the conventional soft chanting from the temples.

Shutters were down and businesses came to a halt. There were barricades and posts to hold people back. Heads with saffron bands popping here and there moved ceaselessly like a growing flame that would soon engulf the town. The hairbands were the markers provided by the VHP office. They had 'Jai Shri Ram' printed on them, with a tiny image of the future Ram Temple as the monogram.

To distinguish between the locals and visitors, they had badges for the latter with a different shade of saffron. 'This differentiation helped us to identify those who were first-timers in our city,' explains Avadesh.

Gaurav Tiwari, a social worker from Ayodhya, who was in high school in 1992 and had participated in the karseva, adds, 'We felt so proud with the band around our heads. We had also explained to the (VHP) leaders that we would prefer wearing shorts to dhotis that day as that would help in being more mobile and faster. The leaders agreed.'

Among the youngsters like Avadesh and Gaurav, the favourite slogan was: '*Jis Hindu ka khoon na khawla, khoon nahi woh paani hai, jis Hindu ki bhuja na pharke, uski bekar jawani hai* (The Hindu whose blood does not boil, has water in his body; the Hindu whose muscles don't ripple, his youth is worthless).'

Though Gaurav was completely disillusioned by the merciless acts of the karsevaks later that day, he says, 'I remember that, during those days, all of us were so enthused by our leaders that we were ready to give up our lives to liberate Ram. We were so charged and almost delirious that we had stopped thinking logically.'

The training of the karsevaks was taken up mainly by the Bajrang Dal. The BJP supervised the work. Anyone keen to be a volunteer would be inducted into these camps. During the earlier training, people were made familiar with the internal roads that led to the Ram Chabootra. In those years, VHP leaders like Acharya Giriraj Kishore made it a point to visit Bajrang Dal camps across the country with the motive to encourage and train the eager youngsters for the 'andolan'.

The founder-president of Bajrang Dal, Vinay Katiyar, tells me that for the karseva of December 1992 there was no registration. 'It was not practically feasible as there were so many Rambhakts streaming into the city each day. We initiated them on the basis of their faith and devotion towards Ram Lalla so that they could tender their bit for a divine cause in the land of Ram.'

Most local karsevaks remember how the leaders assured them, '*Ram Mandir awashya banayenge, mandir wahi banayenge, bhavya banayenge* (A temple for Ram will be constructed, we shall build it at the exact spot, and it will be a grand temple).' During the press conferences held almost daily for a month before 6 December, the VHP proclaimed that no power could come in the way of the karseva.

For the leaders, a pulpit was constructed at the Ram Katha Kunj, near the Babri Masjid, to address the volunteers. The chieftains were driven in around 11 a.m. and headed for the stage. Most were accustomed to addressing the crowd from here as it was used on previous occasions. Then, they educated the people on the vile deeds committed by the Muslims on the innocent and submissive Hindus in the sixteenth century. And, of course, on the need to 'liberate Ram'.

This was a vantage point, 20 feet from the Pooja Sthal (Prayer Area) and 600 feet from the site set aside for the karsevaks. The position gave the senior leaders a clear view of the proceedings below.

On the stage were Advani, Joshi, Vijaya Raje Scindia and Uma Bharti. Later, Singhal joined them, after which the door leading up to the *manch* (podium) was closed. There was a stairway leading to the dais, which had a door that could be locked when necessary. This was the only place with loudspeakers that morning.

The karseva began at 10.30 a.m. in a pious manner with holy intonations and bhajans around a havan in front of the Ram Chabootra. This space included the outer courtyard of the mosque, which had a small raised platform usually used by the Rambhakts who congregated to offer prayers and recite devotional songs. It was at this spot that the idol of Ram Lalla had sat for centuries till he was moved under what had been the *mihrab* (the area of the mosque which is the same as the sanctum sanctorum in a temple) of the Babri Masjid on the night of 22 December 1949.

The havan was conducted by the mahant of the Ram Janmabhoomi movement—Mahant Avaidyanath of Gorakshpeeth, who was the guru of present-day chief minister of Uttar Pradesh, Yogi Adityanath. Others included Ram Vilas Vedanti, Mahant Ram Chandra Paramhans and Mahant Nritya Gopal Das, who is the appointed head of the newly created trust, Shri Ram Janmabhoomi Teerth Kshetra.

Besides, there were other Hindus pining for a role in what was being considered as the most sacrosanct ceremony taking place in the nation. These included the thousands of sadhus from across the country, who nudged and elbowed to get closer to the holy fire. With no loudspeaker, the celestial mantras remained unheard, and the terrestrial political speeches boomed loud and clear.

The netas took turns to produce sensational lines. The *bhashans*, (speeches) were belted out non-stop from the stage. In about an hour, the leaders realized that no one from the sea of karsevaks below was interested either in the serious speeches or in the spiritual soiree.

And then, suddenly, as if from out of nowhere, a karsevak with the alacrity of an acrobat jumped over a high barricade and landed straight within the 'forbidden space'. He flung his hands up in the air like a victorious conqueror and shouted out, 'Jai Shri Ram.'

The floodgates opened, and others followed him. Soon there was pandemonium. Many journalists and locals still remember this scene which had taken place just before noon 'when a teenage karsevak made headway towards the disputed structure and around hundred-odd followed him'. Avadesh remembers, 'We wanted to feel like martyrs for a noble and sacred cause; we immediately rushed towards the mosque.'

'There was complete chaos. The appeals from the dais requesting people to concentrate on the puja and the karseva fell on deaf ears.

No one cared. Appeals for caution from the senior leaders were blown away by the loud slogans and desperate actions,' remembers another local karsevak, who too had broken through the security cordon.

On 6 December 2020, I call Katiyar. 'I am in Ayodhya, but there is no function happening. Usually, we celebrate Shaurya Diwas (Victory Day) to commemorate the demolition of the disputed structure. But this year, we didn't as the administration asked the residents not to have any public activity because of the pandemic.'

I ask him about reports that mentioned him as playing a huge role in the demolition and training of the Bajrang Dal volunteers, who committed the act. 'None of the leaders wanted to bring down the mosque. You are right; there are rumours about us and that the Bajrang Dal preplanned the destruction of the vivadit dhancha.' He explains how onc of the karsevaks dared to climb the dome and then others followed suit. Katiyar says that there were half a dozen men who rolled down from the top and fell behind the structure. Three of them fell straight on the barbed wires and lost their lives. After this, people from the crowd climbed up with feelings of vengeance, anger and frustration. He confesses, 'It became impossible for us to take control of the mob.'

Later, in front of the Liberhan Commission, Giriraj Kishore blamed the mob for what happened. 'The youngsters felt they had to do something more than just attending meetings; they were impatient.'

When asked about the frenzy, Avadesh reminiscences, 'We were excited. After a point, we saw our comrades digging out the huge wooden poles that were used for barricades. We joined the "fun", least realizing what their intention was. The fence and grill surrounding the temple inside the mosque area were dismantled as well.' Avadesh shows me an iron angle that he has preserved as a memoir.

Vishal Srivastava, now an advocate in Ayodhya, also showed me an iron pole that he carried back as a 'prasada'. The pole stands tall on his terrace and holds the TV antenna. Vishal was twelve in 1992. He recollects, 'The city was like on an ongoing *dharmik mela* (religious fair) during those days.' He could not volunteer as a karsevak because of his age. But as soon as the reports of the first dome coming down reached his mohalla, he ran the one and a half kilometres to reach the spot.

'I guess I wanted to be a part of this historical event,' he analyses after eighteen years. That afternoon he joined a few crusaders and pulled out an iron pole from the grill in front of the chabootra and, with hundred others, bashed the mosque. 'Others climbed on the top of the poles and clambered up to the dome. From below, people gave them the saffron flags. They were hailed as heroes as they swayed them from the top of the mosque.'

'Out of the crowd,' recollects a karsevak from Ayodhya, 'the ones who displayed maximum strength and defiance were those who had come from Hissar, a city in Haryana in northern India. Tall and sturdy, they took no time in pulling out the wooden poles.'

The Liberhan Commission, which was set up on 16 December 1992 by the Union home ministry to look into the details of the event, said that the security forces deployed in Ayodhya consisted of thirty-five companies of the Provincial Armed Constabulary (PAC), four companies of the Central Reserve Police Force (CRPF), including a women's wing squad, fifteen tear-gas squads, fifteen police inspectors, thirty sub-inspectors of police, 2,300 police constables, a bomb-disposal squad, sniffer-dog squads, fire brigade and ambulances.

These forces faded out in front of the infuriated mob. Carl Jung, who explained mob mentality in his book, *The Archetypes and the Collective Unconscious*, explains, 'A group experience takes place on a lower level of consciousness than the experience of an individual.

This is due to the fact that when many people gather together to share one common emotion, the total psyche emerging from the group is below the level of the individual psyche. If it is a very large group, the collective psyche will be more like the psyche of an animal, which is the reason why the ethical attitude of large organisations is always doubtful.' Jung further expounds, 'If therefore, I have a so-called collective experience as a member of a group, it takes place on a lower level of consciousness than if I had the experience by myself alone.'[10]

When the security forced tried to intervene, a group of karsevaks kept them at bay. Stones were showered at the law-keepers who fled. 'Most left behind their batons and riot shields. Thinking back, we feel they were more concerned with their revolvers, which they carried with them,' says Gaurav Tiwari.

These local participants recollect how the cops who stayed back surrendered to the mob. 'They stood and watched like hypnotized statues. Forgetting their roles, a few joined the crowd and even shouted slogans. The chants of "Jai Shri Ram" pervaded the afternoon air.'

'Their batons and riot shields proved useful to the karsevaks,' admits Avadesh. The other tools that the mob had included spades, shovels, hammers and pickaxes. Iron tongs and tridents were used by the holy men. Mahant Dharam Das of the Nirvani Akhara discloses, 'Tridents were brought from the local houses and even the Hanumangarhi Temple store.' One of the locals chips in, 'The barbed fence was uprooted, and the iron angles were used to both climb and break.'

It is strange how the karsevaks feel proud of their defiant and law-breaking actions. Says Avadesh with a tone of self-importance, 'We fail to understand why people discuss the coming down of the domes. We should be given maximum credit. Had we not weakened the base (of the mosque), the domes would never have crumbled down.' He describes the scene. The determined karsevaks took the wooden poles from the barricade, ran back 10 feet, and then, with full fervour, used the poles as battering rams to hit hard at the mosque's walls.

Usually, one gets to hear the phrase, *dum laaga ke haisha*, in India, which is chanted by groups that collectively try to pull, push or lift heavy things. In Ayodhya, on that morning, the phrases used instead were 'Jai Shri Ram' and '*Mandir yahin banayenge*'.

'When I reached the spot fifteen minutes past noon, I saw hundreds of karsevaks on top of the mosque, waving saffron flags. It was like a fort captured in a medieval battle,' adds another karsevak. A dozen karsevaks came rolling down with the boulders. The ones who were standing below realized the dangers. They picked up the riot shields and held them together to save those who tumbled down. It was like acrobats falling off a trapeze and being caught by the safety net below.

Prashant in his book, *That Which Is Unseen*, also gives an eyewitness account of the scenes that occurred one after the other. He writes how a crowd of karsevaks suddenly appeared atop the domes of the Babri Masjid holding saffron flags. Some of them were equipped with iron rods, pickaxes and hammers. 'Advani and H.V. Seshadri looked on with some trepidation as it became clear that the Kar Sevaks were not going to listen to their feeble announcements on the PA system to come down. Soon the assault on the domes was in full swing. It was by now clear that Advani was no longer in command of the beast he had unleashed. Meanwhile the other leaders on the stage were cheering and had started up the chant "*Ek dhakka aur do, Babri Masjid tod do* (Give it one more push, bring the Babri Masjid down)".'[11]

Officials at the site watched the events like unflappable birds. It took five hours for the mosque to crumble down. Till the previous day, it was one of the largest mosques in Uttar Pradesh.

The design and pattern were taken from the architectural school of Jaunpur Sultanate.

Graham Pickford, an architect to William Bentinck (1828–1833), writes in his book, *Historic Structures of Oudh*, 'A whisper from the Babri Masjid Mihrab could be heard clearly at the other end, 200 feet (60 m) away and through the length and breadth of the centre court.'

Modern architects attribute this acoustic feature to a recess in the wall of the mihrab, and several recesses in the surrounding walls, which functioned as resonators. This design helped everyone hear the speaker at the mihrab.[12]

Perhaps these recesses within the walls made it easier for the religious militants to bring down the mosque in a few hours.

I meet photographer Pramod Pushkarna, in Delhi, who was present in Ayodhya on 6 December 1992, working for *India Today*. He touches the left side of his chest, 'This is a carryback from there. Someone threw a huge stone that came with great speed and hit me. I carry the two pains from that day—watching secularism battered and the physical ache in my lowest rib.'

I listen to more details that Pramod shares, 'Most journalists reached Ayodhya before 6 December. The hotels were full. People had to share rooms. There were media persons from India and abroad. On the night before, the district administration announced that we had to procure identity cards. One of the journalists from the foreign media team was found missing. To top it all, a call came to enquire about the names of journalists at one of the hotels. A few media persons met Vinay Katiyar to find out if there was any news about the missing journalist. The way Katiyar responded, it was evident that the idea was to scare us.'

He continues, 'Hanging their I-cards, the journalists left early to reach the site of the karseva. By 10 a.m., arrangements for the havan started with Sadhvi Ritambara, Acharya Dharmendra and Uma

Bharti. It was difficult to find a place to take photographs. There was palpable fury in the crowd against the journalists. They were cursing and threatening all, especially the cameramen.'

To ensure that they were not identified by the karsevaks, the scribes hid their identity cards, pens, notebooks and cameras. Ritambara and Dharamcharya had their eyes glued on the journalists. 'Amidst this din, we learnt that Dieter Ludwig, a photographer of *Time* magazine, had to run for his life as huge boulders were hurled at him. The photographers became conspicuous because of their cameras, etc.,' recollects Pramod.

Most of my ex-colleagues who witnessed the scenes remember how a few journalists mustered courage and threw stones back at the karsevaks, who shouted slogans like '*Patrakar murdabad* (Down with journalists).' Pramod swung his camera at one of them. 'This kept me safe. The camera I loved so much became my weapon.' He ran till he reached a small temple with a shivling inside. He placed his camera, left everything to chance, bolted the door from outside, and returned back to the crowd like an ordinary spectator.

The victims who were targeted the most were mainly foreign journalists. Mark Tully explains the reason. On 5 December, the BBC had aired a story on Ayodhya where it used footage from 1990 but did not clarify the date. When telecast, it seemed as if the riot footage was current and not of two years ago. There was no rioting going on when the story was shown. Sir Tully believes that perhaps this was the reason why there was a lot of ill will and anger directed towards the foreign media like BBC. He tried to remedy the situation but in vain, 'When I got to know, I looked out for Advani but could not find him. I spoke to the then editor of *Organiser* (RSS magazine), and he said that the karsevaks were there only to perform shilanyas. Soon after, I bumped into senior RSS leader, Sudarshan, and he too paid no heed to my concerns.'

From the spot Tully chose, the karsevaks got hold of him and kept him locked inside a temple. He tells me what followed thereon, 'The SDM, who learnt about our plight, requested the mahant of the adjacent temple to release us. We were set free after an hour and stationed ourselves at the mahant's temple. Later, a truck was sent for us, and we got into it to get back to Faizabad that evening.'

Journalists were not the only ones concerned about their safety. There were those who were worried about Ram Lalla. Mahant Dharam Das tells me how his focus was to protect the idol inside the mosque. 'Compared to the risks my guru-ji, Abhiram Das, took to place it inside, mine was not a big job,' he says.

It was in the evening, at 5 p.m., that the earlier slogans of the karsevaks changed—it was repeatedly announced that the army would arrive and people were asked to return home. The locals blocked the roads that led to Ayodhya from the nearby towns of Faizabad, Gonda and Sultanpur. They were determined to ensure safe passage for those responsible for the demolition and delay the entry of security forces.

Ram Lalla was shifted to a makeshift temple by 8 p.m. that evening. As per Dharam Das's version, it was under his supervision that a group of karsevaks used spades and shovels, this time to clear the rubble. From the heap, several pieces were also picked up by the Rambhakts to take back home as mementos. Within a couple of hours, a makeshift temple was ready—a crude platform with a few steps, a plastic canopy and an 8-feet-high brick wall. When the chief priest of the Ram Temple, Satyendra Das, listens to Dharam Das's story, he scoffs at him and calls him a liar. He then immediately makes up with a little bit of understanding, 'Most often the youngest siblings (as Dharam is his youngest guru-bhai) are a little naughty. Anyway, I shall relate to you what actually happened.' According to him, after the two domes had been demolished, Satyendra Das had felt that it was time to bring Ram Lalla, who was seated under the central dome, out. 'We were five (priests) in number, and we took Lord Ram and placed him under a neem tree which was the safest place on the north-eastern side of the chabootra. A few karsevaks had helped us. Some of them helped to pull out the wooden throne where Ram Lalla was seated while many of them joined us to remove the huge boulders and debris. It took a good two hours to clean the chosen spot for the makeshift temple.

'It was only after 7 p.m. that with the help of bamboo poles and a huge cloth covering we could re-install Ram Lalla and his three brothers, Lakshman, Bharat, Shatrughan in a temporary home where he lived for the next twenty-eight long years.' Satyendra Das tells me, 'We quickly did some necessary shopping as soon as the curfew was called off after 7 p.m. We bought a large pink silk cloth to cover the mandap (sacred tent). We also purchased sweets and flowers for offerings. A puja was conducted at sharp 8 p.m. with several devotees joining us in the celebration. The town was still teeming with thousands of karsevaks.'

According to some locals, 'Two kinds of celebrations were taking place simultaneously that day. There were those who wanted to rejoice at the setting up of a new (temporary) space for Ram Lalla. And there were those who pined to paint a few more strokes of vengeance to commemorate the coming down of the Babri Masjid.' I was told that the latter were majorly Rambhakts who were from outstation and had stayed back in Ayodhya after the demolition. Their hullabaloo started late in the afternoon. Their torches alight, they went scorching as many Muslim houses as they could.

According to an article published in *The Hindu* on 10 December 2017, 'Much of the Muslim population in the town had fled a week prior to the demolition. However, at least 17 persons were killed, over 250 homes and shops gutted, damaged or looted in the mayhem that followed in the narrow gullies near the disputed site over the next 24 hours. Going by local accounts, two dozen mosques and over 100 tombs were desecrated and damaged by the mob.'[13]

Humanity was lost.

The old, helpless and invalid were burnt alive. The Muslims who fled were safe. That evening, no muezzin call could be heard; chants of 'Jai Shri Ram' dominated the dark wintry air.

It was a new celebration in the name of Ram. No regrets, no pain. The propagandists of Hindutva showed brazen faces. A leader later counter-questioned, 'Did Hanuman-ji ever decide to set fire on Lanka before he reached Ravan's kingdom? The need of the hour had prompted him and his *vanar sena* (monkey army) to burn the kingdom of the demons.'

The demolition of one religious structure paved the way to build a greater temple two decades later.

Epilogue

Ayodhya—Ram ki Nagri

On the Sarayu River's left bank stands Chhoti Chhavni, a huge mansion of great importance. Only three years ago, reaching up to its towering doorway seemed like an impossible task. Cars used to queue up bumper-to-bumper and there was constant VIP movement. All these movements kept the security officials on their toes while the devotees were pushed away to wait for hours till their turn arrived.

It is not the same any more—not at all. The street seems abandoned. The mansion is quiet. It is so quiet and still that it creates an eerie spell. To say it differently, the building is in a state of 'kenopsia'. The old master lies silent, oblivious to the progress of his dream mega project. The V-class security that always stood alert next to the entrance door is missing. Their post has shifted to a remote corner—a balcony at the end of a corridor on the left side of the main temple hall.

Everything here, in Mahant Nritya Gopal Das's citadel, has changed beyond recognition. The number of visitors has reduced to a mere handful of pilgrims and devotees. The priest who read from the

Ramcharitmanas round the clock is missing and so is the tiny marble statue of Hanuman that would give him company. There is an uncanny and discomforting lull. Most visitors, these days, after having offered prayers and looked around the temple, move towards the passage on the left side that leads to a hall converted to a makeshift ICU. The pilgrims are allowed to stand quietly at a distance and pay obeisance to the president of the Ram Teerth Khsetra Trust, who lies almost as inert as the building. He was the mastermind behind the bhavya Ram Mandir, now under construction. But he cannot see the activity; he cannot direct the construction that was always so dear to him.

It's not just the mahant's life that has changed. Almost everything looks and feels different in Ayodhya in 2022.

Revisiting Ayodhya after three years and witnessing one of the most vocal, active and pompous movers and shakers of the Ram Janmabhoomi temple lying inert makes me speculate on the effervescent lives we mere mortals live. The glory and power are all so temporary.

Further down the road, I take a peep inside the Nirmohi Akhara. Here too, the old familiar hustle-bustle is missing. The building is being renovated and, right now, looks dilapidated and cuts a sorry picture.

It is about noon. The head of the akhara has stepped out for some work. I notice that despite the hour there is a dim lamp lit in the portico. Besides this artificial light, everything else looks drab and desolate. I enquire about Durgesh Shukla, the mahant's firebrand secretary. I am told that he succumbed to a cardiac arrest. There are no bhakts or shishyas lotering around. Like in the case of Chhoti Chhavni, a pall of gloom seems to have replaced the hectic activity here as well.

From there I move towards the temple karyashala, my usual route in this town. I spot Anubhai Sompura, who has been the supervisor here for three decades, loitering around the pillars, which seem fewer in number than on my earlier visits. I am told that many of these have been shifted to the construction site of the Ram Mandir. Some visitors, as always, are busy taking selfies with the stacks of pillars as the backdrop while others are touching their foreheads to the tall piles of bricks here that have been collected from Rambhakts over decades!

On the right side of the gate, and towards the centre, a huge temporary building stands, with a board proclaiming it as the office of the Trust—Shri Ram Janmabhoomi Teerth Kshetra. Suddenly, a white sedan enters the gate. The guards at the doorway take positions to welcome the visitor. A man dressed in crisp white steps out. I recognize him, and move towards him. But he sees through everyone and heads straight to the door that is shut brusquely immediately after he and a few followers have passed through it.

Champat Rai, the VHP leader, who serves as the general secretary of Ram Janmabhoomi Trust, is a changed personality. Before he held the post, one could meet him in person and talk over the phone. Now, he chooses to speak to the press only when he thinks it is necessary to pass some information. Otherwise, he has no time. And like him, there is a visible difference in the other VHP leaders in Karsevakpuram. They too, like Champat, would earlier share their views and emotions about the 'Bhavya Mandir'. Now, they contend that they have little to do with the temple construction.

Senior VHP leader Puroshottam-ji continues to be affable but avoids discussing the construction. When I ask him a few questions about the Ram Mandir, his curt reply is: '*Aap ko koi aur baat karna hai toh hum kar sakte hain. Ab hamari umar ho chuki hai aur in sab prashan ka jawab hum nahi de payenge.* (If you want to talk on any other topic, I am willing to talk. I am too old, and I cannot answer these questions on the Ram Temple).' The spark that I had noticed three years ago is gone; then he was full of enthusiasm as he eagerly looked forward to the construction. Not any longer. Another senior VHP leader, a warm person who helped Ram Lalla to get back his land, is missing. Triloki Nath, Lord Ram's best friend in the court cases, is no longer alive. His seat is empty and the walls with racks holding his favourite deities, the posters of Bharat Mata, Lord Ram, Lakshman, Sita and Hanuman, besides other artefacts, are empty and whitewashed.

Nobody even talks about him. He is history. As the sun slowly sinks, the open field at Karsevakpuram is bare. On the main street of this enclosure, a cowherd on his bicycle leads the herd of bovines back to the gaushala. The only sound that is heard is the bored and long mooing of the cows, interrupted by the tinkling of their bells. A dog scampers along, wagging its tail—the sole happy symbol that I see.

Next, I plan to meet Dharam Das, but he is busy at Gandhi Ashram, Naya Ghat, at a bhajan ceremony. We talk over the phone and decide to catch up some other time.

On my way back to the hotel, I feel caught up by the stillness that I encountered everywhere. It haunts me. I feel disturbed.

Ayodhya to the visitors always offered soothing sounds of chants and bhajans, flowing into the streets from thousands of temples big and small, in sync with the rhythmic soft sound of bells and dholaks. Most of the small and little-known temples are now gone, razed to the ground. The small temples are being taken over by the Ram Janmabhoomi Trust. Ratan Gupta, a brassware trader, shares what the people there are surmising, 'They may compensate the owners of these temples either by paying all the money in one go or pay in small instalments or by employing one of their family members as a priest.' He further informs, 'Two ancient temples, namely, Sundar Sadan and Kaushalya Bhavan, have been bought by the RJB Trust by paying around Rs 2 to 3 crore to the respective mahants. Such old temples are being bought mainly because they are coming in the way of expanding the Ram Mandir Parisar.'

I return to my hotel room.This time it is not in Faizabad but in the pilgrim town itself. It is a newly constructed property, well done up, very comfortable, with the latest amenities. Back here, I want to get rid of the strange sadness that has slowly gripped me. I realize I loved the old, slightly rustic, simple yet charming Ayodhya. All through the day I only got to see that avatar fast disappearing, being replaced with all things ultra-modern and very urban. I need distraction. I decide to watch a film. I call the reception for the internet password. He tells me that it's Jai Shri Ram. He explains that since it's a Hindu holy phrase, all words begin with a capital letter. Ram Lalla, in this new hotel, has been given charge of the internet space!

The next morning, a Tuesday, a day dedicated to Hanuman, I visit the Hanumangarhi locality. Even this turf lacks the usual buzz. Most shops have their shutters down. '*Hamari dukan pehle 22 feet ki thi, ab 8 feet baki hai. Aur iske badle mein jo muafza ke paise diye gaye hain lagta hai jaise koi bheek de rahe hain. Yeh sarkar Tana Shahi hai aur yeh goonda raj hai.* (Earlier my shop measured 22 feet, now after they broke it down, it measures only 8 feet. The paltry amount they have doled out as compensation appears as if they are giving us some alms. This government is dictatorial),' deplores Ramji Nigam, who owns a local footwear store here. Ajay Kumar Gupta, who runs a sweet shop, explains that the compensations given by the government are meant only for the owners. For his sweet shop, a sum of Rs 5,87,000 was offered in lieu of the part-destruction in the 400 sq. ft area. Despite this amount, Gupta is full of grievances, 'This sum will just about help me build a new façade and redo the interiors, which were pulled down.' Pointing towards the white ceiling and the walls, he tearfully states that he had revamped the shop three years back, and almost half of it has been pulled down by the administration. He informs, 'No compensation is given for the land the government takes away. I had taken this shop on rent from one of the mahants of Hanumangahi. Most shops here are owned by them. They are being compensated but what happens to us?' asks Gupta.

In contrast to the dark mood of the shopkeepers sway hundreds of brightly coloured saffron flags. These new additions have varied prints: some have the bow and arrow, others have Hanuman carrying the Sanjeevani Parvat, and many show the trio—Lord Ram, Sita and Lakshman. Along with these, in every nook and corner of the town, there are flags with images of the 'stern' Lord Hanuman. This offbeat creation by a Bangalore-based graphic artist, Karan Acharya, has taken over maximum space among its equals in the temple town.

As mentioned earlier, the image was appreciated by Prime Minister Modi when it was designed—the creator had even stated that the image was unfinished when it became popular, in 2015.

The stern-looking Hanuman was given an important status in Ayodhya around 5 August 2020, when PM Narendra Modi visited the place to lay down the foundation stone of the new Ram Mandir. On that occasion, the Saket University was done up like never before, and news channels competed with each other to get a footage of the three helicopters landing in Ayodhya. The news channels did a good job in churning the Hindutva emotions before the landing climax. Finally, the premier stepped out, masked, ensuring that emotions were covered up and the virus was kept at bay. The bhagwa theme was well maintained as he donned a yellow kurta and carried a saffron stole. On the helipad, Chief Minister Yogi Adityanath waited excitedly. A huge national construction was soon going to take off amidst a global pandemic.

The temple town was decked with orange and yellow marigold flowers, besides pink and white lotuses (which happens to be the symbol of the ruling party), roses and carnations. Some of these flowers had 'Jai Shri Ram' embossed on them, which were specially created and flown in from different cities. As many as 3,500 security personnel were deployed that morning. Keeping to the tradition of Ayodhya, the PM set out for the site of the temporary Ram Mandir after visiting Hanumangarhi temple. Once the Bhoomi Puja was over, he gave a speech where he announced that this auspicious occasion will start a 'glorious chapter in the history of India'. He compared it with the day the country gained independence. Yogi Adityanath reiterated the same views when he declared that the

Ram Mandir will be India's national symbol. It was interesting to note that Narendra Modi hailed the name of the Lord using the softer and less-aggressive expression, 'Jai Siya Ram', in contrast to the more masculine phrase, 'Jai Shri Ram'. A postage stamp with images from the epic Ramayana was released by the PM. The RSS chief, Mohan Bhagwat, present at the function, stated that finally the 'hopes and aspirations' of the Hindus which they had nurtured for centuries had become a reality.

The PM also proclaimed, '*Is mandir ke banne ke baad Ayodhya ki sirf bhavyata hi nahi badhegi, iss kshetra ka poora arthatantra bhi badal jayega. Yahan har kshetra mein naye awsar banenge, har kshetra mein awsar badhenge. Poori duniya se log yahan aayenge … kitna kuch badal jayega yahan* (After this temple is built, Ayodhya will not only be known for its grandness, the area's economy will change for the better: there will be an opportunity for everyone in every field. People from all over the world will visit this town … so much will change).'[1]

'Oh yes, so much will change,' retorts the president of the Vyapar Mandal, Nand Kumar Gupta, sarcastically. He adds in the same tone, 'Of course, they are redefining and creating a new kind of Ram Rajya! Can't you see how excited the common people are? Some of us, who are anxious about losing our daily bread, have even landed in hospitals with hypertension and heart issues. But who cares?' Other locals, especially from the trading class, scoff at the euphoria of the leaders. 'What the netas perceive is going to be very different from the Ram Rajya as described in the epic.' Both men and women, who love their Ayodhya dearly and whose households have been here for several decades, now feel the town may change beyond recognition. They understand that while their land will become an important global tourism centre, their lives and dreams will be lost in all the new bling and bizarreness.

These folks are not too far from the truth. The simple and small town-like Indianness of this pilgrim place will possibly only remain in the old photo albums, films and books. The commercial upsurge will increase the schism between different communities and classes, as the residents believe that the locals will feel ousted, and the rich and famous will gradually settle here. As Nand Kumar explains, 'You see most of the ancient religious shrines are run by different Trusts, be it Mata Vaishno Devi in Jammu, Tirupati in Andhra Pradesh, Shirdi Sai Baba in Nashik, and Siddhi Vinayak Temple in Mumbai, to name a few. In the case of the Ram Janmabhoomi Temple, the VHP and Trust are one and the same. So, you see the intention? We will be sidelined totally, as the bhagwas are taking over.'

While the Hindus in Ayodhya look at the VHP suspiciously, the Muslims have turned completely nonchalant and moved on with life. They prefer not to voice their concerns and wish not to be harassed any more. When I pay a visit to Iqbal, Hashim Ansari's son, his house looks very quiet: there are no visitors inside, no sentry is visible outside. Iqbal seems to have lost the puissance of a neta, which he displayed in full throttle three years ago. He appears to have put all his yearnings to be a small-time celebrity on the back burner. Now he pays more attention to the motor repair garage he owns. The workshop ironically is right in front of his house, the same place which he was earlier willing to donate for the construction of a mosque. His statements too have changed drastically. When asked about the new mosque that is being made in Ayodhya's Dhannipur village, pat comes the reply, 'Who has the time to invest in a mosque that is 22 km away from here? Babri Masjid is a closed chapter for us locals.'

Mohammed Yaqoob, a voluntary caretaker of the mosques and graveyards in the town, arrives at the scene. He needs a break from the August humidity and heat. He chips in, 'There are so many mosques here. Has the government ever paid attention to any of them or bothered about their upkeep?' He voices his fear, 'We will be boycotted once the temple is built. The sages will bring an end to all the love and brotherhood that was there between the two communities. We will have no options but to stay quiet and take a back seat.' He finally adds that he feels the present government does not really support the Muslims.

Historian Banke Bihari Mani Tripathi from Ayodhya believes that the apprehension and insecurity of the people are a natural phenomenon, 'Such reactions are bound to take place whenever a change occurs.' He adds, 'There is no doubt that preferences are being given to religious tourists from all over the world. When this town becomes one of the most important holy places along with the added opulence, it is obvious that there will be more traffic and movement. So the government has no choice but to widen the roads for which old buildings need to be pulled down, and so on.' He adds more logic: 'Besides, the businessmen have no true cause to worry. If you visit any temple town, you will notice that big and small shops co-exist; after all, pilgrims come from varied walks of life and have different affordability.' But Tripathi also believes that the ethos of Ayodhya should not be tampered with. '*Purana Ayodhya ka swaroop kayam rakhna chahiye* (The identity of the old Ayodhya should be retained).'

On this trip, three years after my previous one, I decide to visit the temporary wooden Ram Temple, mainly on the insistence of the main priest Mahant Satendra Das. The well-organized system in the temple premises take me by surprise. Small shops selling prasada are lined up on both sides of the entrance road. There are bright saffron flags all around for sale and décor purposes. Once again prints of the 'stern' Hanuman stare back from everywhere. The passage to the temple is well lit by neon and sodium lamps, even during the day. The security people are polite and kind as they frisk the pilgrims. As I stand in front of the temple, I observe the changes: The Ram Lalla idol is placed under a prettily carved wooden roof. In front of his throne stands his three brothers, Lakshman, Shatrughan and Bharat. To their left, Hanuman is seated with folded hands. And a little behind him is a prominent shivaling.

The last, a new addition, catches my attention. Acharya Satyendra Das explains the inclusion, 'This shivaling is addressed as Narmadeshwaar.' He further explains, '*Ek bhakt isko le kar aaya aur suraksha karmi ko diya ki yeh Ram Mandir ke liye hai. Suraksha karmi ne phir prashasan ko saari baat batayi aur uske baad hum ne shivaling sthapit kar diya Ram Lalla ke saath* (A devotee brought this shivaling for the Ram Mandir and handed it over to a security guard, who communicated this to the administration. After that the shivaling was installed beside Ram Lalla).' As I probe further, the high priest cites a shloka from the *Ramcharitmanas*, as if to put a pause to any further queries, '*Shiva drohi mam bhagat kahawa. So nar sapne hoon mohi na pawa* (The devotee who has no love and devotion for Lord Shiva and calls himself my devotee, that person can never be mine even in his dreams).'

A new addition. A reiteration of Lord Shiva's importance among all Hindu gods by Ram himself. This resonated with the recent demand of the Gyanvapi Masjid. 'Those people claiming it to be their worship place are fools. Gyanvapi is a Sanskrit phrase meaning "well of knowledge". The name itself indicates that it belonged to the Hindus. How can there be a mosque with a Hindu name?' asks the acharya.

As I take leave, Satyendra Das raises his hand and hails Ram with the usual 'Jai Shri Ram'. This time he adds, 'Har Har Mahadev.' He gives an inexplicable smile as he confirms the mood of most saffronized people, 'You see the *andolan* (struggle) that began in the early eighties was not for Ayodhya and Ram alone, the objective was always to get (similar) claims over the temples in Kashi and Mathura.'

To prove his point, he dramatically calls out the slogan that was synonymous with the Ram Janmabhoomi movement: '*Yeh toh jhanki hai, Kashi, Mathura baaki hai* (This is only the trailer, Kashi and Mathura are still left).'

There couldn't be a more obvious prediction!

Acknowledgements

I am truly grateful to Krishan Chopra who decided that I could write about Ayodhya the way I saw it over the last two decades, and a little more. The main heroes and heroines of this book are the people of Ayodhya. The raison d'être is my desire to help people see beyond the politics and the courts and understand the lives, challenges and courage of the simple folks of this town.

In the course of writing this book, I renewed old relations with several mahants as well as Muslim and VHP leaders. The best part was that they came ahead with full cooperation. After the lockdown due to the Covid-19 pandemic, my contacts were available for long telephone chats. Without them, completing the book would not have been possible under those strange and unknown circumstances. I would especially like to mention Gaurav Tiwari from Ayodhya, besides the mahants and many other locals.

Kameshwar Choupal spent hours taking me through certain phases of the Ram Janmabhoomi saga and Vinay Katiyar was always available for any information I needed.

I want to thank senior advocates Zafaryab Jilani and I.B. Singh, who have been easily accessible to share details whenever required. My associates from *Outlook* days Alam Srinivas and Prashant Panjiar were always available for any advice or inputs I required from them.

I feel very grateful towards everyone at HarperCollins India who put together their expertise and time to shape up my book. I would especially like to thank associate publisher Swati Chopra and my editors, Amrita Mukerji and Paloma Dutta, for all the help and guidance that they have continuously extended.

Most importantly, this book would have never been completed without the constant support of my family, their patience and encouragement. They helped me with everything from books, access to online libraries and academic sites to suggestions, both criticism and appreciation, tolerance—the list can go on and on—whenever I needed, and that was pretty much often.

Notes

Introduction: Ayodhya: Divided It Still Stands

1. B.B. Lal (ed.), *Indian Archaeology, 1969–70: A Review*, Archaeological Survey of India, p. 40.
2. 'Jain Dharma and Lord Rishabhdev'. https://encyclopediaofjainism.com/jain_dharma_and_lord_rishabhdev/
3. 'Shree Abhinandan Swami Bhagvan'. http://www.jaintirth.in/24-tirthankara/shree-abhinandan-swami-bhagvan
4. Chistu Rajamony, 'Sacred Sites and International Law: A Case Study of Ayodhya Dispute', PhD dissertation, Oxford Brookes University, 2007.
5. Ibid.
6. Zainab Sikander, 'Yogi Adityanath's Mughal hatred based on Jizya. But BJP has many modern versions for Muslims', The Print, 21 September 2020. https://theprint.in/opinion/yogi-adityanaths-mughal-hatred-based-on-jizya-but-bjp-has-many-modern-versions-for-muslims/506656/
7. Prabhash K. Dutta, 'Ayodhya: When Mulayam Singh Yadav ordered police firing on karsevaks heading to Babri Masjid', *India Today*, 9 November 2019.

   indiatoday.in/india/story/ayodhya-when-mulayam-singh-yadav-ordered-police-firing-on-karsevaks-heading-to-babri-masjid-1614033-2019-10-30

1: The Polestar of Faith and Belief

1. Shripad Ramchandra Tikekar (ed.), *Epigrams from Gandhiji*, Publications Division Ministry of Information & Broadcasting, 2017.
2. *Tansen Sen, The Travel Records of Chinese Pilgrims Faxian, Xuanzang, and Yijing: Education About Asia*, Vol. 11, Number 3, Winter 2006. http://afe.easia.columbia.edu/special/travel_records.pdf
3. Shripad Ramchandra Tikekar (ed.), *Epigrams from Gandhiji*, Publications Division Ministry of Information & Broadcasting, 2017.
4. Shaman Hwui Li, *The Life of Hiuen-Tsiang*, p. 83. https://library.um.edu.mo/ebooks/b25788693.pdf
5. Ibid. pp. 87–88.
6. Supreme Court (SC) verdict, p. 63. https://www.sci.gov.in/pdf/JUD_2.pdf
7. William Foster (ed.), *Early Travels in India*. https://archive.org/stream/earlytravelsinin00fostuoft/earlytravelsinin00fostuoft_djvu.txt
8. Asha Kiran, *Ram Mandir*, Lakshay Books, 2018, p. 95.
9. SC verdict, p. 126. https://www.sci.gov.in/pdf/JUD_2.pdf
10. Nikhila Henry, 'Ayodhya Explained: Supreme Court Chose Faith Over Law, Jurist Faizan Mustafa Says', HuffPost, 9 November 2019. https://www.huffingtonpost.in/entry/ayodhya-explained-supreme-court-faizan-mustafa-says_in_5dc694b5e4b02bf 57940668f
11. *Sunni Central Board of Wakf vs Sri Gopal Singh Visharad*, Allahabad High Court Order. https://elegalix.allahabadhighcourt.in/elegalix/ayodhyafiles/hondvsj-ann-3.pdf
12. Sutapa Mukherjee, 'More Secrets from the Grave', *Outlook*, 5 May 2003.
13. As quoted in Jaya Menon, Supriya Varma 'Was There a Temple under the Babri Masjid? Reading the Archaeological "Evidence"', *Economic and Political Weekly*, 11 December 2010. https://www.epw.in/journal/2010/50/verdict-ayodhya-special-issues/was-there-temple-under-babri-masjid-reading
14. SC verdict, p. 109. https://www.sci.gov.in/pdf/JUD_2.pdf
15. As quoted in Jaya Menon, Supriya Varma 'Was There a Temple under the Babri Masjid? Reading the Archaeological "Evidence"', *Economic and Political Weekly*, 11 December 2010. https://www.epw.in/

journal/2010/50/verdict-ayodhya-special-issues/was-there-temple-under-babri-masjid-reading

16. Ibid.
17. 'Archeology of Ayodhya'. https://en.wikipedia.org/wiki/Archaeology_of_Ayodhya#cite_note-IT_depths_2003-1
18. Janet Spector, *What This Awl Means*, Minnesota Historical Society Press, 1993.
19. SC verdict, p. 63. https://www.sci.gov.in/pdf/JUD_2.pdf
20. Ajoy Ashirwad Mahaprashasta, 'Ayodhya Dispute Is a Battle Between Faith and Rationality, Says Historian D.N. Jha', The Wire, 9 November 2019. https://thewire.in/communalism/ayodhya-verdict-babri-masjid-ram-temple-dn-jha
21. *M. Siddiq (D) Thr Lrs vs Mahant Suresh Das and Others*. https://www.casemine.com/judgement/in/5dc845d33321bc57007381a1
22. 'Rights of a Deity'. http://www.legalserviceindia.com/legal/article-1199-rights-of-a-deity.html
23. SC verdict, p. 160. https://www.sci.gov.in/pdf/JUD_2.pdf
24. SC verdict, p. 164. https://www.sci.gov.in/pdf/JUD_2.pdf
25. SC verdict, p. 164. https://www.sci.gov.in/pdf/JUD_2.pdf
26. SC verdict, pp. 165–166. https://www.sci.gov.in/pdf/JUD_2.pdf
27. Ratna Kapur, 'A Leap of Faith: The Construction of Hindu Majoritarianism Through Secular Law' in *Religious Rights*, Lorenzo Zucca (ed.), Routledge, 2017, pp. 227–246.

2: Splintered Peace

1. *Collected Works of Mahatma Gandhi*, Vol. 94, 17 February 1947–29 April 1947. https://www.gandhiashramsevagram.org/gandhi-literature/mahatma-gandhi-collected-works-volume-94.pdf
2. Khursheed Akbar, 'Fields Notes on Caste Practices among Muslims of Nohsa Panchayat', Working Paper – 5. https://tiss.edu/uploads/files/Working_Paper_5_Khursheed_Akbar.pdf
3. '"Go to Pakistan": Meerut police officer caught on camera telling anti-CAA protestors', Scroll, 28 December 2019. https://scroll.in/latest/948092/go-to-pakistan-meerut-police-officer-caught-on-camera-telling-anti-caa-protestors

4. Debjani Chatterjee (ed.), 'Naseeruddin Shah, Aamir Khan Are Like "Traitors", Says RSS's Indresh Kumar', NDTV, 29 January 2019. https://www.ndtv.com/india-news/naseeruddin-shah-and-aamir-khan-are-traitors-says-senior-rss-leader-indresh-kumar-1984673
5. 'Thackeray calls Shah Rukh "traitor", no apologies says actor', *India Today*, 6 February 2010. https://www.indiatoday.in/latest-headlines/story/thackeray-calls-shah-rukh-traitor-no-apologies-says-actor-66770-2010-02-05
6. 'Yogi Adityanath slams SRK, compares him with Hafiz Saeed', *The Hindu*, 16 November 2021. https://www.thehindu.com/news/national/Yogi-Adityanath-attacks-Shah-Rukh-Khan-compares-him-with-Hafiz-Saeed/article60270849.ece
7. Salman Khurshid, *Visible Muslims, Invisible Citizens*, Rupa Publications, 2019, p. 158.
8. Interview with Sayyad Muhammad Asif.
9. Reinhard Bernbeck and Susan Pollock, 'Ayodhya, Archaeology, and Identity', *Current Anthropology*, 37, S 1, February 1996.
10. April 1996, Vol. 8, No. 2-C.
11. 'India: Communal Violence and the Denial of Justice', Human Rights Watch, April 1996. https://www.hrw.org/reports/1996/India1.htm
12. Mark Tully and Gillian Wright, *India in Slow Motion*, Penguin Random House, 2003.
13. 'Supreme Court dismisses all review petitions in Ayodhya case judgment', *The Times of India*, 12 December 2019. https://timesofindia.indiatimes.com/india/supreme-court-dismisses-all-review-petitions-in-ayodhya-case-judgment/articleshow/72491042.cms

3: Ram Resurrected

1. Anand Patel, 'As Ram mandir demand shines bright, other Ayodhya temples fade into oblivion', *India Today*, 7 December 2018. https://www.indiatoday.in/india/story/as-ram-mandir-demand-shines-bright-other-ayodhya-temples-fade-into-oblivion-1404173-2018-12-06
2. 'The Difference between Jain and Hindu Ramayana'. https://www.jagranjosh.com/general-knowledge/what-is-the-difference-between-hindu-and-jain-ramayana-in-hindi-1
3. 'Sikh Version Ramayana'. https://www.speakingtree.in/blog/sikh-version-ramayana

4. 'Tribes have their own versions of Ramayana', *Deccan Herald*, 12 April 2014. https://www.deccanherald.com/content/398712/tribes-have-their-own-versions.html
5. Sarvesh Kumar and Rana P.B. Singh, 'Ayodhya, India: Cultural landscape and perspectives for inclusive heritage development', *Context: Built, Living and Natural*, 2017, pp. 21–30.
6. Nikita Mandhani, 'The Indian princess who became a South Korean queen', BBC, 4 November 2018. https://www.bbc.com/news/world-asia-india-46055285
7. Chirali Sharma, 'Could South Koreans Be Descendants if This Indian Princess?'. https://www.youthkiawaaz.com/2018/11/are-south-koreans-born-out-of-this-indian-princess-from-ayodhya/
8. Shashi Tharoor, *Why I am a Hindu*. Oxford University Press, 2018.
9. David Frawley, 'Why a new encounter with Adi Shankaracharya, India's greatest intellectual, is essential', The Print, 1 June 2018. https://theprint.in/pageturner/afterword/why-a-new-encounter-with-adi-shankaracharya-indias-greatest-intellectual-is-essential/65157/
10. Ibid.
11. Hans Teye Bakker, 'Ayodhyā: A Hindu Jerusalem: An investigation of "Holy War" as a religious idea in the light of communal unrest in India', in *Holy Ground: Where Art and Text Meet*, Bril, 2019, pp. 55–78.
12. Shyamlal Yadav, 'Name game: 3,626 villages named after Ram, 3,309 after Krishna', *The Indian Express*, 4 July 2013. http://archive.indianexpress.com/news/name-game-3626-villages-named-after-ram-3309-after-krishna/1137491/0
13. Sanjeev Sanyal, *Land of the Seven Rivers: A Brief History of India's Geography*, Random House India, 2012.
14. Vasudha Paramasivan, 'Between Text and Sect: Early Nineteenth Century Shifts in the Theology of Ram', PhD dissertation, UC Berkeley, 2010.
15. Richard Burghart, 'The Founding of the Ramanandi Sect', *Ethnohistory*, Vol. 25, No. 2, Duke University Press Stable, Spring 1978, pp. 121–139.
16. 'Tridandi-sannyasa'. https://vaniquotes.org/wiki/Tridandi-sannyasa

17. Richard Burghart, 'The Founding of the Ramanandi Sect', *Ethnohistory*, Vol. 25, No. 2, Duke University Press Stable, Spring 1978, pp. 121–139.
18. Ibid. p. 136.
19. Meenakshi Jain, *The Battle for Rama: Case of the Temple at Ayodhya*. Aryan Books International, pp. 41–43, 2017.
20. http://hvk.org/
21. Gyanendra Pandey, 'Modes of History Writing: New Hindu History of Ayodhya', *Economic and Political Weekly*, Vol. 29, No. 25, 18 June 1994, pp. 1523–1528.
22. S.P. Udayakumar, *Presenting the Past: Anxious History and Ancient Future in Hindutva*, Praeger Publishers Inc.
23. '"Biggest Achievement of My Life": "Angry Hanuman" Artist on PM's Praise', NDTV, 8 May 2018. https://www.ndtv.com/india-news/shocked-and-speechless-karan-acharya-creator-of-angry-hanuman-portrait-after-pm-modis-praise-1848637.
24. James D'Angelo, *The Healing Power of the Human Voice: Mantras, Chants, and Seed Sounds for Health and Harmony*, Inner Traditions/Bear & Co., 2005.
25. Arvind Rajagopal, 'Rama Janmabhoomi, Consumer Identity and Image-Based Politics', *Economic and Political Weekly*, Vol. 29, No. 27, 2 July 1994.
26. Burton Stein, *A History of India*, Vol. 9, John Wiley & Sons, 2010, p. 411.
27. John D.H. Downing, Denis McQuail, Philip Schlesinger, Ellen Wartella (ed.), *The SAGE Handbook of Media Studies,* p. 528.
28. 'Shah Rukh Khan reveals his first Guru and role of a monkey in Delhi's Ramleela while shooting for an international chat show', INVC, 14 April 2016. https://www.internationalnewsandviews.com/shah-rukh-khan-reveals-his-first-guru-and-role-of-a-monkey-in-delhis-ramleela-while-shooting-for-an-international-chat-show/

4: Ram's Protégés

1. Dibyesh Anand, 'The Awakened Hindu India: Ayodhya and Gujarat', *Hindu Nationalism in India and the Politics of Fear*, Palgrave Macmillan, New York, 2011, pp. 123–150.

2. Ezra Rashkow, Sanyukta Ghosh and Upal Chakrabarti (ed.), *Memory, Identity and the Colonial Encounter in India: Essays in Honour of Peter Robb*, Routledge, 2018.
3. 'Mahant Narendra Giri new president of All India Akhara Parishad', India.com, 13 March 2016. https://www.india.com/news/india/mahant-narendra-giri-new-president-of-all-india-akhara-parishad-1027778/
4. Dhirendra K. Jha, 'RSS and the akharas', Fountain Ink, 8 March 2019. https://fountainink.in/reportage/rss-and-the-akharas
5. Rajesh Pradhan, 'When the Saints Go Marching In: Sadhus in Democratic Politics in Late 20th Century India', PhD thesis, MIT, February 2009, p. 130, https://core.ac.uk/download/pdf/4417653.pdf
6. Ibid., p. 134.
7. Santosh Kumar Triparti, *Karmyogi, Paramhans, Sri Ram Chandar ji Maharaj*, Shivank Prakashan, 2016.
8. Case numbers 643/98, 644/98, 645/98. Cantonment police station, Ayodhya.
9. 'Sadhu attempts to rape minor boy in Ayodhya, tries to chop off his private part for resisting sexual assault', Mirror Now Digital, 18 August 2020. https://www.timesnownews.com/mirror-now/crime/article/sadhu-attempts-to-rape-minor-boy-in-ayodhya-tries-to-chop-off-his-private-part-for-resisting-sexual-assault/638949
10. Crime number 66/16-Circle Ayodhya, Janpath.
11. Crime number 5110/18, Ayodhya.

5: Legal Trails, Travails and Trials, 1858–1950

1. Shripad Ramchandra Tikekar (ed.), *Epigrams from Gandhiji*, Publications Division, Ministry of Information & Broadcasting, 2017.
2. *Who's Who of Indian Martyrs: Volume Three*, Ministry of Culture, 1973. https://archive.org/stream/whoswhoofindianm03chop/whoswhoofindianm03chop_djvu.txt
3. Shamshul Islam, 'Hindu–Muslims Unity, Participation of Common People and Women in India's First War of Independence', *Amazing Untold Stories of India's First War of Independence, 1857*.
4. 'The Battle of Chinhat'. https://www.tornosindia.com/the-battle-of-chinhat/#.X0dihsgzZPY
5. Kishore Kunal, *Ayodhya Revisited*, p. 381, Prabhat Prakashan, 2016.

6. SC verdict, p. 799. https://www.sci.gov.in/pdf/JUD_2.pdf
7. *M. Siddiq (D) through LRS. vs Mahant Suresh Das & Ors.* https://www.advocatekhoj.com/library/judgments/announcement.php?WID=12230
8. Kishore Kunal, *Ayodhya Revisited*, p. 379, Prabhat Prakashan, 2016.
9. SC Verdict, p. 801. https://www.sci.gov.in/pdf/JUD_2.pdf
10. Nilanjan Mukhopadhyay, *The Demolition: India at the Crossroads*, South Asia Books, 1994, p. 63.
11. SC Verdict, p. 66. https://www.sci.gov.in/pdf/JUD_2.pdf
12. SC Verdict, p. 806. https://www.sci.gov.in/pdf/JUD_2.pdf
13. 'Historic Argument in Shri Ram Janam Bhoomi Babri Masjid Case'. https://archive.org/stream/ParameshwarRamaMandir/Parameshwar-Rama%20mandir_djvu.txt
14. SC Verdict, p. 807. https://www.sci.gov.in/pdf/JUD_2.pdf
15. A.G. Noorani, 'The Babri Masjid-Ram Janmabhoomi Question', *Economic and Political Weekly*, November 4–11, Vol. 24, No. 44/45, 1989, pp. 2461–2466.
16. Sushil Srivastava, 'The Abuse of History: A Study of the White Papers on Ayodhya', *Social Scientist*, Vol. 22, No. 5/6 May–June 1994.
17. Shashank Chaturvedi, David N. Gellner and Sanjay Kumar Pandey, 'Politics in Gorakhpur since the 1920s: The Making of a safe "Hindu" Constituency', Taylor and Francis, 2019, pp. 40–57.
18. Ibid.
19. Krishna Jha and Dhirendra K. Jha, *Ayodhya: The Dark Night*, HarperCollins India, 2012.
20. P.V. Narasimha Rao, *Ayodhya: 6 December 1992*, Penguin Random House India, 2019, p. 6.
21. Ibid, p. 7.
22. 'The Babari Masjid Question: Letters from the Archives'. http://www.vijayvaani.com/ArticleDisplay.aspx?aid=1585
23. P.V. Narasimha Rao, *Ayodhya: 6 December 1992*, Penguin Random House India, 2019, pp. 20–21.
24. 'The Babari Masjid Question: Letters from the Archives'. http://www.vijayvaani.com/ArticleDisplay.aspx?aid=1585

6: Legal Trails, Travails and Trials 1950 to 2019

1. Shripad Ramchandra Tikekar (ed.), *Epigrams from Gandhiji*. Publications Division, Ministry of Information & Broadcasting, 2017.
2. P.V. Narasimha Rao, *Ayodhya: 6 December 1992*, Penguin Random House India, 2019, p. 12.
3. SC Verdict, p. 34. https://www.sci.gov.in/pdf/JUD_2.pdf
4. Hilal Ahmed, *Muslim Political Discourse in Postcolonial India: Monuments, Memory, Contestation*, Routlegde, 2014.
5. Ghansham Shah, 'Revolution, Reform, or Protest? A Study of the Bihar Movement', *Economic and Political Weekly*, Vol. 12, No. 15, 9 April 1977, pp. 605–614.
6. Ibid.
7. Robert Graeme Salter, 'Swaraj and Sweepers: The JP Movement and the Future of Transformational Politics', PhD thesis, Victoria University of Technology.
8. Ibid.
9. Lal Krishna Advani, *My Take*, Prabhat Prakashan, 2021, p. 141.
10. 'RSS led the unprecedented movement against Emergency', Vishwa Samvada Kendram Kerala, 25 June 2019. https://vskkerala.com/english/article/1751/rss-led-the-unprecedented-movement-against-emergency/
11. Ratan Sharda, *RSS 360: Demystifying Rashtriya Swayamsevak Sangh*, Bloomsbury, 2018.
12. V. Krishna Ananth, *India since Independence: Making Sense of Indian Politics*, Pearson, p. 242.
13. Joshil K. Abraham, Judith Misrahi-Barak (ed.), *Dalit Literatures in India*, Routledge, 2018.
14. Ram Puniyani (ed.), *Religion, Power and Violence: Expression of Politics in Contemporary Times*, Sage Publications India, 2005, p. 187.
15. Sumit Mitra, 'Virat Hindu Samaj holds massive rally to protest against conversion of Harijans to Islam', *India Today*, 15 November 1981. https://www.indiatoday.in/magazine/religion/story/19811115-virat-hindu-samaj-holds-massive-rally-to-protest-against-conversion-of-harijans-to-islam-773435-2013-10-28
16. David N. Lorenzen, *Who Invented Hinduism: Essays on Religion in History*, Yoda Press, 2006.

17. Prema Kurien, *A Place at the Multicultural Table: The Development of an American Hinduism*, Rutgers University Press, 2007.
18. 'Yatra in Hinduism'. https://www.hinduscriptures.in/vedic-lifestyle/beginners-guide/importance-of-pilgrimage-yatra
19. Sumit Mitra, 'VHP-organised Ekaimata Yagna to roll across India with 92 religious caravans', *India Today*, 30 November 1983. https://www.indiatoday.in/magazine/special-report/story/19831130-vhp-organised-ekaimata-yagna-to-roll-across-india-with-92-religious-caravans-771249-2013-07-12
20. Christophe Jaffrelot, 'The Hindu Nationalist Reinterpretation of Pilgrimage in India: The Limits of Yatra Politics'. https://www.researchgate.net/publication/229611077_The_Hindu_nationalist_reinterpretation_of_pilgrimage_in_India_The_limits_of_Yatra_politics
21. Yubaraj Ghimire, 'Dharma Sansad emerges as flagship of Hindutva movement', *India Today*, 30 April 1994. https://www.indiatoday.in/magazine/special-report/story/19940430-dharma-sansad-emerges-as-flagship-of-hindutva-movement-809078-1994-04-30
22. Lubna Mustafa, 'Religion as a factor: A study of parliamentary elections in UP since 1984', PhD thesis, Aligarh Muslim University, 2007. https://shodhganga.inflibnet.ac.in/bitstream/10603/183827/6/05%20chapter%201.pdf
23. 'Reclaiming Sacred Hindu Space at Ayodhya', *India Today*, 31 May 1986.
24. Rajesh Pradhan, 'When the Saints Go Marching In: Sadhus in Democratic Politics in Late 20th Century India', PhD thesis, MIT, February 2009, p. 163. https://core.ac.uk/download/pdf/4417653.pdf
25. Pankaj Pachauri, 'Ramjanmabhoomi-Babri Masjid row: Govt faces a tough challenge', *India Today*, 15 December 1989. https://www.indiatoday.in/magazine/special-report/story/19891215-ramjanmabhoomi-babri-masjid-row-govt-faces-a-tough-challenge-816834-1989-12-15
26. Wajahat Habibullah, *My Years with Rajiv: Triumph and Tragedy*, Westland Books, 2020, p. 111, pp.124–125.
27. 'Rath Yatra Mahajan's Brainchild', *Hindustan Times*, 9 May 2006. https://www.hindustantimes.com/india/rath-yatra-mahajan-s-brainchild-advani/story-0lVHI6IR7fZC8YEOF85vXI.html
28. 'RAM RATH YATRA', Bharatiya Janata Party. https://www.bjp.org/ram-rath-yatra

29. Andrea Marion Pinkney and John Whalen-Bridge (ed.), *Religious Journeys in India: Pilgrims, Tourists, and Travelers*, SUNY Press, 2018.
30. *Dr M. Ismail Frauqui and Ors. vs Union Of India (UoI) and Ors.* on 24 October 1994. https://indiankanoon.org/doc/52822922/
31. 'Babri Masjid Demolition: A Timeline of the Ram Janmabhoomi Dispute Case', *Outlook*, 31 August 2022. https://www.outlookindia.com/national/babri-masjid-demolition-a-timeline-of-the-ram-janmabhoomi-dispute-case-news-220247
32. J. Venkatesan, 'Supreme Court stays Allahabad High Court verdict on Ayodhya', *The Hindu*, 9 May 2011. https://www.thehindu.com/news/national//article60590301.ece

7: Machine on a Mission

1. Shripad Ramchandra Tikekar (ed.), *Epigrams from Gandhiji*, Publications Division, Ministry of Information & Broadcasting, 2017.
2. M.S. Golwalkar, *Bunch of Thoughts*, Vikrama Prakashan, 1968, pp. 174–175.
3. Saba Naqvi, 'Storm Troopers', *Outlook*, 5 February 2022. https://magazine.outlookindia.com/story/storm-troopers/221825
4. Narendra Modi, *Jyotipunj*, Prabhat Prakashan, 2015, p. 45. https://cdn.narendramodi.in/ebooks/JyotipunjEng.pdf
5. Walter K. Andersen and Shridhar D. Damle, *The Brotherhood in Saffron: The Rashtriya Swayamsevak Sangh and Hindu Revivalism*, Penguin, 2019.
6. Christophe Jaffrelot, *Religion, Caste, and Politics in India*, Primus Books, 2010.
7. Jacqueline Suthren Hirst and John Zavos, *Religious Traditions in Modern South Asia*, p. 85. http://opac.lib.idu.ac.id/unhan-ebook/assets/uploads/files/b45a6-112.religious-traditions-in-modern-south-asia.pdf
8. Mani Shankar Aiyar, 'Secular fundamentalism in a time of bhoomi pujan', *The Hindu*, 6 August 2020. https://www.thehindu.com/opinion/lead/secular-fundamentalism-in-a-time-of-bhoomi-pujan/article32279876.ece
9. Wajahat Habibullah, *My Years with Rajiv: Triumph and Tragedy*, Westland Books, 2020.
10. Thomas Blom Hansen, *The Saffron Wave: Democracy and Hindu Nationalism in Modern India*, Princeton University Press, 1999.

11. A.G. Noorani, 'Ayodhya: Deceit and Force', Frontline, 28 April 2017. *https://frontline.thehindu.com/the-nation/ayodhya-deceit-and-force/article9632163.ece*
12. Ibid.
13. Sutapa Mukherjee, '"The Temple Is Another VHP Stunt"', *Outlook*, 5 February 2022. https://magazine.outlookindia.com/story/the-temple-is-another-vhp-stunt/210820

8: Demolition Day

1. Shripad Ramchandra Tikekar (ed.), *Epigrams from Gandhiji*. Publications Division, Ministry of Information & Broadcasting, 2017.
2. 'Background Note on National Integration Council'. mha.gov.in
3. Reinhard Bernbeck and Susan Pollock, 'Ayodhya, Archaeology, and Identity', *Current Anthropology*, 37, S 1, February 1996.
4. Prashant Panjiar, *That Which Is Unseen*, Navajivan Trust, 2021.
5. Saba Naqvi, 'Hour of Janus', Outlook, 28 March 2017. https://www.outlookindia.com/magazine/story/hour-of-janus/226634
6. Ibid.
7. A.G. Noorani, 'Silent Spectator', Frontline, 2 June 2006. https://frontline.thehindu.com/other/article30209549.ece
8. Ibid.
9. '1.5 lakh kar sevaks, 2,300 police constables, 1 mosque: How Babri Masjid fell on December 6, 1992', *India Today,* 6 December 2017. https://www.indiatoday.in/india/story/how-babri-masjid-fell-on-december-6-1992-1101318-2017-12-06
10. Carl Gustav Jung, *The Archetypes and the Collective Unconscious*, Routledge, 2014.
11. Prashant Panjiar, *That Which Is Unseen,* Navajivan Trust, 2021.
12. 'Babri Masjid'. https://www.discoveredindia.com/uttar-pradesh/attractions/mosques/babri-masjid.htm
13. Omar Rashid, 'What happened that December night in Ayodhya', *The Hindu*, 10 December 2017. https://www.thehindu.com/news/national/what-happened-that-december-night-in-ayodhya/article21383162.ece?homepage=true

Epilogue: Ayodhya—Ram ki Nagri

1. https://www.youtube.com/watch?v=IyQtaDvuN3g

Index

About the Author

Sutapa Mukherjee has worked as a full-time journalist with *The Pioneer* and *Outlook*, and as a stringer with Associated Press, Agece France-Presse and BBC online. She has written widely on various subjects that include politics, gender issues, wildlife, travel and lifestyle.

30 Years *of*

HarperCollins *Publishers* India

At HarperCollins, we believe in telling the best stories and finding the widest possible readership for our books in every format possible. We started publishing 30 years ago; a great deal has changed since then, but what has remained constant is the passion with which our authors write their books, the love with which readers receive them, and the sheer joy and excitement that we as publishers feel in being a part of the publishing process.

Over the years, we've had the pleasure of publishing some of the finest writing from the subcontinent and around the world, and some of the biggest bestsellers in India's publishing history. Our books and authors have won a phenomenal range of awards, and we ourselves have been named Publisher of the Year the greatest number of times. But nothing has meant more to us than the fact that millions of people have read the books we published, and somewhere, a book of ours might have made a difference.

As we step into our fourth decade, we go back to that one word – a word which has been a driving force for us all these years.

Read.